DATE DUE

DEMCO 38-296

GARLAND STUDIES IN

AMERICAN POPULAR HISTORY AND CULTURE

edited by

JEROME NADELHAFT
UNIVERSITY OF MAINE

A GARLAND SERIES

Garland Studies in American Popular History and Culture

Jerome Nadelhaft, series editor

THE FLAMINGO IN THE GARDEN

AMERICAN YARD ART AND THE VERNACULAR LANDSCAPE

COLLEEN J. SHEEHY

GARLAND PUBLISHING, INC.
A MEMBER OF THE TAYLOR & FRANCIS GROUP
NEW YORK & LONDON / 1998

Copyright © 1998 Colleen J. Sheehy

ng-in-Publication Data

Sheehy, Colleen Josephine.
    The flamingo in the garden : American yard art and the
vernacular culture / Colleen J. Sheehy.
        p.   cm. — (Garland studies in American popular history
and culture)
    Includes bibliographical references and index.
    ISBN 0-8153-2914-8 (alk. paper)
    1. Decorative arts—United States—History—20th century.
2. Garden ornaments and furniture—United States.   I. Title.
II. Series.
NK808.S53 1997
645'.8—dc21   97-23689

Printed on acid-free, 250-year-life paper
Manufactured in the United States of America

For Peter, Brigid, Annie, and Mae

and

For all those who enliven
our landscapes, especially those interviewed for
this study

Contents

Illustrations

Introduction:
The Flamingo in the Garden
American Yard Art and the Vernacular Landscape

Over and over again I have said that the commonplace aspects of the
contemporary landscape, the streets and houses and fields and places
of work, could teach us a great deal not only about American history
and American society but about ourselves and how we relate to the
world.

J.B. Jackson
Discovering the Vernacular Landscape

In every community across the United States today, one can find an
array of popular sculpture and outdoor decoration in American yards. In
Minneapolis, for instance, Werner Muense has built his own wooden
deer that leaps over a log in his front yard. In Philadelphia, Eileen
Szewczak's hand-painted ceramic rabbit sits in the midst of her
postage-stamp-sized yard. In Atlanta, Estelle Smith has constructed a
miniature sculpture garden, filled with pint-sized copies of the classical
statuary one might find in gardens of the rich, here sitting alongside
cement deer and storybook frogs. And in Los Angeles, Harriet
Bagasao's yard teems with animal ornaments, religious statuary, and
two pink plastic flamingos.

The flamingo in the garden and other ubiquitous objects adorning
yards, gardens, porches, and front stoops have much to tell us about
American culture. They reveal attitudes and values about our places,
homes, neighborhoods, and communities. They reveal ways in which
Americans mediate relationships between culture and nature in their
own back—and front—yards. They tell us about how Americans
negotiate consumer culture through purchase, placement, alteration, and
reuse of mass-produced things, and about how in the midst of a culture
of mass production, the handmade object remains an important element

in our domestic spaces. Yard ornaments and statuary can express religious, ethnic, regional, and other affiliations. And they tell us about what people consider beautiful, for American yard art, at bottom, is about creating scenes of aesthetic pleasure and enjoyment.

This book documents a wide range of American yard art in both imagery and scale of execution, and it discusses the behavior and practices connected with these materials, undertakings that have not been done before to the extent that I do here. Yet this is not an exhaustive study of American yard art, a project that would be of Herculean proportions. This work began with several basic questions: What do Americans put in their yards? How are we to account for this? What meanings does it have? My documentation and study of contemporary sites in several parts of the United States serve as the basis for this work. Yet even more importantly, I attempt to explore the larger significance and meanings behind these objects to understand the perspectives of their creators and the dynamics of the cultures in which these objects operate. Fieldwork led me to consider historical precedents and explanations. I move, therefore, between discussions of contemporary and historical sites and issues. Yet I have not tried to construct a strictly chronological treatment of American yard art. Rather, I explore the central issues that emerged as I engaged in this work in order to suggest some ways of understanding this cultural phenomenon. What results is a study that takes these objects and their creators with an utter seriousness and at the same time recognizes the humor and good fun that can be involved with pink flamingos or herds of fleece-covered sheep arrayed in front yards.

The pink plastic flamingo is one of the most vivid objects in contemporary American yard statuary. Yet as noted in the examples above, American yards are hosts to a melange of vernacular imagery: classical statuary, duck families, cement deer, wishing wells, gnomes, Dutch windmills, barefoot boys with fishing poles, black jockeys and white jockeys, miniature barns, fleece-covered sheep, and life-size Holsteins. These diverse images have emerged from a variety of sources over the past century and a half of American cultural history. Some come from European aristocratic traditions, others from American popular culture; other images make references to idealized landscapes, and some reflect Americans' ideas about what constitutes culture and taste.

Vernacular statuary installed in American yards intersects with the long and lofty history of garden sculpture but gives it a saucy, slang twist. That longer history of garden statuary lies predominantly within the realm of aristocrats, who could enlist servants or slaves for manual labor and who could commission sculptures from artists and artisans.[1] This held true at least until the nineteenth century, when a middle-class developed that had disposable income and leisure time to devote to ornamental gardens. In post–Civil War America, industrialization brought factory-made decorative objects, including garden statuary and furniture, within pocketbook range of the growing middle class. In the twentieth century, even working-class groups have been able to afford houses with small yards, especially with the financial help of savings and loan associations, federal funding programs, and tax incentives. Working- and middle-class residents adorn their gardens with statuary in plastic, plaster, and cement, with strings of electric lights for holidays, and with objects created in home workshops.

The imagery in American yards underlines the fact that this space is a symbolic landscape. On one hand, it refers to the agrarian past of the nation and the landscape created by democratic farmers, so extolled by Thomas Jefferson. On the other hand, it condenses the grand estate garden, merging the greensward and garden plots into one space: the lawn and foundation plantings. Miniaturized into an acre spread or a twenty-foot wide lot, the yard boldly asserts middle- and working- class families' claims as landowners. Home is at once a farm and an estate, bringing together democratic and capitalistic features of our society. This is a culturally charged, dense environment to observe and to interpret.

Sculptural imagery in the garden is related to the garden's function as an idealized landscape. It is helpful for our thinking about contemporary yards to remind ourselves of some attributes of gardens in general and of some historical precedents to ornamental gardens today. All gardens attempt to create an idealized space. Gardens are paradigmatic cultural spaces, geographer Yi-Fu Tuan writes, that embody "cosmic values and environmental attitudes."[2] He notes that despite varied designs, scale, and purposes, all gardens express cultural ideals, putting them in the realm of imagination and artifice. Correspondingly, the garden, Tuan writes, is a site of "playfulness . . . not only do people play in the garden, but the garden itself is the product of a proud imagination able to construct a world full of magical and illusory effects."[3] Gardens are places where both adults and children play. As a result, the imagery found there can often be whimsical and humorous, a trait continued today in joking whirligigs and surprising "yard fannies."

In surveying gardens across history, Tuan notes that early Chinese gardens were built to contemplate the natural world in small, highly designed places separated from urban life. Similar separation from the everyday world appeared in European medieval monastery gardens, where high walls made the space suitable for prayer and scrutinizing one's soul. Dramatic change in European garden design occurred during the Renaissance, when aristocratic gardens expanded and opened to provide long vistas of the grounds and horizons. In an era when the perspective of the individual was celebrated in art and politics, vast gardens were expressions of power as well as prosperity. The grounds at Versailles represent the pinnacle of late Renaissance gardens, built for Louis XIV over a forty-year period beginning in 1661. Its expansive boulevards extend to the horizon, creating views that asserted the reach of the Sun King's power. This kind of formal garden was rejected in eighteenth-century England as a more naturalistic garden style developed. In the picturesque landscape, nature was not arranged along a linear axis, as in the classical garden, but was nonetheless improved upon by human efforts to create winding roads, grandiose clumpings of trees, and inspiring outcroppings of rocks.[4]

These versions of paradise were embodied not only in the design of the garden and its vegetation but also in sculpture placed in the landscape. Much garden sculpture alludes to idealized times, places, and figures. Renaissance gardens refer to the authority and grandeur of classical Greece and Rome. Sculpture of Apollo, Aphrodite, Flora, mythological creatures, and fluttering *putti*—sometimes copies of Greek and Roman statuary, sometimes new interpretations of the subjects—attempted to recreate the order of the classical past. Royalty and aristocrats demonstrated their cultivation and power through art in estate gardens as much as by the art inside their palaces and villas. When Louis XIV used the Greek sun god Apollo as the dominant motif in the gardens at Versailles, no one dared dispute his own appellation as the divine Sun King. In England, the eighteenth-century picturesque garden retained classical references in sculptures of such subjects as Venus, Adonis, and the Dying Gladiator, even while the amount of statuary decreased from earlier formal gardens. Architectural "ruins" or "follies," usually copies of classical or Gothic buildings, were popular elements in the picturesque landscape. These buildings appealed to the Romantic cult of melancholy, which valued natural and artificial landscapes able to evoke bittersweet emotions and thoughtful reflections. These ersatz ruins, with their references to the passing of great civilizations, did just that.[5]

American vernacular gardens and yards, like their grander antecedents, are idealized spaces. They refer to several landscape models. The agrarian landscape—the "middle landscape" of yeoman farmers—acts as one ideal reference in the domestic scene. Drawing from the nation's predominantly agrarian past, landscape historian John Stilgoe writes that the yard embodies the American "epitome of 'the good life.'" The strong pastoralism in American culture has undergirded suburban development, with its requisite grassy yard, now the dominant model for domestic landscapes in the United States. If Jefferson's vision of a nation of yeoman farmers has acted as one model, much of the American landscape has also been shaped by his rational Enlightenment grid, mandated by the Land Ordinance of 1785. In this, the nation was plotted into rectangular sections. That plan still provides the underlying development pattern for most of the United States. Correspondingly, the plan for most urban and suburban areas breaks the grid into block-size parcels that are further divided into rectangular plots for homes and yards. While some suburbs have taken pains to counter the rectilinear layout with winding roads, curving driveways, and sinuous sidewalks, the grid, nonetheless, remains the dominant pattern of landscape organization in most areas of the nation.[6]

In studying the patterns of the American vernacular landscape, this work is premised on several currents in contemporary scholarship. One stems from the field of material culture studies. Scholars in this field assert that objects are important indices to culture and history that can help us to understand realms of experience that often are overlooked or inaccessible when relying on more conventional written sources of evidence. I have tried to understand culture—behavior, beliefs, and expression—by documenting and analyzing garden adornment and by talking to the people who make, buy, and use these objects, an approach that stems from my interests in folklore, folk arts, and folk cultures. I have also attempted to construct a historical perspective on my subject to understand more fully the American landscape we see around us today, an approach that stems from my training in American studies, with an emphasis on American cultural history.

The American home has become a subject that has increasingly attracted the interest of social, architectural, and landscape historians, and my work also is centrally concerned with the American home.

Scholarship on the domestic sphere emerged in the new social history and feminist studies. Scholars claimed that the home was as worthy of serious examination as political arenas or business worlds. Researchers examined the physical design of houses, their configurations in cities and suburbs, and what these patterns reveal about the society that builds and lives in these structures. According to their analyses, domestic architecture reveals aspirations, moral assumptions, and cultural values as much as it reflects economic constraints. The home thus was reconceptualized as sitting at the center of American culture rather than as acting as an enclave separated from the main currents of life, action, and thought. Indeed, the home is one of the supreme embodiments of cultural thought and behavior in any given period. These ideas provided a context for interpreting yard art as a home-based activity in my work.[7]

Another premise of this study concerns the importance of what is termed "the vernacular landscape." Arrangements of buildings, barns, streets, fences, garages, parking lots, telephone poles, curbs, signs, and other small features that make up larger patterns comprise the vernacular landscape. These patterns emerge in a landscape over time as a result of thousands of decisions made by innumerable people, as creators and users of a landscape. The actors can include homeowners, builders, business owners, consumers, and many others who shape how a landscape looks and how it is used. While the vernacular is bound and influenced by official ordinances and by political and commercial development plans, it is not the high-style landscapes designed by architects. Because the vernacular manifests what are often unspoken ideas, it embodies deeply held cultural values and assumptions, making it especially significant to observe and to analyze.

In the late 1970s, cultural geographers began formulating the notion of "the ordinary landscape" and "the vernacular landscape" as important subjects of study. They looked to the work of pioneering landscape historian and teacher John Brinckerhoff Jackson, who had begun writing about such subjects as front yards, garages, and roads in the American landscape in the 1950s, when he began publishing the journal *Landscape*. He served as a leader in the movement to understand common landscapes and their expression of American culture, and his work guided a new generation of American geographers in exploring common landscapes. Among those, Pierce Lewis posited "axioms for reading the landscape," premises upon which the study of vernacular landscapes rests. These include the assumption that "the culture of any nation is unintentionally reflected in its ordinary vernacular landscape."[8]

In addition to its appropriateness in looking at "homemade" landscapes, the term "vernacular" aids our thinking about complicated cultural processes because of its original meaning in reference to language. The vernacular describes a kind of spoken language. It is the vocabulary, pronunciations, word usage, meanings, and slang that a group of people speak in everyday life. It contrasts with the "Queen's English" or the official language of a nation or group that involves proper rules and grammatical structures. The vernacular develops through people's informal interactions within cultural groups, which give rise to shared expressions and meanings. Applying these ideas more broadly, vernacular culture involves an interplay among varied realms of culture: the "official" culture, sanctioned and promoted by educational, political, religious, and artistic institutions; mass culture, circulated by media organizations or involving mass production; and the culture of everyday life that ordinary people create. In relation to material culture, the term "vernacular" has most often been applied to architecture.[9]

The vernacular aptly describes the practices and processes involved in the landscape of the American yard. The design of yards and gardens, the choice of sculpture, and the seasonal patterns of activities involved in its use do not arise from any kind of formal learning in institutions. Most homeowners do not employ landscape architects, trained in the history of garden design, nor do they study the subject much themselves. But neither are gardens and yards merely products of mass culture, the promotions of garden magazines and manufacturers.[10] Patterns in the vernacular domestic landscape have developed from informal learning situations, from family patterns learned in childhood, from the observation of neighbors and of neighborhoods, and from viewing landscapes both nearby and far away from home (in person and in pictures). Folk cultures—particularly ethnic, religious, and occupational communities—generate and shape yard-art practices to some extent. Yet many practices associated with yard art straddle that fascinating territory where elite culture, mass culture, and folk cultures intersect.

I use the term "yard art" to describe a wide range of objects in domestic environments, from the small scale to the grandiose. The environments themselves are designed and sculpted spaces, where their creators have carefully placed statuary and other decorative objects here or there in relation to the house, street, garden, trees, and other elements. Mass-produced and handmade artifacts and various combinations of them can be found there. As a designed space, the yard at times resembles an outdoor room, an outdoor gallery as it were, with sculpture installed within. Yard art can be considered a form of public art, created for public audiences as well as for the pleasure of its creators. These public features may be most apparent in the elaborate environments that often have an architectural scale, such as Simon Rodia's Watts Towers in Los Angeles or S.P. Dinsmoor's Garden of Eden in Lucas, Kansas, which have received a considerable amount of attention and preservation efforts. These kind of large-scale expressions stand at one end of my spectrum of yard art. They are manifestations that share many cultural and aesthetic impulses more commonly expressed at smaller scales.[11]

I use the term "art" with these objects and environments, working with a much more expansive notion of what constitutes art and culture than is often promoted in our society. Drawing on perspectives from folklore studies, I argue that aesthetics are part of culture and that the impulse for order, design, and beauty is expressed in everyday life. Folklorist Michael Owen Jones, for example, has advanced the idea that art is "a feeling for form" and that it is expressed by ordinary people in such designs as home additions and patterned arrangements of garbage cans.[12] The aesthetic impulse, geographer Yi-Fu Tuan argues, "is taken to be not merely a dimension or aspect of culture, but its emotional-aspirational core, both its drive and its goal." The aesthetic response is fundamental, philosopher Arnold Berleant claims in *The Aesthetics of Environment*, to all human engagement with landscape and our surroundings.[13] It is through the ordering of the domestic landscape that we can see aesthetics at work, through the choice of imagery and materials, through the shaping, altering, and care of the landscape. My interest here is always on the behavior, ideas, and values involved in displaying these objects—in the practice—not just in the objects themselves.

This form of art has its viewers, audiences, and critics who participate in a form of popular criticism. For all of its ordinariness, which can sometimes makes it seem invisible, yard art frequently makes a memorable impact on its viewers. During the course of my research, I received countless suggestions about yards I should visit: "You have to see the yard on Bryant and 40th." "You have to see the one in my neighborhood." "Have you seen the plastic eggs hanging from the tree down the block?" "When I was driving back from Boston, I saw." It seemed that no matter to whom I was talking about my research topic—family, neighbors, students, friends, colleagues, acquaintances, strangers—everyone had at least one yard that was a "must see," a yard in their neighborhood or en route to school or work or along the drive to vacation spots or back to hometowns that was spectacular and memorable. These often came not merely as suggestions but as urgings and demands. In some cases I did jot down the address and headed off to find the home that had made such an impression, that stood out as a landmark in their minds. Clearly this material struck a responsive cord with people from varied backgrounds. These countless comments were testimony to the important role that yard statuary and garden design play on a personal level of experiencing and knowing places. They revealed places made visible and memorable.

Yard art has attracted the attention of other scholars, many of whom I owe debts to not only for the data they have uncovered but also for their intellectual frameworks and interpretive ideas. Some researchers have examined primarily large-scale environments. Others have examined one person's yard or one neighborhood. Others have looked at one particular historical period.[17] At the same time that other work guided my own, I felt a nagging sense that a good deal was missing from the discussion of American yard art—a scope and depth that could illuminate local patterns and individual expressions more fully. My aim here has been to construct a useful framework for understanding and interpreting contemporary places within the context of American cultural history. Understanding American yard art becomes a way, then, of also understanding much broader features of American culture.

To do this, I've taken an interdisciplinary approach to my subject, integrating a wide range of sources and methods. I studied yards and interviewed people in four regions and metropolitan areas including Minneapolis and St. Paul, Philadelphia, Atlanta, and Los Angeles, and to some extent, in the surrounding countrysides and towns. These places were selected to provide a national scope to the study and to allow the opportunity to explore regional variations. I also have employed diverse historical sources—garden histories, popular magazines, trade catalogues, advertisements, tourist brochures, slides, photographs, postcards, and stereographs of gardens, and films, among other sources. Middle- and working-class yard art is not always easy to find in historical literature, which heavily favors the gardens of wealthier groups, necessitating that I employ many strategies and sources to uncover the more buried history. That difficulty also accounts for the different voices heard in contemporary and historical situations. With living creators, I was often able to interview people, but in historical materials the voices and perspectives of individual creators were harder to recover.

In this study I claim the flamingo in the American garden as an important cultural artifact of our times.[15] I explore a number of themes and issues that I found most significant to understand American yard art more fully. I look at the "homegrounds" as a designed landscape, a model shaped by a combination of landscape architects, builders, and middle-class tastemakers and homeowners themselves. A central issue that weaves through the text concerns the relationships between public and private landscapes, which I explore in chapters one and two. We often consider public and private space as opposites, viewing the public landscape as the world of business, politics, and work and the private landscape as the world of the home and family life. Yet landscape analysis demonstrates that the public and private in fact interact with each other. The landscape of home, indeed, reflects concerns with some of the same issues as public landscapes. I look historically at the explicit models for residential landscapes, when public landscapes— rural cemeteries and then public parks—were designed and built that had a profound impact on the ideas concerning residential landscapes.

While public parks and the grounds of world's fairs served as models for yards and gardens in the nineteenth century, new public places influenced imagery in American yards over the course of the twentieth century. New forms of leisure such as amusement parks, miniature golf courses, and roadside attractions introduced and inspired new kinds of imagery and new forms of home ornamentation. Increased travel took Americans to faraway settings and climes, and tourists took home souvenirs that circulated exotic imagery, like the pink flamingo, to new regions. Electricity, often showcased in extravagant glory through lighting designs at world's fairs, was adapted not only to buildings in urban centers but also to decorative purposes at home, especially for holiday displays. Other holiday customs for home displays, like those associated with Halloween and Christmas traditions, evolved in this country among immigrant groups, who adapted folk cultures to new settings. Americans have sometimes embraced and embellished these immigrant customs, making them a more widely shared tradition.

Chapter three continues the examination of the impact of travel on American yards in a discussion of the pink flamingo. Here, in terms of the imagery of yard statuary, I explore the pink flamingo in most depth. Iconographic analysis traces the natural history of the bird itself, its presence in American zoos, its cultural representations in Florida souvenirs, architectural details, interior decor, American films, and the pink plastic yard ornament itself. I also note historical changes in its meanings, making use of first-person interviews with people enamored with the bird today. In the latter, I discovered how the iconography is manipulated and altered by users who create new designs for the object. The iconography of the pink flamingo suggests avenues that could be applied to other subjects in the American yard, several others of which I treat only briefly here, as for instance, the black jockey and the gazing globe.

Some of the earliest pink flamingo ornaments were created by industrious homeowners. In chapter four, I consider the creation of yard art as a facet of handiwork in the home. The domestic setting has, in fact, remained a place where handiwork is an important practice and where homemade things are prized possessions, despite the modernization of the home in the twentieth century. In discussing the homemade, this study sketches in some realms of consumer culture that have not been adequately recognized as significant continuations of handcraft traditions. The "do-it-yourself" ethic of American homeowners has been manifest by countless plans to improve and decorate homes and gardens and promoted in a vast prescriptive literature running for a century and a half from the nineteenth-century's *Godey's Ladies Book* to today's *Country Home*. This literature advises homeowners—men and women—from Victorian times to our fin-de-siècle on "how to"—how to make bedroom curtains, how to redecorate the bathroom, how to fix the bathroom plumbing, how to bake a good apple pie, how to design a garden or make a garden bird bath. Countless articles advise consumers on how to use mass-produced products and adapt them to their own homes, and indeed these mass magazines exist in large part to sell those very products to their readers. In these texts, the home is conceived of as a pliable, malleable realm, where older values concerning productivity and handwork coexist with values espousing technological devices and modern styles. These practices make the home an important site for the production of things—and culture—and an important part of what I examine in terms of yard art.

In the final chapter, I note contemporary similarities and differences in contemporary yard art by region, class, religious affiliation, ethnicity, and age. Interestingly, my research challenges the stereotypic image of lawn ornaments enshrined in suburban yards. To the contrary, I found the display of yard statuary crossed boundaries of city, suburb, small town, or rural location and that the suburbs were not necessarily its most favored spot. Other factors, such as age, ethnicity, and class, were stronger factors in its use than municipal status alone. The discussion in this chapter argues that material culture has great power in communicating a complex code of messages and meanings that we read subliminally.

In examining the American yard and its adornments, this study identifies significant features of a shared national culture. The landscapes we live in and care for today were shaped significantly during the nineteenth century, when patterns of land use and an aesthetic for landscapes evolved. Today these deep-seated patterns are inflected by social and cultural factors that spark variations in yard art across the nation, but the underlying patterns remain. I hope that by looking closely at the American yard, we can become more skilled readers of landscape and more appreciative of the aesthetics of our everyday lives.

Notes

1. See Christopher Thacker, *The History of Gardens* (Los Angeles: University of California, 1979) and Derek Clifford, *A History of Garden Design* (New York: Frederick A Praeger, 1963); on American middle-class gardens, see Patricia Tice, *Gardening in America, 1830-1910* (Rochester, NY: The Strong Museum, 1984).

2. Yi-Fu Tuan, *Topophilia* (Englewood Cliffs, NJ: Prentice Hall, 1974), 138.

3. Tuan, *Dominance and Affection: The Making of Pets* (New Haven: Yale University Press, 1984), 29-31.

4. Ibid., 137-49.

5. On Versailles, see Thacker, 147-62. On sculpture and architecture in English gardens, see Paul Edwards, *English Garden Ornament* (London: G. Bell & Sons, 1965), 17-55, 86-119. For discussion of the cult of melancholy and its impact on cemetery and garden design, see Blanche M.G. Linden,

"Death and the Garden; The Cult of the Melancholy and the 'Rural' Cemetery," Ph.D. Dissertation, Harvard University, 1981. Linden explores the intersections between gardens and rural cemeteries in Britain and the United States.

6. John R. Stilgoe, *Common Landscapes of America, 1580-1845* (New Haven: Yale University Press, 1982), 342. On the Land Ordinance of 1785 and the grid as embodiment of Enlightenment thought, see Stilgoe, 87-107; J.B. Jackson, "The Order of the Landscape: Reason and Religion in Newtonian America," in *The Interpretation of Ordinary Landscapes: Geographical Essays*, edited by D.W. Meinig (New York: Oxford Press, 1979), 153-163. Idealized notions about the American home have found ample expression on a popular level. In 1925, Chesla Sherlock, editor of *Better Homes and Gardens*, closed his paean to home ownership, "I Want To Build," with the sentiments: "I want to build a garden where Loveliness dwells. A garden where the lingering pictures of Memory's eyes come into being and all the dreams I have dreamed of Paradise nestle at my feet in my own door yard." See *BH&G,* Dec. 1925, 2.

7. For a discussion on the scholarship concerning the home, see the introduction by Thomas Schlereth for *American Home Life, 1880-1930: A Social History of Spaces and Services* (Knoxville: University of Tennessee Press, 1992), 1-19. In addition, the following have contributed to my thoughts about the American home: Gwendolyn Wright, *Building the Dream: A Social History of Housing in America* (Cambridge, MA: MIT Press, 1981); Delores Hayden, *The Grand Domestic Revolution: A History of Feminist Designs for American Homes, Neighborhoods, and Cities* (Cambridge, MA: MIT Press, 19810; *Redesigning the American Dream: The Future of Housing, Work, and Family Life* (Princeton, NJ: Princeton University, 1977); David Handlin, *The American Home: Architecture and Society, 1815-1915* (Boston: Little, Brown & Co., 1979); Constance Perin, *Everything in Its Place: Social Order and Land Use in America* (Princeton, NJ: Princeton University Press, 1977); Kenneth Jackson, *The Crabgrass Frontier: The Suburbanization of the United States* (New York: Oxford University Press, 1985); Clifford Clark, *The American Family Home 1800-1960* (Chapel Hill, NC: University of North Carolina, 1986); Alan Gowans, *The Comfortable House: North American Suburban Architecture, 1880-1960* (Cambridge, MA: MIT, 1986).

8. See especially J.B. Jackson, *Discovering the Vernacular Landscape (New Haven, Yale University Press,* 1984), John Stilgoe, *Common Landscapes of America, 1580-1845* (New Haven: Yale University Press, 1982), and Pierce F. Lewis, "Axioms for Reading the Landscape: Some Guides to the American Scene" in D.W. Meinig, ed., *The Interpretation of Ordinary Landscapes: Geographical Essays* (New York: Oxford University Press, 1979), 11-32.

9. On vernacular architecture, see Dell Upton and John Michael Vlach, *Common Landscapes of America: Readings in American Vernacular Architecture* (Athens, GA: University of Georgia Press, 1986), and John A. Cuthbert, Barry Ward, and Maggie Keeler, *Vernacular Architecture in America: A Selective Bibliography* (Boston: G.K. Hall & Co., 1985).

10. Virginia Scott Jenkins argues in her book, *The Lawn: A History of an American Obsession* (Washington, D.C.: Smithsonian, 1994), that the well-mown lawn made up of a single species of grass came about because of promotional work of the U.S. Golf Association, the U.S. Department of Agriculture, and home magazines. While I think that Jenkins has done terrific work at charting the development of the lawn and documenting the influences of these organizations and businesses, she fails to account for the reasons that homeowners *wanted* a grassy yard.

11. On large-scale yard art, see John Beardsley, *Gardens of Revelation: Environments by Visionary Artists* (New York: Abbeville Press, 1995); *Naives and Visionaries* (Minneapolis: Walker Art Center with E.P. Dutton, 1974). I trace some of my interest in more commonplace yards to my experience as an intern and tour guide for the *Naives and Visionaries* exhibition at the Walker Art Center.

12. Michael Owen Jones, "Modern Arts and Arcane Concepts: Expanding Folk Art Study" in *Abstracts of Papers Delivered at A Midwestern Conference on Folk Arts and Museums*, Jean E. Spraker, ed. (St. Paul: Minnesota Historical Society Educational Division, 1980), 13-17. Jones refers to an idea voiced by anthropologist Franz Boas, who studied the Northwest Coast Indian cultures in the early twentieth century and argued that their cultural artifacts were "art." On folk cultures and aesthetics, see also Simon Bronner, *The Chain Carvers: Old Men Crafting Meaning* (Lexington, KY: University of Lexington Press, 1985) and *Grasping Things: Folk Material Culture and Mass Society in America* (Lexington, KY: University of Kentucky, 1986).

13. Yi-Fu Tuan, *Passing Strange and Wonderful: Aesthetics, Nature, and Culture* (Washington, D.C.: Island Press, 1994), 2; Arnold Berleant, *The Aesthetics of Environment* (Philadelphia: Temple University, 1992), 1-13.

14. These studies include *Naives and Visionaries*, John Beardsley's *Gardens of Revelations* (cited above), Simon Bronner's discussion of Cal in a Harrisburg, Pennsylvania neighborhood in *Grasping Things* (cited above), 63-86; Daniel Franklin Ward, ed., *Personal Places: Perspectives on Informal Art Environments* (Bowling Green, OH: Bowling Green State University, 1984), Helen Bradley Griebel, "Worldview on the Landscape: A Regional Yard Art Study," *Pennsylvania Folklife* 36 (Autumn 1986): 39-48; Jack Santino, "Halloween in America: Contemporary Customs and Performances," *Western*

Folklore XLII, no. 1 (January 1983): 1-20; Fred Schroeder, "The Democratic Yard and Garden" in *Outlaw Aesthetics: Art and the Public Mind* (Bowling Green, OH: Bowling Green State University, 1977), 94-122; Steven Ohrn, "Gifts to the Street: Landscaping with Yard Art" in *Passing Time and Tradition: Contemporary Iowa Folk Arts* (Des Moines: Iowa Arts Council and Ames, IA: Iowa State University Press, 1984), 84-90; Patricia Grattan, *Flights of Fancy: Newfoundland Yard Art* (St. John's, Newfoundland: Art Gallery of Memorial University, 1983). Little historical research has been done on popular gardens and garden sculpture. Most studies deal only with gardens of the wealthy. Patricia Tice, curator at The Strong Museum in Rochester, has published useful and enlightening work in *Gardening in America, 1830-1910* (Rochester: The Strong Museum, 1984) and in "Gardens of Change," *American Home Life, 1880-1930*, Thomas J. Schlereth, ed., (Knoxville, TN: University of Tennessee, 1992), 190-210.

15. Though focused primarily on literature, scholars of the myth and symbol school of American studies analyzed some artifacts as indices of cultural meaning. See Leo Marx, *The Machine in the Garden: Technology and the Pastoral Ideal in America* (New York: Oxford University, 1964). Alan Trachtenberg explores the history and cultural meanings of an artifact, the Brooklyn Bridge, in *Brooklyn Bridge: Fact and Symbol* (Chicago: University of Chicago Press, 1965). Both of them address issues of landscape—in Marx, the rural landscape, and in Trachtenberg, the urban landscape.

Acknowledgments

Folklorist Ellen Stekert and art historian Karal Ann Marling, both at the University of Minnesota, provided the academic inspiration for this study. Professor Marling's bold, unconventional take on American culture as well as her ongoing support and sharp wit have sustained me over many years now. Judith Martin, Marion Nelson, and David Noble provided guidance and commentary during the course of this work. I am grateful, too, to a number of University of Minnesota faculty members who guided earlier research, or read early versions of this work, or discussed the topic with me. Yi-Fu Tuan, with whom I was fortunate enough to work early in my graduate school days, was enormously influential. Others to thank include John Archer, Gary Alan Fine, Lary May, Rob Silberman, John S.Wright, Gayle Graham Yates, and Lyndel King. Other colleagues who have helped to shape this work include Kate Ratcliff, Shirley Wajda, Betty Bergland, and Jean Spraker.

I would also like to acknowledge the assistance and advice of many people in the areas I traveled for fieldwork. My work would not have been as fruitful or as efficient or as much fun without their help. In Philadelphia, I am grateful to M. Sue Kendall and her husband, Phil, for serving as hosts and guides; to Shirley Wajda for our long, late night conversations; to Gail Stern at the Balch Institute for Ethnic Studies; to Charles Blockson at the Blockson Collection, Temple University; to Janet Evans at the Philadelphia Horticultural Society; to Enola Teeter at the Longwood Gardens Library, to staff at Winterthur Museum Library, to Dorothy Noyes of the Philadelphia Folklife Project for advice on Italian-American neighborhoods and customs, and to my late aunt Ag Duffy and my Duffy cousins, who were helpful aids and generous hosts. In Atlanta, I am grateful for fieldwork suggestions from Dana White professor of American Studies at Emory University; Annie Archibald at the Georgia Folklife Program, and geographer Truman Hartshorn at Georgia State University. Reginald McGhee, an independent curator, generously advised me on neighborhoods to study and introduced me to C.R. Jordan. Thanks also go to Lillian Salter for help and conversation at the Atlanta Historical Society and to Cris Levenduski for her good cheer and hospitality. My travels in Los Angeles were greatly aided by Michael Owen Jones, professor of folklore at University of California-Los Angeles, who provided fieldwork suggestions, contacts, and references; by Mary de la Pena Brown, who served as a guide to East Los Angeles; by Seymour Rosen at SPACES, who shared research materials and fieldwork suggestions; by the late David Gebhard at University of California-Santa Barbara, who offered his general enthusiasm and interest to the project, and by Bill Horrigan, friend, host, guide, and cultural critic. In Washington, D.C., the staff at the Horticulture Library at the Smithsonian Institution were critical to my research there. Neal Johnson and Kate Plaisir lent their inimitable hospitality, support, and friendship.

Research and writing of this work has been supported by a Summer Stipend from the National Endowment for the Humanities, a Work-in-Progress Grant from the Minnesota Humanities Commission, a University of Minnesota Graduate School Dissertation Special Grant, a quarter-leave for professional development through the University of Minnesota Art Museum (now the Frederick R. Weisman Art Museum), and a grant from the Kansas Grassroots Art Association.

I am grateful to the helpful support and advice provided by the staff at Garland Publishing, especially editors Kristi Long and Jerry Nadelhaft and technical assistant Chuck Bartelt. I also owe a great debt to Kathryn (Kay) Hong for her superb editing skills and advice and her generosity.

This work could never have been completed without the extraordinary patience and support of my husband Peter Murphy, the tolerance and good humor of my two daughters Brigid and Annie Rose, and the contributions of my mother Mae, who helped out in innumerable ways, big and small.

Finally, my heartfelt thanks to all of those who let me into their homes and talked to me about their yards and their lives.

The Flamingo in the Garden

I

Yard Art as Public Art
Contemporary Scenes and Historical Antecedents

Harriet Bagasao's yard on a busy corner in Santa Monica, California, features her own unique design of plastic raccoons, plaster cats, cement deer, and pink flamingos. Yet yards resembling hers can be found across the American landscape in cities, suburbs, small towns, and countryside. Many more yards feature similar imagery on perhaps a more modest scale. At her ranch-style home, the narrow plots at the front and sides of the house are entirely devoted to installations of animal statuary, appearing like cartoon versions of museum dioramas. Different species comprise clearly defined spaces. A variety of rabbits inhabit "Bunny Boulevard," and a deer family gathers around a tree stump, with a family of squirrels frolicking nearby. Each ensemble is set off by beds of varicolored garden rocks and by the scalloped edging tiles that enclose each group. Bushy begonias and colorful impatiens grow alongside plastic roses and daisies. Combining all of these elements, Bagasao's yard shows evidence of careful design. Her home serves as a useful model for discussing the public dimensions of American yards, made more vivid and attractive through the display of garden statuary. Using this one California yard as a contemporary starting point, we can explore its historical antecedents—the intellectual, aesthetic, and physical developments that shaped the design of the American landscape we see today.

With its appealing display, Harriet Bagasao's yard functions as a local landmark, moving it from the realm of the strictly personal and private into the public domain. She has, in fact, designed and redesigned the yard with the public view in mind, clearly orienting it to the street. Judging from the responses of neighbors and passersby, the yard succeeds in drawing and delighting many admirers. Bagasao's yard can be considered a vernacular form of public art, of aesthetic expression that appeals to the tastes and pleasures of community audiences.

The concept of public art provides one useful way to think about American yards and the objects displayed there. Until recently, most discussions of public art dealt exclusively with institutional projects— sculptures and murals, primarily, that adorn government and corporate buildings or the grounds of museums and parks and that are created primarily by artists trained in the academy.[1] A shift in public art practice has spurred critical reconsideration of what the "public" dimension of public art entails. Rather than being defined primarily by a work's location and its availability to a public audience (i.e., sited outdoors or in a public building), the location becomes secondary to the relationship of a work to the people who live and work in its vicinity. Artists have become more concerned with working closely with communities. Along with this, interest has grown in community aesthetics, in the process of creating viable public art, and in building mutually beneficial relationships between artists and audiences rather than in perpetuating antagonistic relationships, fostered under modernism, between avant-garde artists and the public.

Yard art—the design of the domestic environment with its embellishments of plants, putti, wishing wells, pink flamingos, and more—acts as a vernacular form of aesthetic expression that engages public audiences. By awakening to the beauty and expressiveness of the everyday environment, we can enrich our ideas about public art, about community aesthetics, and about the public realm.[2] This approach gives us a new view of our domestic spaces, as we see them not strictly divided from the public arena but as participating in civic life and public discourse.

To investigate what constitutes a public sphere, to discover the similarities between public and private American landscapes, this examination takes us from the contemporary west coast to the eastern seaboard of the United States in the mid-to-late nineteenth century. It was then that ideas and designs for prototypical American yards were being formulated by such theorists and practitioners as Andre Parmentier, Andrew Jackson Downing, Frederick Law Olmsted, and Frank Scott, ideas that would have profound impact on the designs and aesthetics of the American landscape for decades to come. These became deeply ingrained and widely accepted landscape patterns, so much so that today, they often become most vividly and fiercely articulated when the aesthetic codes are violated. Before we retrace these developments, Harriet Bagasao's yard warrants a fuller examination.

HARRIET BAGASAO'S YARD AND PUBLIC ART

The public nature of Harriet Bagasao's front yard can be discerned from her own actions and intentions as well as from the reactions of neighbors and other viewers. Bagasao's life story proves her to be an active, involved member of her community, not an isolated eccentric, as vernacular artists are often described.[3] Bagasao is a generous soul who rarely has had an idle moment, even since retiring from the General Telephone Company after twenty-three years of service.[4] She plays organ at Pilgrim Lutheran Church, works with many community and church organizations, invites senior citizen groups to her home, and writes each month to dozens of friends all over the world. Her two sons and their families live in the Los Angeles area and get a good deal of her time and attention. She lives alone now, since the death of her husband in 1985, but she is not isolated from family or friends.

Bagasao began transforming her front yard to its current state after her husband died. Needing activities to fill time previously devoted to her invalid spouse, she was inspired to redesign her yard, which up until then had been filled with simple flower beds. Her initial impulse to redo the yard took more concrete form as she thought about her neighborhood and her grandchildren. "I think the reason I did all this was because of the children," she reflects. After considering what children like, she purchased a cement deer. "I know how much children love them from the Bambi film," Bagasao comments. The neighborhood kids and her own grandchildren *did* love the deer, prompting Bagasao to add more child-friendly statuary, bought at garden supply stores—frogs, "kitty cats," "bunny rabbits," as she describes them, using the language of children.

Bagasao has always been one to immerse herself in home decorating projects, whether wallpapering a bedroom or embroidering a wall hanging. She took to redesigning the yard with the same energy. She pulled out the existing flower beds and covered the ground with white and tan rocks, as some other Los Angelenos do. The rocks would save on the requisite upkeep, a task that would only get harder for a sixty-eight-year-old woman. She bought animal ornaments and

Figure 1. Racoon family in Harriet Bagasao's yard, Los Angeles, California.

arranged them within the yard. Lastly, Bagasao added a religious scene in the corner nearest the street, placing a small statue of Saint Joseph holding the Christ child in the center, flanked by cast plaster cherubs. She reads the figures, however, as Jesus holding a child, creating a display that expresses her love of children. To complete the scene, she added a cast iron plaque featuring a popular garden poem that closes with the line: "One is closer to God in a garden than anywhere else on earth."

Her arrangements of statuary and other elements reveal her careful deliberations. "I'm very particular when it comes to decorating. I always have been," Bagasao says, referring to both her yard and her home interior. Yet she designed the yard with her audience's perspective in mind, not the view from within the house. All animal statuary is positioned to peer out at passersby. On her design process, Bagasao remarks that after she adds an ornament or section to the yard, she walks along the sidewalk to gauge the view from that angle and "to see that everything's in the right place to attract people." Her comment reveals that she did want other people to find it appealing. The proper balance among pieces in each scene and within the yard as a whole are important factors. She fiddles with the placement of each piece to get everything "just right" and often works late in the evenings, when fewer people will interrupt her.

Bagasao's yard art has made her home a focal point in the neighborhood and Bagasao herself into somewhat of a community celebrity. A steady stream of people walk by and comment on her yard to each other or to her if she happens to be outside. Several elementary school teachers bring their students by, and a nursery school instructor uses the display to teach animal names to the children. Strangers have knocked on her door, Bagasao says, "thanking me for a yard like this for the children to enjoy." Others driving by the corner lot stop their cars to get a closer look and sometimes to gather ideas for their own yards. One woman stopped to say that she was making a yard just like Bagasao's and wanted to know how she designed it. At the local drugstore, neighbors recognize her: "Aren't you the lady with all the animals?" Bagasao proudly relates that "just a few weeks ago I had a grandpa and parents and five kids stop. The little girl said, 'Mommy, look, look, there's Bambi.' The parents get so lighted up, too." Her yard has attracted the attention of several reporters and the interests of a curator from the Getty Museum of Art. As far as Bagasao knows, she has not appeared in any publications.[5] "I didn't do it to get publicity,"

Harriet Bagasao modestly insists, "though I have met a lot of wonderful, wonderful people through my yard."

With its inviting imagery and attractive design, Bagasao's yard has become a public site, a place of interaction between the homeowner, neighbors, and the wider community. It is oriented to an audience that responds readily to its imagery and formal design. They show their appreciation by their engagement with the yard, through simple praises—"I like it!"—and with appreciative laughter. This is a vernacular art form that is not articulated in highly sophisticated terms by either its creators or its appreciators. Yet their aesthetic responses clearly convey enjoyment. "I hope they have a sense of humor," Bagasao says about her neighbors.

While Bagasao's yard is not entirely "public"—it still remains private property and is protected from trespass by a cast iron fence—it functions in many ways as a public site and her display functions as public art. The public nature of Harriet Bagasao's yard in Los Angeles does not exist as an isolated example, but is typical of many yardscapes found throughout the nation, even while her yard reflects a regional practice of using colored rocks instead of the more typical green turf. Historians Roy Rosenzweig and Elizabeth Blackmar have recognized the permutations that exist in American ideas and use of "public" space. In discussing Central Park, they argue that even property that is government-owned, which constitutes one notion of public space, has restrictions placed on its use. They identify a "cultural public," the people who claim a space as public through patterns of use, and they discuss how Central Park attracted varied cultural publics that used the park in different ways at different times. In a related way, the viewers and appreciators of yard art constitute a cultural public for the domestic landscape, transforming private property into public space.[6]

THE AMERICAN YARD AND THE PUBLIC SPHERE

That Harriet Bagasao's yard and, in fact, American yards in general serve as communal aesthetic expressions arises from a long cultural history of the front yard as public-oriented space. As it developed in the United States from the mid-nineteenth century onwards, the front yard was oriented to outsiders, served as a site of communication and interaction, and acted as a public expression on the part of the owner. Unlike many cultures that build houses bordering the street or oriented to an interior courtyard, American homes developed historically with an inviting front facing the street and a yard providing a border of green space. A practice that began with country estates of the well-to-do was adopted as a middle-class norm and also influenced the domestic landscape of the American working class. Yards that feature statuary and other decorative elements along with floral displays communicate a heightened sense of the public function of the home exterior. The public nature of the front yard was strengthened by its visual affinities to nineteenth-century public landscapes—the rural cemetery and the public park—that embodied related aesthetic and civic values. The relationships between public and private spaces suggest that it is misleading to draw strict divisions between these two landscape categories. More fluid divisions actually exist between American domestic or private space and public or civic space.[7]

A number of American landscape scholars have noted that the house situated in the midst of a grassy yard open to public view is a unique feature of the American landscape. "Front yards are a national institution—essential to every home," landscape historian John Brinkerhoff Jackson wrote in 1951. More recently, Jackson re-emphasized that idea, calling the front yard "a national space."[8] Front yards and their proper upkeep serve as signs of citizenship and expressions of beauty, representing the idealized landscape of the farm meadow in miniature. That model finds its most typical presentation and duplication in the suburban home, the house in the midst of an expanse of green turf, which now is the most common dwelling in the United States.[9] Historian Kenneth Jackson has argued that the American domestic landscape actually constitutes a new ecosystem comprised of yards, houses, and roads, especially characteristic of the suburb. Garden historian Ann Leighton has noted that the open American front yard, with foundation shrubbery near the house as a kind of framing device, is a characteristically American landscape feature, as is the practice of uniting front yards to create the look of a neighborhood park. Historian Virginia Scott Jenkins recently has traced in considerable detail the emergence of a singularly American "obsession": the lawn. And Fred E.H. Schroeder, a specialist in American popular culture, has traced the front yard aesthetic as part of the vernacular landscape.[10]

The American landscape features noted by these scholars were first espoused in the rhetoric of budding landscape architects in the eastern United States during the middle decades of the nineteenth century, as the nation expanded and settlers built homes. The physical designs they promoted were slowly adopted in practice, first by the wealthier classes on large-scale estates, but eventually becoming a standard design for the built environment.[11] In colonial times and in the early years of the republic, ornamental green space around the home was not emphasized. Most houses were built along the street with side and rear gardens to provide herbs and vegetables. In rural areas, farm yards were work spaces, not areas of aesthetic display. In the mid-nineteenth century, a larger and ornamental green space around the home developed into the American yard. An English term, "yard" originally meant the areas in front of and at the side and back of a dwelling, while "garden" referred to the plantings in the yard. In the United States, yard and garden have merged to include the standard features of a lawn, foundation shrubs and gardens, border plantings, and trees. The garden brought with it traditions of ornamental plantings and statuary.[12] American homegrounds were regarded as public and civic responsibilities. Such figures as Andre Parmentier and Andrew Jackson Downing, though working primarily for the wealthy, were instrumental in promoting a new landscape aesthetic for the general American populace.

Country estates of the wealthy served as exemplary landscapes for the American populace. Many were modeled on the English country home, with grounds designed in the new style of "the picturesque." Dr. David Hossack, a New York civic leader, created one such estate in his Hyde Park. In 1828, Hossack purchased seven hundred acres on the Hudson River and enlisted the Belgian landscape architect Andre Parmentier to design his grounds. By that time, Parmentier had established a nursery business in Brooklyn. Hired to design grounds for numerous country homes in addition to Hossack's along the eastern seaboard, Parmentier employed picturesque principles in designing these landscapes.

Borrowing ideas from British landscape architects such as Lancelot "Capability" Brown and William Kent, Parmentier adapted principles from landscape painting to remold the land itself. Landscapes were to provide "prospects" to a viewer just as a landscape painting presented attractive "views" of a scene. The picturesque abandoned the rectilinear designs of earlier classical Italian and French gardens in favor of a more naturalistic design that was, nonetheless, nature manipulated to create a more heightened view than might appear without human intervention. Entire large trees might be dug up and moved, brooks and streams might be rerouted, and hills recontoured to create a more pleasing scene. In the picturesque, the curvilinear ruled, but it was a line curved by human effort, not necessarily by nature.

On American soil, another idea befitting a democracy was emphasized in the rhetoric on the domestic landscape. The notion that the homes of its citizens should be open to public view has had a lasting impact on the design of residential landscapes. Parmentier himself promoted this idea, thinking that a person's character needed to be expressed in a public manner. In his influential essay, "Landscape and Picturesque Gardens," Parmentier argued that "the front of the house ought always to be *uncovered* . . . A vast idea of the proprietor should be given . . . A row of trees should never be planted in front of the house, particularly when the house has been built in good taste, and at great expense." This idea was echoed and strengthened in subsequent writings on the design of homes, an issue of increasing concern as the nation expanded and built new structures. Corresponding to the vigorous discussions among politicians, artists, and intellectuals about what constituted an American national culture, the ideas about the appearance of homes strengthened the notion that in a democratic society, citizens needed to be involved in civic life and engage in public discussion of ideas. Words were not the only way to express those ideas. They could be embodied in material things—Greek architecture, for instance—but also more broadly in the landscapes and buildings of a republic.[13]

Parmentier introduced principles of the picturesque to the American landscape, but it was Andrew Jackson Downing—architect, nurseryman, landscape designer, and tastemaker—who became its chief proponent and popularizer. Downing designed numerous estate grounds in the eastern United States that served as models for other landscape architects. More importantly, he published several popular books on architecture and landscape design and reached even larger audiences through the magazine *The Horticulturalist: A Journal of Rural Art and Rural Taste*, begun in the 1840s. With articles on growing quinces, strawberries, grapes, and geraniums, instructions for draining swampy grounds, and lyrical essays on the English cottage, *The Horticulturalist* demonstrated that Americans at mid-century were not only eager for scientific and practical knowledge about horticulture but also receptive to instructions on the proper aesthetics for the domestic landscape. Downing designed grounds primarily for wealthy or upper-middle-class patrons who could afford country houses or homes in the early romantic suburbs. Yet he addressed people of more modest means in

The Horticulturalist and in a section on cottages in *The Architecture of Country Houses.*

Downing's work had a profound impact on the development of the American home and its function as an element in public discourse. He promoted the notion that the home publicly expressed the character of its owner. Recasting ideas from John Ruskin in England about the moral purpose of architecture, Downing believed that the appearance of the home—its architectural style and its grounds—should convey to the community evidence of an educated sensibility. The home expressed the owner's character to a public audience. As such, it had a social purpose. Maintaining that Americans "should have good houses," Downing stated, "There is a moral influence in a country home—when, among educated, truthful, and refined people, it is an echo of their character—which is more powerful than any mere oral teaching of virtue and morality." Promoted when Americans were building more homes than ever before, this notion that a home's prospect and appearance had a role to play in the public life of the nation became a critical element embodied in its design.[14]

In Downing's view, the setting for the home was as important as its architecture. Landscape gardening could enhance the public appearance of the home and the views afforded as one approached it. In his first publication, *A Treatise on the Theory and Practice of Landscape Gardening as Adapted to North America* of 1841, Downing discussed landscape gardening as more than the growing of plants: it was the artful design of the homegrounds. Downing advocated the use of ornament or "embellishment," as he called it—such things as shrubbery, vines, flower gardens, and statuary—to define the home, making it an appealing domestic scene for visitors. "When I see the humblest dwelling," he wrote, "adorned by shrubbery and flowers, however small, laid out and preserved in order and neatness, I consider it a good mark . . . and I enter it with pleasant anticipations, but when I see another dwelling . . . a mere ostentatious mass of bricks and mortar, surrounded by grounds, however spacious, slovenly kept, and barren of the fruits of gentle civilization . . . I approach the entrance with distrust."[15]

Downing's design principles were graphically demonstrated in the numerous "before and after" images of houses that illustrated his publications. In these transformation pictures, he typically presented a plain, squared-off house with no yard or other ornamental effects as the "before" image. Then he demonstrated what could be done to infuse the scene with "a little feeling" by adding vines, bay windows, brackets, overhanging eaves, turf, and flowers. The embellishments created the appealing "after" image—a house that looked *homey* and welcoming, showing signs of care and comfort. The profuse illustrations in Downing's works pictured houses open to general view, with families enjoying the yards and gardens.[16] That Downing's aesthetic principles were adopted as the idealized design of the domestic landscape is shown by the incidence of such scenes in the work of the popular printmakers Currier & Ives. The 1869 print entitled *Pleasures of the Country: Sweet Home* shows an ivy-covered house, grassy yard, and happy family closely resembling Downing's earlier prescriptive images. These were pictures of homes that looked outward to the street. The domestic scene could be appreciated from that perspective.

In the post–Civil War era, Frank Jessup Scott further popularized Downing's notions about the visual impact of the homegrounds in his book of 1870, *Victorian Gardens: The Art of Beautifying the Suburban Homegrounds*, which was dedicated to Downing. Writing for "persons of moderate income" rather than to Downing's country gentlemen, Scott adapted the style of the picturesque landscape for businessmen moving to the streetcar suburbs of the 1870s and 1880s. Echoing the notion that the domestic landscape should provide "views" or "frames" to an onlooker, Scott advocated that the homegrounds be designed like a picture with views aimed at neighbors. The "arts of arrangement" needed to be mastered first as the basis of landscape design. Then the reader could move on to plan decorative gardening. Foremost in the aesthetics of this arrangement was the public face of the home. "The beauty obtained by throwing front grounds open together," Scott wrote, "enriches all who take part in the exchange and makes no man poorer." Scott added a tone of moral urgency to the endeavor. "It is unchristian to hedge from the sight of others the beauties of nature which it has been our good fortune to create or secure," he declared, and he called high fences, walls, hedges, and tree rows that blocked out neighbors "unchristian and unneighborly."[17]

Frank Scott was instrumental in making the well-mowed lawn a key landscape feature of the domestic scene, advocating that "a smooth, closely shaven surface of grass is by far the most essential beauty on the grounds of a suburban home"[18] Like carpeting in a nicely appointed room, the lawn provided a finishing touch to the picture presented by the home. Scott advised that the grass be cut at least once a week. Thanks to the development of an inexpensive lawnmower, a closely cropped area of "turf" was feasible by the time Scott was writing. Before 1870, when the Excelsior lawnmower was marketed by Chadborn and Caldwell Manufacturing Company of Newburgh, New York, homeowners had to mow grass with a scythe, an activity usually delegated to servants on large estates or accomplished only once or twice a summer by middle-class homeowners. The services of a family cow or goat could sometimes be called upon to keep grass from growing too high. But the lawnmower helped to accentuate the public nature of the front of the house by making a neat expanse of grass the customary foreground.[19]

Along with a green carpet lawn, ornamental gardening, in general, achieved greater popularity in the post–Civil War era as more middle-class households moved to new ring suburbs bordering city limits. Historian Sam Bass Warner has noted in his classic study of the growth of streetcar suburbs in Boston that the rural ideal of green space surrounding the house, an ideal filtered through Downing and his country residences, was an important factor influencing decisions to move from city to suburb.[20]

Downing's and Scott's ideas continued to be espoused by writers on the domestic scene and by manufacturers of lawn and garden supplies well into the twentieth century in tracts that combined practical advice with philosophical perspectives. We hear those echoes in the words of Leonard Barron in *Lawns and How to Make Them,* a book published in 1906 intended to promote "more and better suburban gardens." Barron devotes a chapter to the making of "lawn pictures," stating, "The greensward is as the canvas on which the artist paints with living trees and shrubs as his pigments. After all the grass is not the picture but only the setting." Similarly, the Long-Bell Lumber Company waxed poetic about lawn furniture in their 1925 catalogue. On the need for an embellished yard, their copy went, "There is a home, somewhere, which offers you an unspoken but tempting invitation to enter, every time you pass it. Its lawn and garden seem to say, 'Come in and rest, or come and play. You're very welcome.' And you want to accept the invitation. It is not a pretentious home. Neither are its lawn and garden large, nor do they bespeak extravagance. What, then, makes it so alluring?" Their products, of course—lawn furniture, pergolas, trellises, and the like.[21]

The lawn was a key element in the visual aesthetic of the home, but it was also a setting for family life. Increasingly in this century, Americans thought of their yards as extensions of the house and discussed yards as outdoor rooms. A lawn was the necessary "carpet" for that room. Using that trope, the authors of *The Outdoor Living Room* (1932) devoted an entire chapter to "A Carpet of Sod":

> There is sure to be a good deal of walking about in the outdoor living room so the flooring and carpeting of our room is an important consideration. And just the same as in the indoor room, the richness and beauty of the carpet will greatly influence the appearance and attractiveness of the room . . . And if we analyze an attractive outdoor room we are sure to agree that there is no one element which contributes more toward its beauty than the carpet of green which extends from border to border. In sunlight and in shadow its cool soothing green is ever a joy to the eye and there is no carpet more delightful to walk upon than a good grass turf.[22]

The aesthetic appeal of turf, then, involved not solely its attractive appearance but also included its appeal to other senses—its luxurious feel underfoot as children and adults worked, played, or relaxed outdoors.

That these aesthetic principles were widely implemented by the turn of the century can be seen in visual sources outside of the popular magazines in which writers espoused home design principles. Judge Hilliarson of Des Moines, Iowa, documented one example of the wide acceptance of the landscape styles in a stereograph of his home and yard taken at the turn of the century. The judge is seen proudly posing with his family in the front yard of their modest wood frame house. The mown yard with its ornamental gardens and urns asserts that these are cultured midwesterners, even if living in the relative wilds of Iowa. Viewed by the judge's neighbors or by complete strangers far from Iowa, this stereograph is one in a genre of Victorian stereographs of middle-class homes and more lavish estates. Nearly every Victorian parlor included a stereoscope, a device that created a slightly three-dimensional view of the image. Cultural historian Shirley Wadja has argued that these artifacts reflected the interests, preoccupations, values, and emerging sensibilities of middle-class Americans, who displayed them and viewed them in Victorian parlors for entertainment and instruction.[23] Stereographs of attractive yards both reflected and promoted a shared aesthetic for the home landscape.

Images of attractive American yards also circulated in postcard form. In his 1910 postcard, an Austin, Texas, man identified as "Oscar"

wrote to his "dear friend" Miss Signe Swanson in Chicago, praising the
beauty of middle-class front yards in her city. "This is one of those
great views I told you about sometime ago," he wrote, describing the
photograph of Chicago's Humboldt Boulevard, where well-mown
lawns and neat flower gardens fronted middle-class homes all down the
block.[24] Postcards featuring estate gardens of the wealthy were popular,
too, well into the twentieth century. The Swan House in Atlanta,
Georgia was one such site enshrined through the postcard, featuring its
Italianate gardens with classical statuary arranged on terraces and near
pools. A tourist to Tarrytown-on-Hudson in 1908 could impress a
friend back home with a postcard of the elaborate grounds of
Rockwood Hall, the residence of William Rockefeller. By the 1930s,
travelers were buying postcards with views of homes of the new
aristocracy, such as Paramount star Claudette Colbert's gardens and
home overlooking Hollywood. Whether of middle-class home or estate
grounds, postcards circulated models of impressive homegrounds to
average folks around the nation. They demonstrate that designs of
private homes, yards, and gardens participated in a public culture that
was able to capture the public eye and pocketbook. That discourse on
the home and yard was a facet of community life also noted by
sociologists Robert Lynd and Helen Merrell Lynd in their in-depth
study of Muncie, Indiana, in the 1920s and revisited in the mid-1930s.[25]

EMBELLISHMENTS IN THE YARD AND GARDEN

The cultivated homegrounds espoused by Downing, Scott, and later
writers was an art in itself, and it was also a place for art. Gardens, after
all, have served throughout history as outdoor galleries. Compared to
Renaissance and classical gardens, those in the picturesque style
reduced the quantity of statuary in order to accent natural features—
albeit natural features artificially shaped and refined. The picturesque
garden still made a place for statuary and other accents and adornments
as well as for architecture in miniature in the forms of old mills,
hermitages, classical temples, ornamental farms, and grottoes. Downing
devoted an entire chapter of *Landscape Gardening* to the subject of
these "embellishments," the features that added a finishing touch to the
grounds themselves. Embellishments could include natural plantings
like flower gardens and parterres, functional objects like rustic benches
and baskets, and pure ornament like statuary and urns. These features

contributed richness and unity to the scene, more fully integrating the aesthetics of the house with those of the yard.

Art in American gardens borrowed readily from varied cultural traditions, including both Renaissance and English picturesque gardens styles. When yards became an expected part of the American domestic landscape in Victorian times, the garden was to be a setting for art as it was in Europe, and an easy way to achieve refinement was to incorporate artistic elements from European culture. "Culture" with a capital "C" was at the time considered to be European. That was where American artists went to get training, where artistic styles offered models for untrained American artists, where the latest fashions originated, and where wealthy travelers on the Grand Tour achieved refinement.

Some garden sculpture was imported from abroad, like those written about by Gertrude Jekyll, the British gardener and writer. Widely read and admired in America, Jekyll did much to circulate knowledge of European gardens in her publications. While she is now credited primarily with promoting the perennial border garden and influencing Americans to adopt a more simplified, informal garden design, she also promoted high-style gardens and garden sculpture from Europe's grandest estates. Her 1918 book, *Garden Ornament*, featured photographic plates of the gardens of famous European estates, chock full of classical sculpture, such as the marble statue of the Roman god Mercury at Holme Lacy estate or the peasant figures posed in the garden at Tyninghame, Haddingstonshire. Taste makers like Jekyll had a strong impact on Americans, from those who loved her English country garden to those who wanted to emulate the high styles of European gardens.[26]

"Weld" was just such an estate garden, located in Brookline, Massachusetts. During the first half of this century, it was one of the most photographed and well-known private gardens in the United States. Weld was built by millionaires Larz Anderson and Isabel Weld Anderson. Shortly after their marriage in 1897, they purchased a Brookline estate for a summer home as a retreat from their main residence in Washington, D.C. They commissioned architect Charles A. Platt to design gardens and appoint them with European statuary, beginning first with the Italian garden. (Larz Anderson had worked at the American embassy in Italy, and the couple had honeymooned there.) The Andersons planned Weld in multiple stages, eventually building the estate to a total of 78 acres. They brought in other popular interest in things Japanese, and an English garden was built in 1910.[27]

Each section was outfitted with sculpture and architectural features. Antique columns and statuary imported from Rome embellished the Italian gardens. But rather than placing Roman gods on the balustrade in this section, busts of American heroes Abraham Lincoln, George Washington, and Benjamin Franklin were displayed. The Andersons added their own idiosyncratic touches elsewhere in Weld that reflected their interests, alliances, and taste. In the Japanese garden, a bronze eagle with spread wings dominated the bonsai and Buddha statues. In some cases Larz and Isabel themselves bought garden statuary while on tours abroad. Inspired by English and German gardens, Larz Anderson purchased ceramic woodland gnomes in 1917 and began a fairy tale garden in one section of the estate. That was to be a theme that ran through other scenes at Weld, for it corresponded to Isabel's profession as a published writer of fairy stories. The gardens at Weld had a wider impact on American gardens, as many middle-class visitors were welcomed to tour the estate, which Isabel Anderson also opened for theatrical and charity events. Millions more saw photographs, drawings, and plans of Weld's impressive gardens in popular magazines. The eclectic mix of garden styles at Weld represents an American characteristic in garden design and embellishment. The Andersons' proclivity to adopt and absorb wide-ranging styles and images has translated more broadly into vernacular yards, as still seen today in Harriet Bagasao's home landscape.[28]

Few Americans of the Andersons' day were as financially blessed as they were to enlist architects or travel to Europe to purchase statuary. Middle-class homeowners could, by Victorian times, purchase copies of classical statuary in less expensive versions made of cast iron, lead, stone, ceramic, and plaster. Classical figures, urns, and furniture became popular additions to middle-class yards. Many settees in cast iron mimicked natural forms. Iron was molded to look like woven tree branches and vines, similar to the designs of rustic furniture, or they took on the form of grapes and flowers.[29]

American iron foundries had expanded in the mid-nineteenth century when techniques for producing a durable cast iron were perfected. Along with the trains, arch bridges, and machinery needed for an industrializing nation, cast iron was adapted for ornamental purposes. Cast iron was the first popular material for middle-class garden embellishment. J.W. Fiske Ironworks of New York and E.T.

Barnum Wire and Iron Goods of Detroit were just two manufacturers of
a range of yard statuary for a range of income groups. The 1894
catalogue for E.T. Barnum, for instance, featured five-foot-high cast
iron deer that could substitute for the real deer parks of the aristocracy
at ninety-five dollars each, a hefty cost at the time that only the upper-
middle-class or the wealthy could afford. Folks of more middling
income could purchase "wide awake rabbits" for just under two dollars;
several iron bunnies set across the lawn made them "look as natural as
life."[30]

In addition to visiting famous gardens or viewing photographs of
them, Americans learned how to display their newly purchased garden
statuary at garden shows, events that grew to be very popular by the
end of the nineteenth century. Along with presenting new varieties of
plants and flowers, these exhibitions included displays of highly
designed gardens, complete with fountains and garden statuary.
Horticulture buildings at the world's fairs of the era exposed large
audiences to new varieties of plant species, to new garden products, and
to the aesthetics of garden display. At the 1876 Centennial Exposition
in Philadelphia, for example, Horticulture Hall served as a prime
attraction, with displays by seed companies, manufacturers, and florists.
Garden ornaments were featured in its exhibitions. In one section, a
flower display was accented with an Italian terra cotta sculpture of two
waifish children standing under an umbrella, titled "Out in the Rain." It
soon was copied in cast iron by American manufacturers, who adapted
it as a fountain finial, with water spraying from the top of the umbrella,
and sold it to upper-middle-class homeowners.[31]

Late nineteenth-century American artists and manufacturers
increasingly produced their own varieties of garden sculpture rather
than relying on European imports. Their work often did, nonetheless,
retain classical references. Garden statuary thus served as an outdoor
parallel to the mass-produced artworks popular inside the home—
miniature plaster casts of famous statuary from antiquity and
chromolithographs of revered paintings. As evidence of one's
familiarity with art and culture, these objects were valued for their
edifying impact on the domestic scene and for the favorable
impressions they were able to make on one's neighbors, friends, and
business associates.[32]

American garden sculpture continued to reach larger markets well
into the 1920s. This occurred despite the sharpening of lines between
original works of art and reproductions drawn by the cultural elite at the

time. At the turn of the century, American museums and other tastemakers wanted to transform the "fine" arts into a more rarefied pursuit that separated them from the *hoi polloi*. American museums stopped exhibiting plaster casts of famous statuary, a practice that had been central to their earlier policies. In the domestic landscape, however, the display of sculptural reproductions remained a common practice, asserting the popular notion that arts had a necessary place in everyday life. For American sculptors, mass-produced garden statuary provided critical sources of income. In the 1920s, New York City galleries advertised original works by American artists as well as copies of European masterpieces. All could be purchased in expensive bronzes but also in plaster and cement versions for middle-class customers.[33]

In both theory and practice, an aesthetic—ideas, values, and models—for the American domestic landscape was widespread by the turn of the century. It was defined by the single family home in the midst of a public-oriented plot of land, fronted by a well-kept expanse of lawn accented by shrubbery, flower gardens, and garden embellishments. These aesthetic principles were shared between the domestic sphere and public spaces. Downing and his followers worked freely between designing private estates and public grounds. In their views, domestic and public landscapes shared similar principles, with the public spaces executed at larger scale. Both landscape types responded to the growing need for open space, fresh air, and the enjoyment of nature and art. Both were considered appropriate to a democratic society. Despite the different legal status of public and private property, landscapes of the rural cemetery, the public park, the suburb, and the homegrounds were based on similar aesthetic principles.

PUBLIC LANDSCAPES

Most Americans first came into contact with public landscapes that embodied principles of the picturesque through the rural cemetery movement of the 1830s through the 1860s. By the 1830s, many churchyard cemeteries had become overcrowded and could not expand, hemmed in as they were by city streets and buildings. At the same time, municipal leaders and medical experts became increasingly concerned with the spread of disease in urban areas, brought on, in part, by decomposing corpses. New cemeteries built just outside the city, they thought, could help to alleviate these problems. Not "rural" in the sense of being in the open countryside, these sites were built just beyond city borders, where large tracts of land were still available.

Mount Auburn, the first American rural cemetery, opened in Boston in 1831. It was laid out under the leadership of doctor and botanist Jacob Bigelow and paid for by the Massachusetts Horticultural Society. Abandoning the grid layout used in earlier cemetery design, Mount Auburn was modeled on the picturesque English landscape, with winding roads, expanses of grass, and exotic architecture and statuary. The meandering avenues of Mount Auburn were named after trees— Elm, Willow, Cedar (forerunners of street names in suburban subdivisions across the country today). Appealing to romantic sensibilities, the architecture and statuary in Mount Auburn tended toward the exotic: an Egyptian entrance gate, a Gothic chapel, and a sphinx, alongside the more customary gravestones of Boston's civic and religious leaders.[34]

Mount Auburn soon became a retreat for all classes of Bostonians. They visited the cemetery in droves, taking carriages and horse-drawn wagons there not only to visit graves of the deceased but also to relax and socialize in the open air and stroll the grounds, appreciating the greenery and statuary. The cemetery was used as a pleasure-ground soon after it opened. By the 1850s, Mount Auburn had become a local tourist attraction, mentioned in visitors' guides to Boston. By that time, visitors could purchase pocket guides to the grounds and its statuary for twenty cents. Ministers hoped that the grounds would provide moral instruction to its visitors by memorializing the lives of illustrious persons and encouraging reflection on human mortality. If visitor behavior was any indication, however, Mount Auburn was not as edifying as civic leaders may have hoped. Visitors used the place more as a pleasure ground than for moral instruction.[35]

Rural cemeteries were established just outside many American cities in the 1840s and 1850s. Philadelphia opened Laurel Hill in 1836. New York City established Greenwood Cemetery in 1838. Green Mount in Baltimore and Spring Grove in Cincinnati followed. These new public landscapes prompted Andrew Jackson Downing to declare that, in the absence of large public gardens, cemeteries did "a great deal to enlarge and educate the popular taste in rural embellishment." Downing was accurate in thinking that cemeteries would be important magnets for the general public. Over 30,000 people a year flocked to places like Laurel Hill in Philadelphia.[36] As with Mount Auburn, most people visited local cemeteries for a pleasant outing rather than to visit gravesites of friends or relatives.

With their open green spaces and picturesque landscapes, rural cemeteries provided antidotes to urban noise, congestion, and dirt. Cemeteries spurred a movement at mid-century for the establishment of public parks. Andrew Jackson Downing again played an important role in their development and appearance, even though he died in a steamboat accident in 1852, before the great public parks were actually built. Just prior to his death, Downing praised the idea of a major public park for New York City—it would become Central Park—saying that such a place would be "a green oasis for the refreshment of the city's soul and body." He went on to argue that it must comprise at least 500 acres, not the meager 160 that the mayor was proposing.[37] In 1852, 750 acres were set aside for the park.

Downing's partner, Calvert Vaux, went on to work with landscape architect Frederick Law Olmsted, also a friend of Downing, on the winning design in the competition for Central Park in 1858. In the design for Central Park and in his many other major landscape commissions across the continent, Olmsted had an inestimable impact on American landscape design. His work promoted a naturalistic landscape that could offer antidotes to the rigid grid system of cities and to their congestion, noise, and tension. He believed that landscape design could not only create pleasing places but also could have a social impact by offering similar amenities to rich and poor alike and by bringing diverse cultures and classes together in one place.[38] Central Park was completed in 1863. In its design, Olmsted utilized picturesque principles of landscape design—large areas of grassy knolls, winding avenues, forested areas, and greensward accented by pavilions and concert halls. It provided New York's one-and-a-half million residents with opportunities to enjoy an expansive naturalistic setting.

Olmsted insisted that wild nature was not appropriate for parks. They must show the manicured mark of human design on the landscape. Open spaces in parks should not look like unkempt fields but should resemble well-kept lawns. Shrubs, plants, and trees would need pruning, just as they did in home gardens. Olmsted emphasized natural features and kept architectural and sculptural accents to a minimum, believing that what New Yorkers needed most in the park was a respite from city streets through immersion in nature. His and Vaux's plans were altered over the years to accommodate major buildings (among them the Metropolitan Museum of Art), to meet the demands of many civic groups, who added more sculpture, often dedicated to honorary figures, and to respond to new ideas about recreation, resulting in the addition of sports fields. In the post–Civil War period, Central Park became the grand model followed by municipalities throughout the nation as more and more cities built public parks. Olmsted was frequently invited to design them. His major work in Central Park has been called "the greatest civic achievement in the United States in the nineteenth century" and in historian David Schuyler's estimation, "More broadly, the parks, parkways, and park systems it inspired are undoubtedly also that century's greatest contribution to city planning in America."[39]

Public parks served as examples of what the public could do on a smaller scale in the domestic landscape. Parks required the same kind of gardening care demanded by the homegrounds. Visits to public parks and guidebooks published about them acquainted Americans with plant species that could grow in local climates, with pleasing designs, and with garden accents. The correspondence between public parks and residential design took its most common form in the development of American suburbs.[40]

Alexander Jackson Davis had designed the first "romantic suburb," Llewellyn Park, New Jersey, in 1857, working with Llewellyn S. Haskell, a New York businessman who purchased the original 350 acres of what would eventually be a 750-acre planned community located twelve miles west of New York City. Davis was a friend of Downing and an admirer of Olmsted, and he put their ideas into practice in planning Llewellyn Park. The suburb was designed as a naturalistic landscape. With forested areas, winding roads, and planned prospects, it was residential and a "proto-park," a characteristic recognized in its name. One section of Llewellyn Park was designated as a parklike space for its residents, but it was not open to the general public. Haskell had donated a fifty-acre area that was retained as common park space, known as "the Ramble," and this was appointed with architectural and ornamental accents such as summer houses, kiosks, rustic seats, and rustic bridges. Many other suburban communities with parklike features were planned in the 1850s but curtailed by the advent of the Civil War.[41]

Olmsted was indebted to Davis's Llewellyn Park in developing his plan for Riverside, Illinois, just after the war in 1868. Located north of Chicago, Riverside had a parklike landscape, created by large open lots, a large, open parkway system along the Des Plaines River, and small parks dispersed throughout the community. Those features along with curvilinear roadways thickly planted with trees marked a contrast to Chicago's urban grid to the south and created a feeling of rural spaciousness. Even today, when development has surrounded Riverside, its original design still conveys a marked landscape shift from the city. Olmsted designed other suburban communities, such as Roland Park, near Baltimore, Pinehurst, North Carolina, and Tarrytown, New York, but according to Albert Fein, Riverside was his most comprehensive plan and stands as "America's foremost example of nineteenth-century community design. . . . "[42]

By century's end, the picturesque landscape—whether embodied in the domestic landscape, the suburb, the rural cemetery, or the public park—expressed a widespread American response to urbanization. These designed landscapes employed similar natural features and vegetation. Embellishments of statuary, vases, urns, and outdoor furniture were common to both civic and domestic landscapes. Manufacturers of garden statuary and furniture at the time sold their wares to bereaved families, cemetery operators, park managers, and homeowners alike. The American domestic landscape, therefore, was not necessarily a separate spatial category but shared common design aesthetics and ideology with public spaces.[43]

These aesthetic landscape conventions had a major impact on the design of the twentieth-century American landscape. The places designed in that era serve as embodiments of earlier aesthetics and ideologies and as models for later designs. In residential landscapes, the nineteenth-century propensity toward public orientation of American homes continued to serve as the predominant design model for the twentieth century domestic landscape. The public function of homegrounds, particularly of the front yard, has continued to play an important, if overlooked, role in public life. From Muncie, Indiana, in the 1920s and 1930s, as described in Robert and Helen Merrell Lynd's Middletown studies, to the Levittown of post–World War II suburbs, as described by Herbert Gans, the aesthetics of the homegrounds play a significant role in a visual conversation among neighbors in communities across the nation.[44]

In the late twentieth century, the aesthetic conventions established over a hundred years ago still carry immense power as established models for domestic landscapes. Yard design and maintenance continue to physically express a resident's good neighbor status, so much so that diverging from accepted standards can mean legal retribution enforced through local housing inspectors. In recent years, homeowners in some communities have attempted to challenge the national norms for yard upkeep by not mowing their lawns, by letting weeds take over, by planting prairie grasses, and by devoting more front lawn space to ornamental gardens. Many have received harsh comments from neighbors, who express worries about weeds spreading to their yards, attracting garbage and vermin, and lowering the quality of their neighborhood and the resale value of their homes. Some cases have been taken to court to challenge those norms.

These kinds of controversies over the aesthetics of landscape design demonstrate the continued interplay between public and private landscapes. In 1995, when the Minneapolis Park Board decided to save funds by not mowing many park grounds, their plan caused a furor among Minneapolis residents. Letters to the editor in local newspapers argued that unkempt parks encouraged people to throw garbage there, attracted rats and bugs, and prevented them from using the parks for some of their favorite pastimes.[45] The unkempt park land was a visible—and symbolic—sign of the perceived decline of the city, during a summer that also witnessed a record-breaking homicide rate. The Minneapolis Park Board gradually modified their no-mowing plans. As cases like these demonstrate, communities have considerable investment in the aesthetic principles that underlie the design of the public spaces and domestic landscapes.

Some writers and homeowners challenge the existing landscape norms, but most Americans continue to find the mown lawn—J.B. Jackson's "national institution"—a pleasing landscape, despite grumbles about its upkeep. Many Americans hire lawn services in order to maintain the established visual codes and community expectations. Others, especially in drier regions, have taken the route of Harriet Bagasao in Los Angeles, who took out her turf and covered the yard with colored rocks.[46] As this discussion of both aesthetic and democratic principles expressed in the American yard attests, those advocating changes to the landscape conventions established over the past 150 years or more will need to take into account more than ecological issues alone. During its development, the American yard—with its lawn, gardens, embellishments, and statuary—has become more than simply private property or a natural landscape. It is a complex public, civic, and artistic environment. It is one of our most pervasive forms of public art.

NOTES

1. Interest in issues related to institutional works of public art has mushroomed in the past twenty years as "per cent for art" projects have been implemented for new building construction by local, state, and federal governments. A growing body of literature chronicles this movement. Major publications include Erika Doss, *Spirit Poles and Flying Pigs: Public Art and Cultural Democracy in American Communities* (Washington, D.C.: Smithsonian, 1995). Doss critically analyzes the debates about public art, arguing that much of the controversy that public art can generate arises from an erroneous conception of what the "public" in the art involves. She argues for the close involvement of the communities with artists in the creation of public art so that it embodies public interests and aesthetics. Doss addresses the importance of process in the creation of public art. See also *Public Art Review,* a national journal published by FORECAST Public Artwork, a public art organization based in St. Paul, Minnesota. FORECAST has fostered a progressive idea of public art that expands it from being primarily visual art to include art forms such as performance and literature. See also Harriet F. Seinie and Sally Webster, *Critical Issues in Public Art: Content, Context, and Controversy* (New York: HarperCollins, 1992); John Beardsley, *Art in Public Places: A Summary of Community-Sponsored Projects Supported by the National Endowment for the Arts* (Washington, D.C.: Partners for Livable Places, 1981); Patricia Fuller, *Five Artists at NOAA: A Casebook on Art in Public Places* (Seattle: Real Comet Press, 1985). For historical treatment of issues in public art, see Karal Ann Marling, *Wall to Wall America: A Cultural History of Post-Office Murals in the Great Depression* (Minneapolis: University of Minnesota Press, 1982) and Michele H. Bogart, *Public Sculpture and the Civic Ideal in New York City, 1890-1930* (Chicago: University of Chicago Press, 1989).

2. By "vernacular" I mean, following J.B. Jackson, the commonplace landscape created and modified by countless individuals—the general populace—"through local custom, pragmatic adaptation to circumstances, and unpredictable mobility." See the preface to his *Discovering the Vernacular Landscape* (New Haven: Yale University Press, 1984), ix-xii. Folklorists studying folk arts and material culture have turned their attention to the domestic landscape. See, for instance, Simon Bronner, *Grasping Things: Folk Material Culture and Mass Society in America* (Lexington: University Press of Kentucky, 1986), especially chapter "Entering Things," 23-86; Daniel Franklin Ward, ed., *Personal Places: Perspectives on Informal Art Environments* (Bowling Green, OH: Bowling Green State University Popular Press, 1984).

Latter includes diverse essays on public art displays in domestic environments throughout the United States. For suggestive discussion of the importance of vernacular expressions in the urban landscape, see Barbara Kirschenblatt-Gimblett, "The Future of Folklore Study in America: The Urban Frontier," *Folklore Forum* 16 (1983): 214-20.

3. A dominant art world attitude toward vernacular artists has been a romantic kind of primitivizing. Most recently John Beardsley has written about the large-scale environments created by Simon Rodia, S.P. Dinsmore, and Tressa Prisbrey in relationship to the history of fine arts in *Gardens of Revelation: Environments by Visionary Artists* (New York; Abbeville Press, 1995). Following the thinking of surrealist artists earlier in this century, Beardsley argues that the creators of these large-scale sites are alienated from their communities. For an excellent critique of the attitudes that have prevailed toward these artists, see Michael D. Hall and Eugene W. Metcalf, Jr., *The Artist Outsider: Creativity and the Boundaries of Culture* (Washington, D.C.: Smithsonian Press, 1994). In one essay in that volume, Michael Owen Jones argues that because many researchers have not looked for traditions or community ties, these artists have been perceived as isolated eccentrics.

4. Interview with Harriet Bagasao by author, Los Angeles, November 9, 1988. Sadly, in 1995, Harriet Bagasao's family informed me that their mother had died that year and that her house had been sold.

5. Newspapers frequently do feature stories on highly decorated yards, whether with statuary, holiday displays, or flower gardens.

6. Roy Rosenzweig and Elizabeth Blackmar, *The Park and the People: A History of Central Park* (Ithaca: Cornell University Press, 1992), 5-7. The public nature of yard displays has been noted by other scholars, for instance, see Fred E.H. Schroeder, "The Democratic Yard and Garden" in his collection *Outlaw Aesthetics: Art and the Public Mind* (Bowling Green, OH: Bowling Green University Popular Press, 1977), 105; Steven Ohrn, "Gifts to the Street: Landscaping with Yard Art" in *Passing Time and Tradition: Contemporary Iowa Folk Arts* (Des Moines: Iowa Arts Council and Ames, IA: Iowa State University Press, 1984), 84-90; and Patricia Grattan, *Flights of Fancy: Newfoundland Yard Art* (St. John's, Newfoundland: Art Gallery of Memorial University Press, 1983). For discussion of articulation of aesthetics in folk arts, see Michael Owen Jones, *The Handmade Object and Its Maker* (Berkeley: University of California Press, 1975).

7. The problematic notion of the public sphere and even of "the public," concepts central to a democratic society and democratic processes, has been explored in Bruce Robbins, ed., *The Phantom Public Sphere* (Minneapolis: University of Minnesota Press, 1993), especially editor's introduction (vii -

xxvi) and Nancy Fraser, "Rethinking the Public Sphere: A Contribution to the Critique of Actually Existing Democracy," 1-31. Many scholars writing about the single family home have emphasized the isolation of the nuclear family and the separation of domestic and civic space. For instance, see Gwendowlyn Wright, *Building the Dream: A Social History of Housing in America* (NY: Pantheon Books, 1981; rpt.Cambridge, MA: MIT Press, 1983). She notes that the smaller bungalow homes built in the early twentieth century did away with many extra bedrooms and storage areas, which had been necessary to accommodate large numbers of children and extended family in the Victorian home. Hence, the nuclear family of parents and a smaller number of children began to dominate American households during the early part of this century, 171-172. Dolores Hayden recommends that Americans redesign domestic space to overcome the isolation of the single family home, an ideal no longer suited to contemporary life, in *Redesigning the American Dream: The Future of Housing, Work and Family Life* (New York: W.W. Norton, 1984). Architectural historians and geographers interested in environmental perceptions of buildings and designed space have noted the communicative aspects of the front of American homes and of buildings more generally. The best source on this is Amos Rappaport, *The Meaning of the Built Environment: A Nonverbal Communication Approach* (Beverly Hills, CA: Sage Publications, 1982). He discusses the meaning of "front" throughout the work; see for instance, 22, 77, 189.

8. J.B. Jackson, "Ghosts at the Door," *Landscape* Autumn 1951: 3-9. This interview with Jackson appeared in the film *Figure in a Landscape: A Conversation with J.B. Jackson*, produced by Janet Mendelsohn and Claire Marino, 1988. See Jackson's publications, particularly *The Necessity for Ruins* (Amherst, MA: University of Massachusetts Press, 1980) and *Discovering the Vernacular Landscape* (New Haven, CT: Yale University Press, 1984).

9. According to the 1990 U.S. census, more Americans live in suburbs than in urban centers or in rural areas and small towns for the first time in history.

10. Kenneth T. Jackson, "A Nation of Suburbs," *Chicago History*, (Summer 1984): 6-25. For a more fully developed discussion of these ideas, see his chapter "Home, Sweet Home: The House and Yard" in his *Crabgrass Frontier: The Suburbanization of the United States* (New York: Oxford University Press, 1985), 45-72; John Stilgoe, *Common Landscapes of America, 1580 to 1845* (New Haven, CT: Yale University Press, 1982), 342; Ann Leighton, *American Gardens of the Nineteenth Century* (Amherst, MA: University of Massachusetts Press, 1987), 11; Virginia Scott Jenkins, *The Lawn: A History of an American Obsession* (Washington, D.C.: Smithsonian,

1995). Fred E.H. Schroeder, *Front Yard America: The Evolution and Meanings of a Vernacular Domestic Landscape* (Bowling Green, OH: Bowling Green University Press, 1993).

11. Jenkins argues that, in practice, the lawn did not become the dominant norm for American households until the mid-twentieth century.

12. On gardening in colonial America and in the late eighteenth century, see Ann Leighton, *Early American Gardens: "For Meate or Medicine"* (Boston: Houghton Mifflin, 1970). For the meaning of "yard" see Leighton, *American Gardens of the Nineteenth Century*, 81.

13. Leighton, *American Gardens of the Nineteenth Century*, 130.

14. Downing, *The Architecture of Country Houses* (New York: Dover Publications, 1969; repr., D. Appleton & Co., 1850), xviii.

15. "Notes on the State of Rural Arts," *The Horticulturalist* I (September 1846): 111.

16. For examples of "before" and "after" illustrations, see Downing, *The Architecture of County Houses*, 78-80; and Downing, "The New England Suburban Dwelling," *The Horticulturalist* II (December 1847): 31-32.

17. Frank Jessup Scott, *Victorian Gardens: The Art of Beautifying the Suburban HomeGrounds* (Watkins Glen, NY: American Life Books, 1982; repr., D. Appleton & Co., 1870), 60-61. According to David Schuyler in his introduction to the facsimile reprint, Scott's book endured in popularity: It was reprinted in 1872, 1873, 1881, and 1886.

18. Scott, 107.

19. Patricia Tice, *Gardening in America, 1830-1910* (Rochester, N.Y.: The Strong Museum, 1984), 65; M. Christine Klim Doell, *Gardens of the Gilded Age: Nineteenth-Century Gardens and Homegrounds of New York State* (Syracuse, N.Y.: Syracuse University Press, 1984), 33.

20. Sam Bass Warner, *Streetcar Suburbs: The Process of Growth in Boston (1870-1900)* , 2d ed. (Cambridge: Harvard University Press, 1980), 11-14, 143-45.

21. Leonard Barron, *Lawns and How to Make Them,* (New York: Doubleday, Page & Co., 1914; repr. 1906), preface, n.p. and 135, and *The Book of Lawn Furniture* (Kansas City, Mo.: Long-Bell Lumber Company, 1925). The latter is from the trade catalogue collections of Winterthur Museum Library.

22. Leonidas W. Ramsey and Charles H. Lawrence, *The Outdoor Living Room* (New York: Macmillan Co. 1932), 87.

23. Shirley Wajda, "A Room with a Viewer: The Parlor Stereoscope, Comic Stereographs, and the Psychic Role of Play in Victorian America" in

Hard at Play: Leisure in America, 1840-1940, Catherine Grover, ed., (Amherst: University of Massachusetts Press with The Strong Museum, 1992), 112-38.

24. This and other stereographs and postcards discussed below in the collections of the Horticulture Library, Office of Horticulture, Smithsonian Institution.

25. Robert Lynd and Helen Merrell Lynd, *Middletown: A Study in American Culture* (New York: Harcourt Brace & Co, 1929), 93-104; and *Middletown in Transition: A Study in Cultural Conflicts* (New York: Harcourt, Brace and Co., 1937), 144-45 and 250-52.

26. On this shift, see Patricia Tice, "Gardens of Change," in *American Home Life, 1880-1930*, Thomas Schlereth, ed. (University of Tennessee Press, 1992), 190-210. Gertrude Jekyll, *Garden Ornament.*, (London: George Newnes, Ltd, 1918; reprinted by Antique Collectors Club, 1982).

27. Richard G. Kenworthy, "Bringing the World to Brookline: The Gardens of Larz and Isabel Anderson," *Journal of Garden History*, II, 4 (1991): 224-41.

28. Ibid., 224. Despite the importance of Weld to American garden history, it was destroyed after Isabel Anderson's death in 1948, eleven years after her husband died. Without heirs, she willed the estate to the city of Brookline, which neglected the property for years, finally razing the house and abandoning the gardens. Little of Weld is left today. See Kenworthy's account.

29. Ellen Marie Snyder, "Victory Over Nature: Victorian Cast-Iron Seating," *Winterthur Portfolio* 20 (Winter 1985): 221-42.

30. Leighton, *American Gardens of the Nineteenth Century*, 230-34. On the creation of garden statuary by American sculptors for private estates, see Michele H. Bogart, *Fauns and Fountains: American Garden Statuary, 1890-1930* (Southampton, N.Y.: The Parrish Museum, 1985), n.p. E.T. Barnum Wire & Iron Goods, Detroit Michigan, 1894 catalogue, 6-10 (The Strong Museum Library, Rochester, N.Y.); Doell, 82.

31. On children as popular subjects in garden statuary, see Bogart, *Fauns and Fountains,* n.p.; Doell, 62; on "Out in the Rain" fountain, see Tice, 66. Children were also popular subjects in Victorian cemetery sculpture; see Ellen Marie Snyder, "Innocents in a Worldly World: Victorian Children's Gravemarkers," in *Cemeteries and Grave Markers: Voices of American Culture,* edited by Richard E. Meyer (Ann Arbor: UMI Press, 1989), 11-29.

32. In addition to Western European influences, Chinese and Japanese garden styles have influenced American gardens periodically (outside of their creation by Chinese and Japanese-Americans). See, for instance, Ann Leighton on "specialty gardens" in her book *American Gardens of the Nineteenth Century*, 287-290. On popular art in the nineteenth-century home, see Kenneth

Ames, et al., *Accumulation & Display: Mass Marketing Household Goods 1880-1920* (Wilmington, DE: The Henry Francis du Pont Winterthur Museum, 1986), 97-107. According to art historian Michele Bogart, garden statuary served an important role in the process of legitimation for American sculptors. See her essay in *Fauns and Fountains: American Garden Statuary, 1890-1930*. In another piece Bogart argues that most Americans bought sculpture to show others that they were cultured. See "The Development of a Popular Market for Sculpture in America, 1850-1880," *Journal of American Culture* 4 (Spring 1981), 23. M. Christine Doell points out that the Victorian garden was a place for the arts in general: middle- and upper-class households staged musical and dramatic performances with family members in the home garden and used it as a setting for reading, painting and drawing, see *Gardens of the Gilded Age* (Syracuse, NY: Syracuse University Press, 1984), 113.

33. On the changing cultural order that widened distinctions between popular and high arts, see Lawrence Levine, *Highbrow and Lowbrow: The Emergence of Cultural Hierarchy In America* (Cambridge: Harvard University Press, 1988), esp. 146-164 on museum practices. On popular sculpture, see Bogart, "The Development of a Popular Market for Sculpture."

34. Leighton, *American Gardens of the Nineteenth Century*, 136-38; David Schuyler, *The New Urban Landscape: The Redefinition of City Form in Nineteenth-Century America* (Baltimore: Johns Hopkins University Press, 1986), 37-56; Thomas Bender, "The 'Rural' Cemetery Movement: Urban Travail and the Appeal of Nature," in *Material Life in America,* Robert Blair St. George and Dell Upton, ed., (Boston: Northeastern University Press, 1988), 505-18; and Blanche M.G. Linden, "Death and the Garden: The Cult of Melancholy and the 'Rural' Cemetery" (Ph.D. Dissertation, Harvard University Press, 1981), 310-480.

35. Blanche Linden-Warden, "Strange but Genteel Pleasure Grounds: Tourist and Leisure Uses of Nineteenth-Century Rural Cemeteries" in *Cemeteries and Grave Markers: Voices of American Culture*, Richard E. Meyer, ed., (Ann Arbor: UMI Research Press, 1989), 295-300.

36. Leighton, 140-41.

37. Downing, "The New-York Park," *The Horticulturalist* XI (August 1, 1851), 345. On relationships between the rural cemetery and public park movements, see Bender, 513.

38. Albert Fein, *Frederick Law Olmsted and the American Environmental Tradition* (New York: George Braziller, 1972), 8-10. Rosensweig and Blackmar offer a different picture of Olmsted's intentions, not quite as populist as represented by Fein. See pp. 238-41.

39. For the changes wrought on Central Park after Olmsted's involvement, see Rosensweig and Blackmar, Section IV, "Redefining Central Park," 263-340. Olmsted's other commissions included Prospect Park in Brooklyn, Belle Isle in Detroit, several parks and a parkway system in Boston, Delaware Park in Buffalo, Seneca Park, Rochester, see Fein's section of illustrations, "V. Olmsted and the Planning of Cities," n.p.; Schuyler, *The New Urban Landscape*, 149.

40. On the development of Central Park, see Rosensweig and Blackmar, *The Park and the People: A History of Central Park*, cited above; David Schuyler, 59-101; Leighton, 141-43; 186-95; Julius G. Fabos, et al., *Frederick Law Olmsted, Sr., Founder of Landscape Architecture in America* (Amherst: University of Massachusetts Press, 1968), 17-21; for Olmsted's thoughts on the aesthetics of public parks, see excerpt from his essay, "Architectural Fitness," *Garden and Forest*, August 19, 1891, reprinted in S.B. Sutton, *Civilizing American Cities: A Selection of Frederick Law Olmsted's Writings on City Landscapes*, (Cambridge, Mass.: MIT Press, 1971), 13-18. For impact of public parks on domestic landscapes, see Doell, 6.

41. Schuyler, 156-60; Fein, 32-34.

42. Fein, 33-35; Schuyler, 162-67.

43. Trade catalogs for garden and lawn suppliers attest to the interplay among home gardens, parks, and cemetery statuary; the Winterthur Library, Wilmington, Delaware, holds a collection of these. For instance, the 1871 catalog for Miller Iron of Rhode Island and the 1895 catalog for M.D. Jones & Co. of Boston both feature statuary and outdoor furniture for lawns, gardens, parks, and cemeteries.

44. *Middletown*, 93-104; and *Middletown in Transition*, 144-45 and 250-52. Herbert Gans, *The Levittowners: Ways of Life and Politics in a New Suburban Community* (New York: Pantheon Books, 1967), 48,176-78.

45. Virginia Scott Jenkins in *The Lawn*, for instance, argues that Americans need to rethink their requirements for a well-mown yard of one plant species, because of the environmental impact and cost in time and money to homeowners. For other discussions of changing practices for the American yard, see Jerry Adler, "Bye-Bye, Suburban Dream," *Newsweek*, May 15, 1995, 41-53. Michael Pollan, "Why Mow? The Case Against Lawns," *New York Times Magazine*, May 28, 1989, 23-26, 41-44; and Karin Winegar, "Ideological turf war pits chemical lawn care against natural," *Twin Cities Star Tribune*, June 20, 1992, 1E, 2E. Yard statuary can sometimes attract the wrath of neighbors, although this usually happens when a piece takes a unique form. It is rare to find housing inspectors called for displays of traditional yard ornaments, however profuse. For an instance of protest by neighbors in one area of

Minneapolis, see the case of Paul Wychor, truck driver, handyman, and amateur sculptor, whose ten-foot-high cement sculpture "Sleeping Doors" drew a round of calls to the city's housing inspector. Wychor intended the piece as a human figure pushing open a door, but neighbors could not recognize the imagery. Some fearfully concluded that Wychor might belong to a religious cult and called Minneapolis housing inspectors to force its removal. See Jim Klobuchar, "Man's home is castle, but yard. . . . " *Twin Cities Star Tribune,* October 1, 1989, 1B, 7B.

46. For problems with upkeep of the lawn and arguments about its future, see Virginia Scott Jenkins, "The War Between Man and Nature" and "The Age of High-Tech Horticulture" in *The Lawn,* 133-81; and Fred E.H. Schroeder, "Myths and Anxieties" and "Front Yard Futures" in his *Front Yard America: The Evolution and Meanings of a Vernacular Domestic Landscape,* 121-54.

II

Travel, Play, and Celebration in American Landscapes

Just as the rural cemetery and the public park served as models for domestic landscapes during the nineteenth century, new landscape types have influenced the design and art in American yards in this century, resulting in a wider variety of subjects, materials, and designs. The home landscapes we see today testify to the inspiration provided by new forms of public spaces that are less sedate, more fanciful, and more commercial than public parks or cemeteries. Visual affinities can be seen to amusement parks, miniature golf courses, roadside attractions, and Disneyland. Their visual correspondences demonstrate a continuing interchange between landscape types, between domestic and public spaces.

Many new kinds of spaces emerged to attract and serve tourists as travel became a defining feature of modern life, particularly since the 1920s when car travel exploded. The new public landscapes have generally been commercial sites that served as new gathering places. The artifactual vocabulary of their built environments aimed to communicate to travelers, urging them to stop and enjoy a promised delight, an experience or a product. The commercial vocabulary at first relied on elements from domestic landscapes and, in turn, also influenced later designs and imagery for homegrounds. Most tourist sites emphasize celebratory space that is set off from daily routines for leisure and enjoyment, while the home landscape emphasizes an annual cycle of seasonal change and holiday celebrations. Domestic landscapes borrow some artifactual vocabulary of tourist landscapes to celebrate holidays in particular. The adoption of this artifactual vocabulary coincided with the spread of homeownership to broader portions of the American populace. Working- and middle-class homeowners readily adopted the designs, imagery, and materials from new public spaces for their holiday displays and year-round yard art.

Albert "Mike" Schack's yard in Grand Rapids, Minnesota, offers an instructive model and starting point for this discussion, because it distills a number of features characteristic of contemporary yardscapes and illustrates their relationships to other landscape forms.

"MIKE'S WORLD" OR "YOU CAN'T IMAGINE HOW PEOPLE CAME DOWN HERE TO SEE THAT THING . . . "

Visitors come from near and far to visit Mike Schack's yard in Grand Rapids, Minnesota, which features a sign calling it "Mike's World," a play on both Disneyworld and Ironworld, an amusement park and museum attraction in a nearby town that celebrates Minnesota's Iron Range. "They have Disneyworld, Ironworld. This is my world," Schack says about his creation. Schack's yard is filled with his own creations, impressive sculptures of a tyrannosaurus rex, a giant mosquito, an alligator, and the cartoon character Popeye, along with a scene of the Blessed Virgin, Snow White and the Seven Dwarfs, antique wood stoves for flowers stands, whirligigs hanging from trees, and knock-out flower gardens.[1] Oriented to the public view rather than to an interior vantage point, Schack's yard shouts a beckoning welcome to friends and strangers, to the appreciative and the merely curious. A profuse border of cosmos begins a block away from the yard, drawing the eyes of passersby. When they see Schack's sign that warns, "Caution: Dinosaur and Mosquito Crossing," they know more than a mere flower garden awaits their visit. It's worth a stop off Highway 2 to take a closer look, and many people do. Over the years, "Mike's World" has become a free roadside attraction.

Mike Schack began decorating his yard in the mid-1950s when he and his wife, Ann, moved to town from a nearby farm. But it was his creation of the giant mosquito that brought a regular stream of visitors to his home. Just prior to his retirement in 1980 from Hanna Mining Company, where he had worked as an electrician, Schack built the giant mosquito—his first wooden sculpture—which joined his unique bird bath made with a crank shaft for its base. His inspiration for the mosquito came from a common Minnesota experience: while working outside one evening, he was swamped by the persistent pests. Once he decided he wanted to build the sculpture for his yard, he studied the bug's anatomy "from life," so to speak, slapping them gently so that he could see how they were put together. Then he built the mosquito, using a cedar pole for the body, sheet metal for wings, and wire conduit for the antennae and legs. The finished bug stood over four feet high and ten feet long. After setting it out in the yard, he said, "It even surprised me, it looked so good."

The mosquito marked the beginning of hundreds of visits from Grand Rapids neighbors and from tourists vacationing in this resort district of Minnesota. Mike Schack says, "You can't imagine how people came down here to see that thing . . . That was really the laugh of Grand Rapids that first year . . . That's the fun part, when other people get a laugh." Visitors appreciate the garden, the sculptures, and the humor, chatting with Schack and taking pictures. Via family vacation photos, the mosquito has appeared in print as far away as France, when a photograph taken by a French visitor was printed in a local newspaper as testimony to the wonders of the New World. Along with their snapshots, visitors leave with bouquets of flowers that Schack hands out. In the late 1980s, he added a guest book for visitors to record their names and addresses.

Like Harriet Bagasao in Los Angeles, Mike Schack explicitly aims his yard at a public audience. "I don't know how to say it," he said about his design process, "What I do every once in a while is to go out there on the road so I can see what the people see, and look at it. Sometimes I have to fill in the bare spots . . . so I have to do something to fill it in." Though not working with a master plan in mind, his yard exhibits aesthetic principles through its overall design and through the individual sculptures that adorn the space. When asked if there can be too much in the yard, Schack says, "No, you just have to keep it orderly, otherwise it doesn't look good." Many people comment to him on the difficulty of mowing the grass with so many sculptures in place, but Schack insists that for him, "It's not really that bad."

The resulting design of Schack's yard is certainly an extravagant example of yard art. Yet, importantly, it shares elements with many neighboring yards. In yards just down the street, giant wooden butterflies adorn fronts of houses, colossal plastic daisies spin next to natural flowers, and recycled objects, such as washing machine tubs, have been transformed into novelty flower pots. Elaborate sites like Mike Schack's are not isolated aberrations but concentrated distillations of local landscape practices. They amplify and make more visible landscape elements that are often otherwise read on a subconscious level. Their colorful and fanciful imagery draw visitors and tourists, showing that they utilize landscape strategies often borrowed from public sites that aim to attract public audiences.

To understand the aesthetics and the dynamics of Mike Schack's yard and others like his, we need to explore some of the historical origins of tourist landscapes, places created to appeal to public audiences. This endeavor will take us from wilderness landscapes to the grounds of world's fairs to amusement parks, the roadside and its attractions, and the development of outdoor Christmas displays.

TOURISM AND LANDSCAPE

Appealing and inspiring landscapes have attracted tourists for several centuries in the West. Beginning in the eighteenth century, the wealthy classes, particularly in England, embarked on their Grand Tour to see awesome views of natural scenes, like the Alps, or equally stirring historic places, like the ruins of Rome. The emergence of landscape as an independent subject for painting, in fact, had roots in artists' ventures to those foreign locales.

In the United States, grand landscapes became tourist destinations during the first decades of the nineteenth century. Well-to-do and middle-class Americans ventured off to see the wonders of their new republic. Niagara Falls was the foremost tourist attraction of the time. The expansive topography and pounding torrents at the falls offered an experience of the sublime and inspired thoughts of divine power. Its appeal would be matched later in the century by other wilderness spots further west, such as Yellowstone and Yosemite. Tourists also were attracted to cultivated landscapes, like those in the Connecticut or Hudson river valleys. The view from Mount Holyoke, where a visitor could gaze out at settlements along the oxbow of the Connecticut, was a sight many traveled to see, among them artists who captured the scene in painting. These were picturesque views, more akin to the aesthetics of Andrew Jackson Downing, who helped to design many estate grounds along the Hudson.

"Tourism is a principal means by which modern people define for themselves a sense of identity," writes geographer John Jakle in his book on travel in North America. Through their visits to tourist sites, Americans of the nineteenth century had begun to define a national culture through landscape.[2] And, indeed, as travel became easier, faster, more comfortable, and more affordable through the development of the steamboat, train, and automobile, tourism became a defining feature of modern lives.

Anthropologist Dean MacCannell has argued that modern people attempt to integrate fragmented experiences into a unified whole through tourism.[3] If that is the case, then the ambitious world's fairs of the late nineteenth century and early decades of this century were primary sites for such integration to occur. The fairs attracted millions of tourists, who witnessed their grand efforts to represent the whole of Western art, culture, and industry. In elaborate settings that combined architecture, sculpture, and landscape, world's fairs served as three-dimensional encyclopedias of Western civilization and enterprise. World expositions were wondrous places, certainly parallel to natural wonders in their ability to inspire awe in their visitors. In their size, design, and complexity, world's fair grounds were equivalent to sublime natural landscapes, such as Niagara Falls, representing a kind of cultural and technological sublime.[4] And indeed, at a time when natural landscapes still drew most American travelers, the expositions of 1876 in Philadelphia and 1893 in Chicago prompted unprecedented tourism to American cities.

In the United States, the fairgrounds themselves expanded dramatically and became central features of the American fair. In the International Exposition of 1851 in London and that in Paris in 1867, fairs took place for the most part inside immense buildings (the Crystal Palace in London). At American fairs, entirely new environments were built for these celebrations. The Centennial Exposition of 1876 was built in 236 acres of Philadelphia's Fairmount Park and designed by H.J. Schwartzmann, who had designed the original 800-acre park. Dozens of temporary buildings were constructed throughout the park, some devoted to branches of knowledge, such as horticulture, others serving as state and national pavilions. Its display of the gigantic Corliss engine, which provided power for the fair, new manufactured wares, and American colonial scenes, among other displays, were presented in the midst of a highly designed landscape that was adorned by statuary, some of gargantuan proportions. The landscape of the fairgrounds and its accents became part of the attraction. Visitors could climb to the look-out deck in the hand of the Statue of Liberty, which France had sent to the fair while the rest of the statue was still under construction. Or they could gaze in awe at the bronze statue of Pegasus standing in front of Memorial Hall. Other gardens and park areas throughout the fair were dotted with additional statuary of more modest scale.[5]

Central Park and the picturesque aesthetic were the dominant models for the grounds at the Centennial Exposition, although Frederick Law Olmsted's design for Central Park had aimed to minimize the intrusion of statuary and major buildings in the natural landscape. Yet in Chicago in 1893, Olmsted himself designed the grounds for the Columbian Quincentennial Exposition, creating a landscape where nature stood back to emphasize a grand architectural environment. This fair took a whopping 685 acres along Chicago's lakefront. It required three years to completely construct this city-within-a-city, an effort that required extensive land reclamation, road building, and installation of telephone and electrical cables to serve over 200 structures.[6] The White City, as it was called, presented a spectacle of architectural grandeur, albeit of temporary duration, based on Beaux Art styles. The centerpiece of the grounds was the Court of Honor, with its enormous classical-columned buildings surrounding the Great Basin, which itself measured 250 by 2,500 feet. "For the first time," historian David Burg writes, "hundreds of thousands of Americans saw a large group of buildings harmoniously and powerfully arranged in a plan of great variety, perfect balance, and strong climax effect."[7]

Anthropologist Burton Benedict has written that world's fairs were grand educators about modern life, particularly about the world of goods and the cultivation of taste.[8] That claim also applies to the landscape designs of fairgrounds. In Philadelphia, Fairmount Park became an important public park, and in Chicago, the 1893 fair resulted in the establishment of a park and new cultural institutions. Frederick Law Olmsted's designs in Chicago, along with Daniel Burnham's Beaux Art design of the buildings, spurred the City Beautiful movement in urban design in the decades following the fair.[9] Hence, world's-fair grounds were influential design environments for American urban landscapes, particularly the first fairs in the late nineteenth and early twentieth centuries. Fairs offered visitors the experience of a completely designed environment, one that embodied a kind of order lacking in the urban environment. Fairgrounds also offered playful experiences in a fantasy enviroment. Their temporary structures and landscapes offered visual and physical pleasures of architecture, landscape design, sculpture, and light. The appeal of these kinds of large-scale, designed enviroments found at world's fair grounds provides a clue to the continuing appeal of places like Disneyland and Disney World today. Their combination of landscape, architecture, sculpture, and illumination influenced not only American cities but domestic landscapes as well.

ELECTRIC LIGHTS, SPECTACLE, AND URBANISM

Electric illumination played an important role at world's-fair grounds, and it also contributed significantly to modern perceptions and experiences of the urban landscape. The new energy source, harnessed by Thomas Edison in 1879, was put to ceremonial use soon thereafter. In 1883, for instance, when the Brooklyn Bridge opened to great hoopla after thirteen years of construction, electric lights were strung across its cables, articulating the structure itself and its dramatic setting in lower Manhattan. It was the first structure of its size to wear ornamental lighting.[10] At a time when most homes, businesses, and streets were still lit with gas, electric lights on the East River bridge paralleled and amplified the incredible feat of engineering that it embodied.

Decorative lighting on a grand scale was first introduced to large segments of the American public through temporary displays at world's fairs. Electricity lit interiors of fair buildings, and outdoor lighting was used for purely ornamental purposes to showcase the buildings at night. At the 1893 World's Columbian Exposition in Chicago, Westinghouse Company, the primary supplier of electricity for the fair, built a generator with nearly three times the electrical capacity of that used in Chicago's business district, making the exposition the grandest consumer of electrical energy in the nineteenth century. Buildings "bejeweled with glittering crowns" created a nighttime spectacle that contributed to the fair's popular nickname—"the White City." Decorative lighting of fair buildings continued to play an important role in the spectacle of American fairs. At the Pan American Exposition in Buffalo in 1901, a 375-foot tower, dedicated to the Goddess of Light and outlined with thousands of electric bulbs, served as the focal point of the fairgrounds.[11]

Ceremonial lighting at World's fairs provided a vision for the urban landscape, influencing the model of urbanism just as their architecture and landscape design served as models for urban design. In the early decades of this century, when corporate magnates competed for height in their skyscrapers, they also began to want the most spectacularly lit building posed against the night skyline. A dramatic example of the status of light is offered by F.W. Woolworth, who, in 1915, insisted that architect Cass Gilbert make the Woolworth building in New York City fifty feet higher than any other skyscraper. Though it was indeed taller, the building was, according to journalist Charles Person, "swallowed up in darkness and robbed of its glory" at night, especially in comparison to the Singer building, which was "strung and studded with lights." Not to be overshadowed, Woolworth then implemented a plan to form "the most wonderful permanent lighting spectacle in the world" by flooding the top thirty floors of his building with indirect lights, a technique adopted the same year at the Panama Pacific International Exposition in San Francisco to marvelous effect.[12]

The spectacular lighting effects first introduced at international expositions and later replicated in urban centers became key features of the amusement park, a new form of public space that reached its grandest proportions in the early twentieth century. Amusement parks, in fact, owed much of their origins to the midways at world's fairs, the first "Midway Plaisance" having appeared at the 1893 Columbian Exposition in Chicago. At Coney Island, America's premier amusement park area at the turn of the century, electric lighting adorned fantasy architecture, contributing to a dazzling spectacle that drew enormous working-class crowds on weekend escapes from New York City. Opened in 1903, Luna Park boasted a quarter of a million lights that turned an already magical realm into "an enchanted garden" at night. Dreamland, opened at Coney Island in 1905, outdid Luna Park by outlining its structures with a million lights, 100,000 for its central "Beacon Tower" alone. Architecturally, amusements parks looked like miniature cities, and socially, they helped their visitors negotiate the new experiences of urban life—new technology, new gender relations, new social relations—in playful ways. Yet they also offered a critique of real cities, for these were spaces that revealed an architectural and spatial order not always apparent in cities to urban residents. And their fanciful, even outrageous, architecture and sculpture, called "barking architecture" by art historian Michele Bogart, countered the solemnity of didactic statuary on civic buildings, meant to uplift and instruct urban residents.[13]

CELEBRATION ON THE LANDSCAPE

Amusement parks offered a permanent place for fun, available to the public to visit and enjoy when time and money permitted. The lighting spectacles Americans viewed at fairs, amuseument parks, and in downtowns inspired homeowners to adapt elements to their properties. The Christmas season became the focus of home lighting displays, appropriately enough, given that this time of year is regarded as "the season of light" to mark the darkest time of the year and the beginning of longer days. Since prehistory humans have responded to the solstice with displays of light—fires, candles, and other forms of illumination. In this regard, Christmas and Hannukah draw from earlier solstice practices that marked the return of longer periods of sunlight. Once electricity had been shown off as a decorative medium at world's fairs and amusement parks, Americans adopted it at home for the holidays to light up the darkness, to spread holiday cheer, and to attract admiration from neighbors.[14]

By the late nineteenth century, Americans had new attitudes about the observance of Christmas as a religious holiday. This was a far cry from earlier influences of Puritan belief, which held that Christmas trees were pagan and that proper Christians did not celebrate Christmas at all, especially given the Puritan opposition to the Church of England, which did observe Christmas.[15] Debated among colonists and members of the new republic throughout the seventeenth and eighteenth centuries, Christmas became well established by the Victorian era through a combination of factors. New immigrant groups, particularly Germans, brought Christmas holiday practices with them, which were adopted more broadly by other Americans, whose ties to earlier beliefs were weakening. Americans also admired Queen Victoria and Prince Albert, who surprised the royal children in 1844 with a Christmas tree, thereby helping to legitimize and spread the display of Christmas trees in America. By 1870, Protestant Sunday schools actively taught millions of American children about Christmas observances. A sign of the new acceptance of the holiday was reflected in the designation of December 25 as a business holiday by all American states and territories between 1836 and 1890. By 1931, public schools in forty-one states had declared the day a legal holiday.[16]

Outdoor Christmas displays in the United States initially focused on what were called "community trees." Large evergreen trees were installed in parks or squares or near public buildings for everyone to enjoy. The electrically lit civic Christmas tree was popular in many cities by the early twentieth century. In 1913, social crusader Jacob Riis described a "tree of light" in New York's Madison Square for *Ladies Home Journal*, a sight he claimed was repeated "in towns and hamlets all over the land. . . . " In Madison Square, 50,000 children and adults gathered around the tree to sing carols. Riis recommends a community tree such as this one "for their many forgotten poor and lonesome rich . . . the Christmas tree will help them get together which is what they really need." President Cleveland added electric lights to the White House family tree in 1895, but it was President Calvin Coolidge who first switched on the lights of a 45-foot outdoor tree in 1924, starting a tradition followed by every American president since.[17]

Inside American homes, lighting was among the last electrical features to be installed. Electricity made its way into the home in fits and starts, historian David Handlin notes. At first, Americans were hestitant to accept the new energy source wholeheartedly, fearful of the potential for home fires and, on a social level, of how electical conveniences would affect women's roles in the home. Electricity was first used to run small appliances, yet by 1910, electric washing machines and refrigerators were still novelties in most American homes.[18] Soon thereafter, however, a writer for *Scientific American* in 1916 could note that the American home had been "invaded" with electricity. By then, more and more homes in urban centers had been outfitted with electricity for lights and major appliances as well for other conveniences such as fans and toasters.[19]

With the adoption of electricity in the home, Americans soon began to employ its decorative potential, first seen in the celebration of Christmas. Lights on the indoor Christmas tree are, claims one writer, "the uniquely American contribution to the Christmas tree." The first use of electric lights rather than candles to light a tree occurred in 1882, when Edward Johnson, vice president of Thomas Edison's New York City electric company, had bulbs hand-blown and hand-wired to decorate his tree. By 1903, Ever-Ready Company in New York began manufacturing strings of lights, called "festoons" or "outfits," for adorning family trees. Selling for twelve dollars, the equivalent of a worker's average weekly wage, they could only be purchased by the well-to-do to use on their indoor trees.[20]

Denver claims to have been the site of the first *outdoor* electrical lighting on a home Christmas scene. In 1914, David D. Sturgeon, owner of Sturgeon Electric Company, wanted to please his terminally ill son, who was bedridden at Christmas and could not see the family tree. Sturgeon dipped some light bulbs in green and red paint, then strung them on a tree outside his son's room. The display was a hit with the family and neighbors, who began to decorate their homes in a similar manner. Crowds of admirers from all over Denver would visit the neigborhood at holiday time, and eventually a citywide contest for the best Christmas display ensued, hosted by the *Denver Post* and the Denver Electrical League. Soon the decorative uses of electricity in holiday displays increased dramatically, particularly during the 1920s.

Home holiday displays attracted large public audiences just as community trees had done. In 1928, Marion Starkey praised the growing use of electric lights in *American Home* magazine, noting that many Americans were getting involved in "a delightful new art of 'electrical renaissance' . . . the art of Christmas gardening."[21] Starkey describes two gardens near Boston where homeowners had mounted extensive lighting displays for several years. Henry Peckham's house and grounds sported 6,000 lights, while Frank Sloan's display came in second with a mere 3,500 lights. Peckham's superior numbers had been built up over a ten-year period. "They are already quite famous," Starkey wrote about the two homes. "People motor across a state's length at that season to study how they may go and do likewise in their own gardens, and imitations are legion." Home magazines supplied practical advice in articles on the best light sockets and on installing lights. Other articles recommended adding silhouettes of Christmas images—candles and churches—in home windows.[22]

Civic efforts at holiday displays kept pace with the domestic scene. Businesses and city governments used holiday decor to beautify urban landscapes and attract customers to commercial areas. Civic displays became marks of community pride and boosterism, prompting friendly competition between cities. In 1927, the mayor of Minneapolis sent telegrams to ten other cities, declaring itself "the brightest Christmas city" and challenging them to outdo its holiday display. Its downtown streets sported thousands of lights, matched by 10,000 lighted outdoor Christmas trees in residential neighborhoods. Though far from snowy Minneapolis, the city of Phoenix took up the challenge. In 1931, it declared itself "the Outdoor Christmas City" of the nation.[23] The city was divided into districts, and prizes were given to various classes of outdoor decorations. The city installed alternating red and green lights in the downtown street lights, and large wreaths with bows were hung on every post. Merchants competed with each other for the best window decorations. Homeowners had their prize categories, too. *Better Homes and Gardens* commented that the overall effect of "gaiety is contagious," no doubt an even more important element in civic life as the Depression took hold.

In the postwar era, when more prosperous times returned, holiday lighting skyrocketed once again. By 1949, *Life* magazine noted the national infatuation with lit spectacles for civic and commercial buildings. That year merchants in Kansas City, Missouri, invested $15,000 in 20,000 red-and-white lights and 60 miles of wire used to outline the outdoor shopping mall, Country Club Plaza, during the holiday season. The display attracted steady throngs of local shoppers as well as thousands of people from neighboring states. Homeowners across the nation joined in with their own lighting spectacles, as noted by Collier's magazine in a 1954 spread on holiday lights in Cleveland. It is, they said, a form of holiday cheer that could be found in every city and town in the United States. At times, neighbors engaged in friendly competition for the most elaborate spectacle, a humorous side of the holiday, writer Paul C. Law called "the annual Christmas-lights derby" in a 1954 piece for the *Saturday Evening Post*.[24]

Not until the environmental movement of the early 1970s, combined with that era's "oil crisis," did Americans miss a beat with bigger and brighter holiday displays. A growing awareness of Americans' prodigious energy use and conservation efforts combined to dampen holiday light displays, a practice some considered a frivolous use of energy. In 1973, many light switches turned off when President Nixon urged Americans to conserve energy by dispensing with outdoor lighting displays, and many cities and states followed his lead. Since the 1980s, holiday lights have made a comeback, in part due to lessened concern with electricity bills and in part due to the development of more energy-efficient lights.

Urban buildings today continue to employ decorative lighting to assert status and to mark special occasions. Prior to the energy crisis of the 1970s, Minneapolis skyscrapers were outlined in lights every Christmas season. The twinkling lights made the city look like an oversized Main Street, U.S.A., straight from Disneyland, encouraging an affectionate attitude toward what might otherwise have seemed an indifferent, unintimate place. In the 1980s, downtown business groups reinstituted the use of holiday lighting at a more modest scale, most notably on the city's first skyscraper, the Foshay Tower, built in 1929 and modeled on the Washington Monument. The building has been adorned with lights strung from its tip to look like a giant Christmas tree. The effect humanizes the urban environment by accenting community events and marking the passage of seasons. It also draws shoppers and spenders to downtown areas, helping to keep them vital and prosperous.[25]

MIKE SCHACK'S CHRISTMAS SCENE AND HOLIDAY LANDSCAPES

In the contemporary landscape, holiday displays help to clarify the public nature of the home and yard. Throughout the United States, Americans of Christian faiths decorate home interiors and exteriors from Thanksgiving through New Year's Day. The family's indoor Christmas tree is frequently placed in the picture window for neighbors to enjoy and admire. Electric lights line roofs and windows of homes or balustrades of apartment balconies, while other strands of lights twist around pine trees or float in tree branches. Whole urban neighborhoods sometimes don Christmas decorations and lighting displays. And in every city throughout the nation, certain homes boast thousands of lights, filling the night sky like miniature Las Vegas strips. These practices transform the holiday from a private, family-oriented event into a public occasion.

Mike Schack's holiday yards illustrate the relationship between seasonal displays and other forms of yard art. His Christmas scenes were, in fact, his first ventures in yard art. In the early 1970s, he constructed several sculptural pieces for temporary holiday displays. His first project involved the creation of an eight-foot cross made of ice. For weeks Schack froze sheets of ice in cake pans and later stacked them together to build the cross. For the vertical beams, he held ice blocks together with water until they froze, which didn't take long in the frigid weather that winter. Then he created a decorative fence around the cross using large icicles collected in his neighborhood. These were spray-painted red, then stuck in the snow, points up. The crowning touch was his addition of a spotlight with rotating colored gel to create a visual effect similar to the lighting of the St. Paul Winter Carnival Ice Palace, a grand structure made entirely of ice and often lit from within. Schack's display proved to be a highlight of the holiday season in Grand Rapids, attracting streams of admirers, winning an award for best Christmas display from the local Lion's Club, and appearing in the local newspaper.

Mike Schack went on to a new challenge during the next Christmas season, when he constructed a miniature version of the town's St. Joseph Catholic Church. This time, relatives and neighbors pitched in by freezing water in milk cartons. A coworker at the Hanna Mining Company made a customized triangular pan to use in freezing the church steeple. From these contributions, Schack built a four-by-six-foot church, complete with a six-foot high steeple and stained glass windows made of ice. He placed ceramic figurines and dolls inside to represent parishioners, and he lit the interior at night, creating a silvery glow on the ice walls. Shack's ice church once again won him first prize for Christmas displays and a feature story in the newspaper.

As with Shacks' miniature church, the creation of Christmas displays is a shared endeavor in many American communities. Residents work together to construct beautiful lighting displays and holiday scenes, making the neighborhood a communal public art piece. Since the 1930s, one Italian neighborhood in South Philadelphia, for instance, has created a stunning lighting display. Forty families on Colorado Street contribute twenty-five dollars and labor each year toward the neighborhood illumination. The men put up Christmas lights, creating a display that draws admirers from all over Philadelphia. The display itself—lights linked from one rowhouse to another and draped across the streets—physically expresses the tight community bonds that exist in the neighborhood, while its construction promotes and perpetuates the cooperation such a project requires.[26]

Similar traditions persist in other parts of Philadelphia and are practiced in many other parts of the country. In snow-bare Anaheim, just outside of Los Angeles, neighbors in one district work together each year on a Christmas display, making shrubs into snowmen and transforming yards into snow-covered visions by filling them with cotton. The whole neighborhood stages a kind of communal performance complete with kids carolling, holiday music blaring, and adults taking turns playing Santa and passing out candy to visitors, who come from miles around to enjoy the festivities. The residents have dubbed their neighborhood "Candy Cane Lane" for the holiday. "For two weeks out of the year, it's like a fantasy land," as one resident put it. Photographer Christian Patoski has documented holiday displays throughout the United States, from New York City to Florida to Texas and Montana. Snow and cold are not required to complete the holiday scene, as Patoski's images of Christmas lights on palm trees and shell ornaments on evergreen trees in Florida attest.[27]

Even when Christmas displays are not a neighborhood-wide effort, they are, nonetheless, aimed at the community in an effort to spread the Christmas cheer. Paul Pino and his wife, Celeste, in Darby Township of

Philadelphia, create a car-stopping Christmas spectacle by spelling out "Noel" in lights on the roof of the house and filling the yard with holiday figures. Paul Pino says he continues to decorate because it was a tradition from his childhood, growing up in south Philadelphia. At his current home people stop all the time at Christmas and "tell us how much they love the house, how much they enjoy it." In most urban areas in the United States, the trek around town to look at Christmas displays is a common family tradition, encouraged by local newspapers that annually publish itineraries of the most spectacular homes.[28]

Clarence Weidert's home in south Minneapolis appears on many itineraries of Christmas landmarks in the Twin Cities.[29] He and his family put up a spectacular Christmas display every year in a spirit similar to that of Paul Gino of Philadelphia. Thousands of lights adorn his home, creating a beacon that alerts visitors to a quasi-divine revelation before they even see the house. When they arrive, they are not disappointed. The front, side, and back yards of the corner house are filled with figures of carollers, Santas, nativity scenes, and toy soldiers, while an animated jack in the box plays peek-a-boo on the porch.

The Weiderts' public expression of holiday cheer requires a considerable investment in time, energy, and money. Three months are given over to the installation and dismantling. Weidert begins putting up lights in October with his sons and friends (a friend who is a retired fireman puts lights and statutes on the peak of the roof). Besides the higher-than-usual electric bill for lights that outline the entire house and every tree, the Weiderts spend about five hundred dollars each year for the candy bars that Santa gives to visiting kids. Weidert has not kept track of his monetary investment over the years, though he admits to spending a considerable amount for the animated figures, the figures for the holiday scenes in his yard, and the thousands of lights. Yet the monetary and time investments are well worth it, he claims, for all the enjoyment it gives to his visitors, especially the children.

From Thanksgiving through New Year's, his home is visited by thousands of people, locals as well as tourists. Beginning in early December and continuing through Christmas Eve, Weidert plays Santa from five to ten o'clock every evening, handing out a candy bar or some other treat to each child. In 1988 alone, four thousand children sat on Santa's lap and told him their Christmas wishes; the number has reached seven thousand in years past. Every evening, when the sky is lit up and holiday carols from the home stereo pierce the cold night air, a continual stream of cars and folks on foot migrate to the Weidert house, stopping to gaze on the incredible scene. "Look at that," they say, "look at that." Parents bring children to visit Santa for free. Unlike Santa visits at department stores, at Clarence Weidert's, parents may take their own photographs of Santa with the kids. Weidert's house has become so notable—and noticeable—that jets flying into the Twin Cities airport occasionally pass over the place, so pilots can point it out to their passengers.[30]

As these widespread Christmas displays attest, the American home is a site for an annual cycle of publicly oriented holiday decor. Christmas lights and holiday tableaux give way to Valentine hearts in picture windows in February, plastic eggs hanging from trees and bushes for Easter. Each holiday has a repetoire of artifacts and images for decorating the home, yard, and garden. At Halloween, a close second to Christmas in frequency and complexity of outdoor displays, harvest-inspired tableaux combine natural materials—straw bales, corn stalks, and Indian corn—with scary figures—ghosts made from white plastic bags, harvest figures with pumpkins for heads and newspaper-filled clothes for bodies, and storebought goblins and other Halloween spirits.[31] These temporal and temporary holiday yard displays demonstrate the public nature of yard art in general and the role of the American home in public culture. They also demonstrate the strong role the home plays in celebrating the annual cycles of natural seasons and cultural customs.

ROADSIDE ATTRACTIONS AND OTHER SPECTACLES WORTH A STOP

Mike Schack's yard just off Highway 2 in Grand Rapids, Minnesota, offers an eye-catching focal point along the road as locals drive to and from town and as tourists make their way to lakes or into town for groceries. There is a public orientation to his display on a corner lot. Its large, colorful sculptures speak the language of the roadside. With its fantasy animals, pipe-toting Popeye, and demure Snow White with her Seven Dwarfs, Mike Schack's yard mixes the humorous, oversized civic monument common to the Minnesota landscape with the roadside dinosaur park or alligator pit and Disneyland, all forms that promise an out-of-the-ordinary experience to those willing to make the stop.[32] Schack's giant mosquito could be one that bit Paul Bunyan. Its exaggerated size resembles other Minnesota town monuments that

Figure 2. Mike Schack's colossal mosquito in Grand Rapids, Minnesota.

boast of the uniqueness of their community through colossal statuary. In this state, one can find statues of Paul Bunyan himself in Bemidji and in Brainerd, his girlfriend, Lucette Diana Kensack, in Hackensack, and his cradle in Akley. Big fish monuments and other colossal imagery adorn many other Minnesota towns. Schack overtly points to connections between Disney's theme parks and his yard with his sign declaring the spot "Mike's World."

As Schack's yard demonstrates, the twentieth-century American roadside, with its spectacles, surprises, and colorful imagery, is first cousin to the amusement park. The visual aesthetic of the roadside has influenced the appearance of front yards, whether they are located on busy streets or off the beaten track. A reciprocal relationship exists between the domestic landscape and the roadside, as each landscape has borrowed from the other over the course of this century.

In early discussions of the roadside, when roads were being built for carriages and bicycles, we find a concern with the public aspects of roadside space. Writers exhorted property owners to assume a civic duty to keep their roadsides attractive. In *The Road and the Roadside*, Burton Willis Potter argued that roads were an important mark of a civilized nation. Offering both practical and philosophical advice, he commented on a wide range of roadside subjects—their construction and practical upkeep, the placement of guide posts and drinking troughs, and laws governing their use. Potter also promoted the importance of a pleasing aesthetic for the roadside. It was incumbent upon private homeowners to make roadside property attractive to passersby. "Besides the legal duty every dweller by a highway is under to use it with due regard to the rights of the public, he is under a moral and Christian obligation to maintain order and neatness within and without his roadside," Potter wrote. "When one benefits the community in which he lives, he thereby also benefits himself; and when he is possessed of the right kind of public spirit, he will beautify and improve his homestead and his roadside. . . . "[33] A pleasant prospect from the roadside, he insisted, provided a model for neighbors to follow.

Potter wrote primarily to homeowners and farmers, but his principles for roadside etiquette and aesthetics applied equally to business owners. In fact, the commercial roadside initially borrowed from home landscapes to make these new spaces appealing and reassuring. In the early days of highway auto travel during the 1920s, architectural historian Chester Liebs writes, small businesses were eager to make their establishments appear welcoming to folks whizzing by at thirty miles per hour in their Model T's. A chief means of achieving a friendly and familiar look was to appropriate elements of domestic architecture and landscapes. Photographer Dorothea Lange captured the roadside vernacular in her 1939 picture of the Lone Star Inn of Fresno, California, a modified bungalow, selling steak dinners, chili, and hamburgers. Similarly, roadside cabins, gas stations, and restaurants were gussied up with the overhanging eaves and false half-timbering of the Tudor cottage or trimmed with the shutters and flower boxes of the colonial cottage. Gardens and roadside lawns were added that completed the reference to the home scene, and handmade lawn ornaments were often added to complete the reference to home. One popular 1948 tourist stop in St. Albans Bay, Vermont, had converted a high-peaked house into a gas station, then added small cabins at the side, and finished off the scene with a fantasy garden, filled with handmade lawn ornament cut-outs of ducks, pink flamingos, and bonneted kids.[34]

The use of colorful imagery to attract customers harks back to the use of sculptural signs in eighteenth- and nineteenth-century cities, when signs shaped as people, objects, or animals advertised business establishments. Large teapots advertised tea stores. A carved sheep hung outside a woolen shop, and a wooden horse stood in front of a livery stable. Trade signs communicated the business of individual shops quickly and directly to passersby, a function that was particularly important when many Americans were illiterate or only read foreign languages.[35]

What folk sculpture expressed in the nineteenth century transferred to billboards and electric signs in the twentieth-century commercial landscape. In some cases, an entire building has taken the shape of a product, resulting in buildings that are a salient element in the American vernacular landscape. Architects Robert Venturi and Denise Scott Brown argue in *Learning from Las Vegas* that popular imagery effectively attracts people to vernacular architecture, letting them know the function, product, or fantasy experience offered by such structures as the Long Island Duckling, a building in the shape of a giant duck where ducks are sold, or Caesar's Palace in Las Vegas. This has proved to be an effective technique in countless roadside commercial buildings where "form follows function," a prominent modernist adage. But whereas high modernism promoted an intensely rational and stripped-down architecture, programmatic or mimetic architecture plays on the fantastical, the whimsical, and the irrational by making common objects colossal. It takes function literally in that the building often embodies the product for sale—an ice cream cone stand in the shape of an ice cream cone—or it embodies a fantasy experience available there—an exotic vacation spent lodging in a giant elephant's leg.

Many of these buildings have been "homemade" enterprises, vernacular architecture built by enterprising and imaginative individuals. Documented by J.C. Andrews in *The Well Built Elephant and Other Roadside Attractions*, these structures were built nationwide, from Riverhead, New York (home of the Big Duck duck store) to Bena, Minnesota (the Big Fish Supper Club) to Melbourne, Florida (the Oranges fruit stand) to California, host to numerous uniquely shaped buildings, such as the Tail of the Pup hot dog stand in Los Angeles and the Mother Goose Pantry, shaped like Old Mother Hubbard's giant shoe.[36] This genre of pop architecture originated in the late nineteenth century with Lucy the Elephant at Atlantic City, built in 1881 by James B. Lafferty. Lucy was followed by a larger elephant at Coney Island that was big enough to house a small hotel.

These elephant buildings were located at tourist destination sites, but it was car culture that generated numerous mimetic buildings across the United States along roads and highways from 1920 to 1970. To name just two, Paul Newport designed and built a milk bottle dairy store in Spokane, Washington, in 1922 by making a wood frame and covering it with mesh and stucco. And John Tindall, Ed McCreary and Jesse Hood built The Donut Hole buildings in Los Angeles, the first in 1963 and a second in 1968. Customers could drive through the doughnut hole to pick up a fresh, bag of hot pastry. Though many of these structures have fallen into disuse and have been torn down, new ones occasionally appear. More frequently today, the commercial sign takes sculptural form rather than the building itself, which, as noted by architect Robert Venturi, is usually a simple shed design behind the more fanciful sign. Colossal fiberglass chickens for supermarkets signs and giant steers for steak restaurants are just two examples of commercial sculpture found throughout the United States today.

In its ongoing conversation with the home, roadside businesses still make use of domestic imagery to make corporate franchises seem like friendly "Country Kitchens." Or business managers may plant gardens with flowers and statuary to express a cheery neighborliness that invites people to stop by and visit. Lawn ornaments, with their eye-catching appeal, are inexpensive means for small businesses to catch the eyes of passing motorists with whirligigs, windsocks, or statuary. In 1988, a hardware store in Atlanta installed a large display of plastic pink flamingos to stop people driving past on the highway, and a car dealership in that city used a similar technique to make potential customers to take notice and stop.[37]

MINIATURE GOLF AND HOMEMADE THEME PARKS

Historian Virginia Scott Jenkins has argued that the game of golf, with its highly manicured landscape, had a major impact on the development of the American lawn. Golf courses introduced Americans to the high standard of a constantly green, spongy turf that spurred similar desires for home landscapes, first influencing wealthy Americans, who took up golf in the late nineteenth century, and eventually filtering down to a broader public. The United States Golf Association helped to develop new grass species and promoted them for the home landscape.[38]

But the humbler version of the sport—miniature golf—also borrowed and generated ideas for home landscape design and imagery. The pint-sized game of golf began in the 1920s as an inexpensive alternative to the real game for working- and middle-class groups. Golf provided the model for the game itself, but the garden was the model for the landscape of miniature golf. Garden structures and statuary— gazebos and miniature windmills—served as obstacles or hazards for players trying to land their ball in the next hole.

James Barber built the prototype for miniature golf courses at his home in Pinehurst, North Carolina. In 1916, he laid out a course right in his yard, using its gazebos, gates, arbors, and flagstone garden paths for the landscape and hazards. Entrepreneurs copied Barber's plan for minigolf, and the game quickly became a national fad in the 1920s. Enterprising businesspeople Garnet and Frieda Carter, who created a minigolf course at their resort at Lookout Mountain, near Chattanooga, Tennessee in the mid-twenties, did much to popularize the game. Theirs was very much a do-it-yourself affair, with Frieda taking the lead as designer. She had already designed ten cabins at the resort, companions to the main hotel, called "Fairyland," to look like fairy tale cottages. She called them "Mother Goose Village." She extended the theme to her design for a minigolf course on their front lawn, using left-over materials from the cabin-building to make hazard structures and adding statues of gnomes, elves, and storybook figures like Little Red Riding Hood to the scene.[39] When the course caught on like mad, Garnet

Carter saw the opportunity to make money by spreading their formula. He called the enterprise Tom Thumb Golf, taking a storybook character's name, and set up one hundred craftsmen to fabricate the components necessary for a course. He sold these kits to entrepreneurs across the United States.

The miniature golf craze—and it was one of those 1920s-style crazes—peaked in 1930. Just one sign of Americans' intense interest in the sport comes from Los Angeles, where in 1930 alone 584 permits for construction of new minigolf courses were granted.[40] While some minigolf entrepreneurs received prebuilt components for their courses from the manufacturers like Garnet Carter, many more took the do-it-yourself route. They built course furnishings that borrowed from yard sculpture and garden structures—gazebos, wishing wells, Dutch windmills, and fairy tale characters. Magazines like *Popular Mechanics* offered plans and instructions for the handyman to construct a home game of miniature golf for the family.[41]

The game's popularity did not subside before leaving an indelible mark on the American landscape in the many courses built across the country in the 1920s. Interest in the game resumed in the post–World War II era, and its popularity has continued to grow, making minigolf an ongoing part of American leisure and American vacations. Courses operate around the nation in urban settings, in outlying rural areas, and in vacation lands. Current courses take two major variations. Many remain simple ma-and-pa operations that are homemade affairs with handbuilt hazards that resemble garden furnishings. Others have become fantasy environments more akin to amusement parks. Summer vacationers can golf beside a giant tyrannosaurus at Magic Carpet Golf in Key West, Florida, a colossal Guernsey cow at Fairway Golf in St. Paul, Minnesota, and and a dragon at Jockey Ridge's in Nags Head, North Carolina, to name just a few.[42] The landscape of minigolf has always played with scale in fantastical ways, sometimes miniaturizing the colossal by shrinking lighthouses, churches, and old mills, and monumentalizing other imagery, often real or imaginary animals rendered in bright fiberglass colors.

The connections between commercial roadside attractions and ornamented domestic space are underlined by the fact that a good number of roadside stops actually began as do-it-yourself projects in homeowners' private yards that grew and grew, creating spectacles worthy of a visit. These environments dot the American landscape from coast to coast, sometimes called folk art environments or the gardens of naive or visionary artists. They are homegrown roadside attractions, not commercial franchises. Although many eventually have become tourist attractions, they are not built as money-making endeavors.[43]

These vernacular environments have become tourist attractions in part because they embody familiar aesthetics but are carried out on a larger scale than in most yards. George Morris of Raleigh, North Carolina, for instance, bought a few acres outside the city after retiring from his work as a plasterer, and proceeded to fill the landscape with plaster mushrooms, giant dogs, frogs, and lighthouses. Humorously naming it "Gotno Farm," Morris welcomes the many visitors who stop by. Veronica Terrillion created her House and Garden in Lewis County in northern New York State over several decades. The front yard features her own cement statuary in an elaborate environment comprised of many tableaux, including the Our Lady of Fatima group, a menagerie of animals, and water creatures on an island in a pond. In response to her many visitors, whose names Terrillion has recorded in over seven guest books, she has developed a formal tour of the garden and her house. Fred Smith's famous Concrete Park in Phillips, Wisconsin features 250 concrete and glass statues depicting folkloric figures such as Paul Bunyan and Kit Carson alongside scenes of daily life in the region, tableaux that include images of Smith's own friends. Putting up the statuary over a fifteen-year period, Smith used bottles from his tavern business, embedding them into cement figures. Smith called his Concrete Park "the best Goddamn decoration on Highway 13 in the country." While Smith was alive, the park became a roadside stop for those traveling north to the fishing territory of northern Wisconsin's vacationland. The tourist appeal of the site has increased since it was adopted for restoration by the Kohler Foundation, the Wisconsin Arts Board, and the National Endowment for the Arts. The site is now owned by Price County, which conducts public tours of the grounds. Many similar environments are now being designated worthy of historic preservation, a development sure to preserve their function as tourist attractions as well.[44]

DISNEYLAND AND AMERICAN YARDS

Like George Morris, Veronica Terrillion, and Fred Smith, Walt Disney was an avid do-it-yourself handyman. Disneyland itself, architectural historian Derham Groves has argued, grew out of Disney's attraction to miniature railroads, one of which he built in his own Los Angeles backyard before he launched Disneyland. His theme park represents a large-scale fantasy environment in some ways similar to the one he built at his home in Holmby Hills, Los Angeles, a place he bought precisely because it had sufficient room to accommodate his dreams for a backyard railroad. In 1949, Disney began work on his outdoor line, modeling it on the Southern Pacific Railroad. He dubbed his train "the Carolwood Pacific," after Carolwood Avenue, where his new home was located. Soon he had laid a half a mile of track, complete with bridges and tunnels, through and around his wife Lilly's flower gardens. He later added a miniature barn, modeled after his own father's barn and inspired by the barn of Henry Ford's father, which he had seen on a visit to Greenfield Village. Disney used his small barn as a workshop and a "dispatcher's office" for the train. When he began planning Disneyland, the train that would take visitors to different landscape sections became a key element. Bill Evans, the landscape designer who helped Disney on his backyard, was enlisted to design the landscape of Disneyland.[45]

Opened in 1955, Disneyland represents the Versailles of amusement parks: a large-scale physical expression of one person's imagination.[46] In designing the theme park, Walt Disney cleaned up earlier amusement parks and incorporated elements from formal and vernacular gardens. The face of Mickey Mouse appears in flowers at the entrance to Main Street U.S.A. The park is embellished throughout with topiary elephants, hippos, and giraffes in garden settings. Giant whirligigs atop the facade of "It's A Small World" help to draw visitors to that ride.

Disney's theme parks now serve as models for many American yards and gardens. Homeowners often wish to copy on a small scale Walt Disney's creation of an idealized and enchanting environment. The power to shape an environment, whether just shy of two hundred acres, in the case of Disneyland, or a half-acre lot, holds enormous appeal to many landowners. "Brother" C.R. Jordan, a retired landscaper in a working-class suburb of Atlanta, refers to Disney World as a model for his yard. Although he has never been to Disney World, he said "I hear they don't have a cigarette or nothing on the ground. That's how I want my yard—spotless." His impressive front yard—bordered at the roadside with fanciful topiary and whirligigs made from bicycle wheels, filled with begonias and punctuated with religious statuary, woodland animal ornaments, and Biblical messages painted on rocks— expresses Jordan's notions of the ideal landscape: part Disneyland, part heavenly vision. He labored for forty years to create the current landscape, building the house himself and transforming the land from a barren, dusty lot into a lush garden. Jordan spends time working on his yard everyday: "I make things beautiful every chance I get," he adds. The landmark status of his home becomes most apparent when over four thousand tulips bloom there each spring, attracting carloads of visitors and buses from Atlanta nursing and convalescent homes. Imagery from Disneyland and the Disney films serve as models for Werner and Thekla Muense's yard in Minneapolis, where Werner has Snow White and the Seven Dwarfs and Bambi statues in their yard.[47]

As seen in the Muenses' yard art, Disney's imagery has been incorporated into American yards. Snow White, who stands at the waterfall just outside Disneyland's Fantasyland, and her cohorts, the Seven Dwarfs, can be found in cement, made by small ornament companies that do not worry too much about copyright infringement. Unworried about those issues, home handymen fashion plywood cutouts of the group in their own basements. Mike Schack bought his Snow White ensemble from a local senior citizens group that had made them as a money-making hobby. Similarly, doe-eyed Bambis and Thumpers from Disney's cartoon repertory have transformed the naturalistic deer and rabbit lawn statuary from turn-of-the century molds. The bright colors and fairy tale imagery of Disney cartoons have translated into the creation of other cartoon characters for the yard. Mike Schack created his own Warner Brothers cartoon character Popeye from a downed tree branch, and other handymen have created plywood cutouts of such characters as Elmer Fudd and Bugs Bunny.

The visual affinities between the colorful imagery of the commercial roadside, which attempts to attract customers, and the contemporary yard underline the public-oriented focus of the front yard. What's offered in the domestic landscape may be a similar fantastical experience as the roadside. But it's usually offered for free, or perhaps at the price of a friendly chat. Mike Schack's giant mosquito doesn't sit in his yard to sell bug spray. It freely offers a visual joke and allows visitors to laugh about a common human experience and to appreciate the Minnesota humor. The connection between commercial roadside and residential yards demonstrates the common vocabulary of material things. This is not to claim that all American space has become commercialized. Rather, vernacular aesthetics involve reworking familiar images and materials, and, in doing so, speak to public audiences.

The public appeal of the large-scale roadside sites and their more modest counterparts attests to the ability of vernacular landscape traditions to embody the pleasing aesthetics of middle- and working-class groups. Untutored in, though not necessarily unaware of the aesthetics of high art and elite landscape architecture, these groups are nonetheless artifactually conversant with a different aesthetic, one comprised of elements as diverse as do-it-yourself magazines, cartoons and animated films, Disneyland vacations, the American roadside, garden store merchandise, and local public landmarks. People like Harriet Bagasao, Mike Schack, C.R. Jordan, Clarence Weidert, and Paul Pino create public art that expresses a vital connection between these individuals and their communities. This active community involvement is vividly demonstrated by the vigorous interaction between yard artists and their public, relationships that are very often intergenerational, including senior citizens and neighborhood children.

At a time when scholars and leaders worry about increasing privatization of American society and growing segmentation in urban communities, it does us good to look at grassroots activities that, however modest in scope, help to overcome those ills. Vernacular customs that humanize the environment have been receiving increased attention, as J.B. Jackson, who studied commonplace landscapes for over four decades, noted in an article on "The Popular Yard." Some architects and city planners have rewarded the contributions of everyday citizens to the urban landscape, something the FRIDAY Architects/Planners of Philadelphia did when they gave "Building of the Month" prizes in 1976 to one home with an elaborate Christmas light display and to another brick rowhouse ornamented and painted by its owner.[48]

These efforts to recognize contributions of the vernacular landscape to civic life could well be heeded by those involved in institutional public art works, especially given the bitter controversies generated by many civic projects. For example, public art could benefit from more attention to the keen pleasures of yard art: seasonal changes, ephemeral elements, and accretion. The use of objects to mark seasonal change—whether plastic pink flamingos that appear at the first sign of spring or plastic eggs hanging from shrubs at Easter, harvest figures at Halloween or Christmas lights and illuminated Santas after Thanksgiving—connects the artifactual landscape to the natural landscape and to the life cycle, even in urban areas. These reminders of temporal change contradict notions of an inviolate and permanent work of art that will stand through the ages. Seasonal changes often involve an element of performance: to model his or her yard, homeowners sometimes don special costumes and roles for Halloween trick-or-treat or Christmas holidays. The temporal element of yard art also involves an emphasis on the process of creating and dismantling a display. This construction process can be as important as the finished piece itself, something that the public artist, Christo explores in his creation of large-scale, temporary works such as "Running Fence," a twenty-four mile long curtain of white nylon created in the early 1970s in Sonoma and Marin Counties of California.

Twentieth-century yard art also points to the need for more than homage, awe, or seriousness in the public landscape. Too often artists and public officials overlook the need for humor, spectacle, and whimsy in the environment. Like Mike Schack with his Popeye and giant mosquito, Claes Oldenburg, Red Grooms, and Luis Jimenez all have recognized the desire for visual humor, thereby creating some of the most beloved and successful public monuments of recent times. Other public art projects have successfully incorporated vernacular elements, as did the Seattle Arts Commission in its installation of dozens of whirligigs made by Emil and Vera Gehrke along a fence bordering the Viewlands/Hoffman electrical substation in the late 1970s.[49]

Yard art traditions testify to the continued public features of the American home and to the vitality of vernacular aesthetics. While not overturning all private aspects of the home, yard art does help to create an intermediate zone where individuals, families, neighbors, and strangers can interact. Those audiences become "cultural publics" for private yards. Thus yard art overcomes some of the divisions enforced by a built environment constructed primarily of single family homes. By bringing people together to ooh and awe, to exclaim and to laugh, yard art makes cities and suburbs, towns and countrysides friendlier places to live. Through visual affinities with public landscapes, from the public park to the amusement park, yard art demonstrates homeowners' efforts to bridge public and private worlds through the use of artifacts. These domestic landscapes thereby vividly demonstrate the subtlety and the power of material culture. If some social critics despair at Americans' lack of vocabulary for expressing ties to their communities, an examination of our artifactual vocabulary as demonstrated in our yards can be cause for greater optimism.[50]

NOTES

1. Interviews with Mike Schack, Grand Rapids, Minn., August 6, 1987; March 1988; August 18, 1988.

2. John F. Sears, *Sacred Places: American Tourist Attractions in the Nineteenth Century* (New York: Oxford University Press, 1989), 4-5; on Niagara, 12-30; on the Conneticut and Hudson river valleys, 49-71.

3. John Jakle, *The Tourist: Travel in Twentieth-Century North America* (Lincoln: University of Nebraska, Press, 1985), 22. Dean MacCannell, *The Tourist: A New Theory of the Leisure Class* (New York: Schoken Books, 1976), 13.

4. Alan Trachtenburg discusses this idea in relation to the Brooklyn Bridge and Henry Adams' comments on the "dynamo" in American culture. See *Brooklyn Bridge: Fact and Symbol* (Chicago: University of Chicago Press, 1965), 129-39.

5. See Thomas Schlereth, "The Material Universe of American World Expositions," in his *Cultural History and Material Culture: Everyday Life, Landscapes, Museums* (Ann Arbor: UMI Research Press, 1990), 265-302; and *A Facsimile of Frank Leslie's Illustrated Historical Register of the Centennial Exposition 1876,* introduction by Richard Kenin (New York: Paddington Press, 1974).

6. Schlereth, 277.

7. David F. Burg, *Chicago's White City of 1893* (Lexington, KY: University Press of Kentucky, 1976), 118-19.

8. Burton Benedict, *The Anthropology of World's Fairs* (Berkeley: Lowie Museum of Anthropology and Scolar Press, 1893), 2.

9. Albert Fein, *Frederick Law Olmsted and the American Tradition*, 66.

10. David McCullough, *The Great Bridge* (New York: Simon and Schuster, 1972), 524; 538-39.

11. Burg, 98, 111-12, 137, 227; Helen A. Harrison, "The Fair Perceived: Color and Light as Elements in Design and Planning" in her *Dawn of a New Day: The New York World's Fair, 1939/40* (New York: New York University Press and the Queens Museum, 1980), 46-52; Gary Brechin, "Sailing to Byzantium; The Architecture of the Fair" in Burton Benedict's *The Anthropology of World's Fairs: San Francisco's Panama Pacific International Exposition of 1915* (Berkeley: University of California with the Lowie Museum of Anthropology, 1983), 98-10l; Edward Hale Bush, "The Color Treatment of the Pan-American Exposition," *Scientific American*, November 10, 1900, 293-94.

12. Charles W. Person, "New York's Greatest Lighting Spectacle," *Scientific American*, February 20, 1915, 171; Brechin, 98-99. On the importance of lighting in civic architecture, see Richard C. Peters, "Light and Public Places," *Places,* 1 (Winter 1984): 41-47. For a discussion of the conflicting models for the urban landscape embodied in "the White City" of the Columbian Exposition and the Midway Plaisance, see Barbara Rubin, "Aesthetic Ideology and Urban Design" in *Common Places: Readings in American Vernacular Architecture,* edited by Dell Upton and John Michael Vlach (Athens, Ga.: University of Georgia, 1986), 482-507. Rubin argues that the Midway, with its entreprenurial hodgepodge of booths by individual vendors, served as a precursor to later highway strips and strip shopping centers.

13. Russel B. Nye, "Eight Ways of Looking at an Amusement Park," *Journal of Popular Culture* 15 (Summer 1981): 63-65; John Kasson, *Amusing the Million: Coney Island at the Turn of the Century* (New York: Hill & Wang, 1978), 66; Gary Kyriazi, *The Great American Amusement Park* (Secaucus, NJ: Citadel Press, 1976), 66. See Michele H. Bogart, "Barking Architecture: The Sculpture of Coney Island," *Smithsonian Studies in American Art*, 2 (Winter 1988): 3-17 for valuable discussion of relationships between amusement park imagery and the public sculpture of world's fairs.

14. For transformation of Christmas into a "festival of consumption," see Daniel Boorstin, *The Americans: The Democratic Experience* (New York: Random House, 1973), 157-62.

15. "Tree of Christmas," brochure (Washington, D.C.: Smithsonian Natural Museum of History and Technology, 1978) in Vertical files, Office of Horticulture Library, Smithsonian Institution, Washington, D.C.

16. Tristam Potter Coffin, *The Book of Christmas Folklore* (New York: Seabury Press, 1973), 18-19. James Barnett, *The American Christmas: A Study in National Culture* (New York: Macmillan, 1954), 2-8, 19-20, 66.

17. "Origin of Outdoor Christmas Lighting Traced to Denverite," *Colorado History News*, December 1986, 6; Jacob A. Riis, "The New Christmas That Is Spreading All Over Our Country," *Ladies Home Journal,* December 1913, 16. On Coolidge, see "Coolidge Will Light Big Christmas Tree," *New York Times,* December 7, 1924, 2. Interestingly, the article states that Coolidge was invited to light the tree by representatives of the Society for Electrical Development, who thought that a display of one large tree would help conservation efforts to preserve forests.

18. David Handlin, *The American Home: Architecture and Society, 1815-1915* (Boston: Little, Brown and Company, 1979), 419-21, 474-75.

19. "Electrical Invasion of the Home," *Scientific American*, December 2, 1916, 502.

20. Phillip V. Snyder, *The Christmas Tree Book* (New York: Viking Press, 1977), 113-16, 128.

21. "The New Art of Christmas Garden Lighting," *American Home*, December 1928, 235-246.

22. Elmer C. Fewell, "How to Light Your Homegrounds," *Better Homes and Gardens*, December 1930, 67-68.

23. "Minneapolis Claims Brightest Christmas," *New York Times*, December 25, 1927, III, 6. "Let the Whole House Say Merry Christmas" *Better Homes and Gardens*, December 1931, 13-15.

24. "Christmas Lights," *Life*, December 19, 1949, 40-45; "America Lights Up for Christmas," *Colliers,* December 18, 1954, 94-96; Paul C. Law, "Deck the Halls with Frills and Follies," *Saturday Evening Post*, December 18, 1954, 36.

25. The Foshay Tower has worn banners hailing the victories of the local baseball team, the Minnesota Twins, and was wrapped with a gigantic yellow ribbon when the American hostages in Iran were released in 1980. For the importance of marking time and events in the urban environment, see Kevin Lynch, *What Time Is This Place?* (Cambridge: MIT Press, 1980).

26. Mike Capuzzo, "Pulling Together on Colorado Street," *Philadelphia Inquirer*, August 31, 1988, 1C, 4C.

27. For other instances in Philadelphia, see "A Neighborhood Effort," *Philadelphia Inquirer*, December 4, 1987, 1A. Information on customs in Anaheim neighborhood from interview with Judy McCormack, November 9, 1988. Patoski has published her photographs in *Merry Christmas America: A Front Yard View of the Holidays* (Charlottesville, VA: Thomasson-Grant, Inc. 1994).

28. Roy Campbell, "Bright Lights, Big Wonders for Little Town," *Philadelphia Inquirer*, December 24, 1987, D1; for tour itinerary, James Lileks, "'Twas the Light before Christmas," and "66 Places to See Great Lights," *St. Paul Pioneer Press Dispatch*, December 18, 1987, 1B, 2B, 3B. Another elaborate site for holiday displays in Los Angeles is Florencio Morales, documented by Amy Kitchener, *The Holiday Yards of Florencio Morales* (Jackson, MI: University Press of Mississippi, 1994).

29. Interview with Clarence Weidert, Minneapolis, Minn., January 2, 1989. Weidert commented that many visitors appreciate the religious elements of his display, i.e., the nativity creches. The personal expression of religious beliefs remains important in the domestic landscape in a society that attests to the belief in the separation of church and state. Considerable controversy has

been generated by the display of religious symbols related to Christmas and Hanukah on public property. Legal cases have gone as far as the U.S. Supreme Court: on a 1986 case involving a nativity scene, Christmas tree, and Jewish menorah at the Allegheny County Courthouse in Pittsburg, see County of Allegheny v. American Civil Liberties Union Greater Pittsburgh, 106 L Ed 2d, U.S. Supreme Court, 1989.

30. Information on pilots flying over his home supplied by Wiedert in interview; author observed visitors to Weidert home on several occasions, December 1987-90.

31. On Halloween displays, see Jack Santino, "The Folk Assemblages of Autumn: Tradition and Creativity in Halloween Folk Art." *Folk Art and Art Worlds*, John Michael Vlach and Simon Bronner, eds., (Ann Arbor, MI: UMI Press, 1986), 151-69. Halloween displays are discussed in many of the essays in Jack Santino, ed., *Halloween and Other Festivals of Death and Life* (Knoxville: University of Tennessee Press, 1994).

32. For discussion of civic monuments in Minnesota, see Karal Ann Marling, *Colossus of Roads: Myth and Symbol Along the American Highway,* (Minneapolis: University of Minnesota Press, 1984); on relationships between colossal statues and yard art, see Colleen J. Sheehy, "Giant Mosquitos, Eelpout Displays, Pink Flamingos: Some Overlooked and Unexpected Minnesota Folk Arts" in *Circles of Tradition: Folk Arts in Minnesota* (St. Paul: University of Minnesota Art Museum in conjunction with the Minnesota Historical Society Press, 1989), 46-48.

33. Burton Willis Potter, *The Road and the Roadside.* (Boston: Little, Brown and Co, 1893), 113.

34. Chester H. Liebs, *Main Street to Miracle Mile: American Roadside Architecture* (Boston: Little, Brown, 1985), 44-48. For Lange and Vermont photos, see Liebs, 46-47.

35. Robert Bishop, *American Folk Sculpture* (New York: Bonanza Books, 1985), 23-42.

36. On programmatic architecture, see Liebs, 48-53, and David Gebhard's introduction to J.C. Andrew's book, cited below. Robert Venturi, Denise Scott Brown, Steven Izenour, *Learning from Las Vegas: The Forgotten Symbolism of Architectural Form*, rev. ed. (Cambridge: MIT Press, 1977). J.C. Andrews, *The Well-Built Elephant and Other Roadside Attractions* (New York: Congdon & Weed, Inc.,1984).

37. Author observed flamingo ornament display during fieldwork in Atlanta in October 1988 and also had phone interview with Roy Strickland, John Smith Chevrolet in Atlanta, October 26, 1988.

38. Jenkins, *The Lawn*, 52-61.

39. Liebs, 138-39

40. Liebs, 144. See also Karal Ann Marling, *Colossus of Roads*, 35-39.

41. Margolies, 74-76.

42. For images of these, see Margolies, 78-83.

43. I. Sheldon Posen and Daniel Franklin Ward, "Watts Towers and the *Giglio* Tradition," *Folklife Annual* (Library of Congress), 1985: 143-57. There is some disagreement among scholars over what to call these places: folk art environments, visionary environments, gardens of revelation have been some terms used to describe them. In some cases these environments are folk art forms that exhibit ties between an artist and his or her community and reflecting community aesthetics. Even in those cases that at first appear to be idiosyncratic expressions, the artist has utilized folk elements in its construction that may not be at first apparent. Folklorists Daniel Ward and I. Sheldon Posen, for instance, discovered that Simon Rodia's Watts Towers, which have been viewed as thoroughly idiosyncractic, had connections to Italian festival structures. John Beardsley has written about large-scale domestic environments most recently in *Gardens of Revelation,* and he does argue for greater appreciation of the artists and their creations, which are often built as a public gift to the artist's community. Yet his reliance on a model of analysis first developed by surrealist artists, who were interested in subconscious expressions by people characterized as "other," including tribal people and the mentally ill, perpetuates the notion that these sites are eccentric and marginal.

44. These large-scale folk art environments have been documented most vigorously by Seymour Rosen of Los Angeles through the organization SPACES (Saving and Preserving Arts and Cultural Environments), which he founded and directs. Contributions and documentations from scholars and devotees throughout the United States are published in the SPACES quarterly newsletter. On George Morris, see SPACES newsletter, no. 2, 1985, 6 and Roger Manley, *Signs and Wonders: Outsider Art Inside North Carolina* (Raleigh: North Carolina Museum of Art, 1989), 22. On Veronica Terrillion, see Varick A. Chittenden, "Veronica Terillion's 'Woman made' House and Garden" in *Personal Places: Perspectives on Informal Art Environments.* Daniel Franklin Ward, ed., (Bowling Green, OH: Bowling Green University Press, 1984), 41-61. On Fred Smith, see Judith Hoos and Gregg Blasdel, "Fred Smith's Concrete Park" in *Naives and Visionairies* (New York: E.P. Dutton & Co. with the Walker Art Center, 1974), 53-60. Update on the status of Concrete Park in SPACES newsletter, no. 1 (1982), 2, and SPACES newsletter, no. 4 (1982), 4-5. SPACES works to preserve these environments, lobbying for some to be declared historic landmarks. They have met with some success, as with Simon Rodia's Watts Towers in Los Angeles.

45. Derham Groves, "Walt Disney's Backyard," *Exedra: Architecture, Art & Design*, 5, 1 (1994): 29-38.

46. Richard Schickel, *The Disney Version: The Life, Times, and Commerce of Walt Disney*, 2d ed., rev. (New York: Simon & Schuster, 1985), 315.

47. Interview with C.R. Jordan, Atlanta, GA, October 24, 1988. Interview and visits with Muense's, Minneapolis, 1984-1990.

48. J.B. Jackson, "The Popular Yard," *Places* 4 (Spring 1989): 26-31. Jackson concludes that the designed vernacular yard "can give our houses and streets and cities a humanity they badly need." On awards, see David Slovic and Ligia Rave, "Buildings of the Month Awards: Philadelphia," *Places* 1 (Spring 1984): 44-59.

49. Yi-Fu Tuan and J.B. Jackson have both written about historical connections between the garden and theatre in Tuan, *Dominance and Affection: The Making of Pets* (New Haven, Con.: Yale University Press, 1984), 31-35; Jackson, "Landscape as Theatre" in his collection *The Necessity of Ruins and Other Topics* (Amherst: University of Massachusetts Press, 1980), 67-75. Holiday traditions that involve homeowners donning a costume and playing Santa or Dracula are contemporary examples of similar practices, which like earlier traditions, involve elements of trickery and surprise. A riveting account of Christo's process for creating public art is provided in the film *Running Fence* by David and Albert Maysles, 1977. On Claes Oldenburg, see Martin Friedman, *Oldenburg: Six Themes* (Minneapolis: Walker Art Center, 1975); on Red Grooms, Luis Jimenez, and the Seattle Art Commission, see Beardsley, 36, 25, 22, respectively. Richard Sennett discusses the importance of play in public sociability, a quality he sees as suppressed in modern times. See *The Fall of Public Man* (New York: Alfred A. Knopf, 1977), 316-23.

50. Robert Bellah et.al. analyze what Americans have to say about individualism and community in *Habits of the Heart: Individualism and Commitment in American Life* (Berkeley: University of California Press, 1985).

III

The Flamingo in the Garden
An Iconography of American Yard Art

In 1984, "Miami Vice" brought a new style of television drama to the
small screen, a look established immediately in its opening shots.
Borrowing the montage and music combinations popular in music
videos, the show began with the driving beat of Jan Hammer's rock
music, paired with quick-cut shots of Miami. After an initial shot of
towering palm trees, a flock of scurrying pink flamingos opened the
sequence, followed by water rushing under a speeding boat, women in
bikinis walking on the beach, and scenes of postmodern architecture by
the Miami-based firm Arquitectonica. The plot centered on vice cops
Sonny Crocket and Ricardo Tubbs, played by handsome stars Don
Johnson and Philip Michael Thomas, who battled the city's sordid yet
glamorous underworld of drugs, smuggling, and prostitution, all
rendered in an inimitable visual style borrowed from film noir and
given a pastel tint. Most action used the art deco district of south Miami
Beach as its backdrop. This was a place where the dangerous
temptations of sex, drugs, and crime were underscored by a catchy rock
beat, where cops drove Ferraris and wore Giorgio Armani suits, and
where even the police station was housed in an elegant art deco
building, suitably appointed inside in postmodern furniture and colors.

With its hip visual style that thrust flamingos and Florida into the
minds of millions of viewers, "Miami Vice" is widely credited with
spurring a flamingo craze during the 1980s, when sales of the pink
plastic lawn ornament catapulted to unprecedented heights.[1] Miami had
been the virtual birthplace of America's love affair with the flamingo,
and the show's opening images may have made the plastic bird *au
courant*, just as its stars' stylish linen suits influenced men's fashion

and Don Johnson's five o'clock shadow made scruffiness sexy. Yet many other factors converged in the 1980s to make the plastic pink flamingo so popular. By the time "Miami Vice" first aired, consumers from diverse groups were already buying up the garden ornament, some to assert its paradisical associations with the American home and yard, some to express ambivalent attitudes about American culture. The iconography and ethnography of the pink flamingo thus presents a fascinating and useful case study in American yard art.

The flamingo serves as a revealing image to examine at length for its origins and meanings, and it provides a lively object with which to look at consumer practices, which reflect their active and creative manipulation of objects. These uses document the complex interactions and intersections between reality (the real bird), representation (images of the bird) and the social world (people employing the imagery). In this chapter, I examine the iconography of the flamingo in some depth, moving from an examination of the natural history of the bird to its appearance in American zoos to its representation in American art and artifacts and its associations with the home. In more recent years, people in varied groups have used the imagery to express complex and sometimes contradictory ideas and attitudes toward the home, mainstream culture and subcultures, and even about sexuality. The use of interviews and fieldwork yields important inside viewpoints on the contemporary use and display of flamingo imagery and the pink plastic flamingo lawn ornament. Before turning to the flamingo, I consider more briefly several other genres of garden imagery that persist and co-exist in American yards, including the gazing globe, images of children, the black groomsman or jockey, farm imagery and woodland animals. The gazing globe and the black groomsman are given more development in part because their changing status and meanings echo similar dynamics to the pink flamingo.

THE DECLENSION OF THE GAZING GLOBE

In 1920, in the midst of Mrs. Frederick Taylor's Philadelphia estate, Boxly, stood a glass ball with a shimmering, mirrored surface. The shiny globe captured on its circumference a reflection of the magnificent shrub enclosure and surrounding gardens. The box shrub itself had been planted in 1803 in the Chestnut Hill area of the city by one of the estate's early owners, Count Jean Du Barry, who had wanted to plant a garden in remembrance of Versailles. He appointed the garden with fruit trees and with white marble statues, purchased abroad and then placed against the dark green shrubbery. Mr. and Mrs. Frederick W. Taylor moved in nearly a century later in 1901. They took painstaking care to move and revive the stately box and added crossing pathways. The gazing globe, placed in the center of the brick pathways, captured the entire scene in miniature as a shiny orb. Mrs. Taylor's garden demonstrates that the gazing globe was an artifact of impeccable taste in the early decades of this century. The practice of displaying one in the midst of a garden or yard was endorsed by the prestigious Garden Club of America, an organization founded in Philadelphia, for it sung the praises of Boxly in many of its publications.[2]

The gazing globe was indeed a popular accent for upper-class gardens in the early years of this century. But it had mysteriously fallen out of fashion by mid-century and beyond, particularly among the class of consumers who would have eagerly purchased and proudly displayed it in their gardens in an earlier era. The declension of the gazing globe thus presents a fascinating case of an object's shift in value from an elite to a lower-middle- or working-class object. Why and how this happened is a difficult story to fully uncover, a story told mostly through garden catalogues. Yet today many Americans are curious about this object—its name, its origins, and its use. Considering it a curious object and a sign of bad taste, many are surprised to hear that it was once a sign of beauty and cultivation in the gardens of the wealthy.

Evidence indicates that Mrs. Taylor was not alone in her admiration for the gazing globe. A 1904 catalogue for the Galloway Terra-Cotta Company features a reflective gazing globe on a terra-cotta pedestal as part of its garden furnishings. The Philadelphia company had been in business since 1810, and its three awards at international expositions were proof of the quality of its products. The gazing globe was just one of dozens of items made by Galloway Pottery for home decorating. The company's inventory ranged from life-size statues of the Greek goddess Diana and copies of the Venus de Milo to more mundane pots, urns, box planters, and furniture. "Your garden will be improved," the company opined, "with artistic pottery and terra-cotta furniture . . . It may be said that a garden is incomplete without a Sun Dial to mark the sunny hours, while a Gazing Globe is an ideal piece to place amidst the flowers, reflecting their beauty in its mirrored surface."[3] The artfulness of the objects was emphasized in promotional rhetoric. "The garden, even though small, will be improved by the proper placing of artistic pieces," the Galloway Pottery catalogue stated, "while a sundial, bird bath, or gazing globe should form a central point of interest to complete its beauty."[4] Well-to-do Philadephians could purchase a 26-inch gazing globe for twenty-four dollars, a 22-inch orb for twelve dollars, and pedestals in varying heights, priced at four to twelve dollars from Galloway Pottery. One would have had to be comfortable economically to pay even twenty dollars for the globe and stand, when the average earnings of American workers were not even three dollars a day. Its popularity among the upper class can be seen in images of gardens from this era: displayed at the end of a long garden walk at the John Slack home in Pittsburg in 1915, at the center of crossing garden paths at the J.H. Troup house in Harrisburg, Pennsylvania, or in the midst of rose gardens at the W.W. Cummer House in Jacksonville, Florida, in 1924.[5]

Though we do know that the gazing globe was popular in American gardens in the early part of this century, its origins are more difficult to pinpoint. Its form and material suggest that it is related to the hollow, reflective Christmas bulb that had become popular in the United States at the same time. Those decorative objects developed first in late nineteenth-century Germany, arising from competitions among glassblowers, who challenged each other to blow larger orbs as feats of their craft. The blown-glass Christmas bulb originated in the German town of Lauscha in the 1840s. Lauscha's glassblowing cottage industries, in fact, made nearly all blown-glass tree ornaments until just before World War I.

Louis Griener-Schlotfeger of Lauscha is credited with making a reflective silver-nitrate solution for glass blowing, borrowing a recipe from Bohemia bead makers and their silver beads. Lauscha glassblowers were known to amuse themselves by seeing how large a bubble they could blow. These balls were called "kugels." By adding Griener-Schlotfeger's silver solution, the glass attained a reflective quality. In Germany, the balls were hung from the home ceilings at Christmastime, and by 1848, some Germans started hanging them on their Christmas trees. Griener-Schlotfeger perfected a process for making paper-thin kugels and, in 1870, devised a method for molding them into such shapes as pine cones, apples, and ice crystals. By that time, the bulbs were being exported to the United States, brought in great quantities by businessmen like F.W. Woolworth, who first saw them on his buying trips to Europe.[6]

Like the Christmas bulb, the gazing globe was made from blown glass with a reflective surface. The mirrored orb was meant to reflect the beauty of the surrounding landscape. Its reflective qualities mimicked another common garden accent—water—which could be shaped into designed pools, ponds, and fountains. The gazing globe on a pedestal captured the world around it in 360 degrees, condensing the beauty of the surrounding landscape—the garden, house, and sky—into a miniature world. It created in actual form and expressed symbolically idealized sentiments about the home and garden as a perfect world.

By 1920, Galloway Pottery devoted a full page to their gazing globes, which could be set on pedestals of varying styles. "When in the midst of roses or other flowers," they recommended, "the gazing globe has its greatest charm." Prices had increased, with 14-inch globes going for sixty dollars and a 12-inch one for forty-eight dollars.[7] It may have been a Galloway Pottery product that T.H. Mulligan purchased for his garden in nearby and swanky Swarthmore, Pennsylvania, where a gazing globe stood in the center of his garden in the mid-1920s.[8] Yet by that time these objects were also beginning to grace the yards and gardens of a growing number of middle-class homeowners. The Long-Bell Lumber Company of Kansas City, Missouri capitalized on the growing market in its 1925 catalogue, *The Book of Lawn Furniture*. Gazing globes were available, along with their trellises, arbors, and benches, to create "a much admired" garden.[9]

The era's nouveaux riches adopted gazing globes, along with other artifacts, as signs that they had arrived into a world of achievement and taste. The candy millionaire, Milton S. Hershey, for instance, had a gazing globe placed in the midst of the lavish three-acre rose garden he commissioned to be built just south of the Hershey Hotel in his company town of Hershey, Pennsylvania. When the garden opened to the public in May 1937, the gazing globe was surrounded by 12,000 roses in 112 varieties. More than 200,000 people visited the gardens that first season, and by 1941, the Hershey Rose Garden drew nearly half a million visitors each year.[10]

At about the same time, the garden supply company of Stumpp & Walter Company, headquartered in New York City with branch stores scattered along the eastern seaboard, promoted their "Sloane gazing-globe" as "an attractive lawn ornament" for a reasonable fifteen dollars in its 1931 catalogue. Whimsy rather than art was conveyed in its selection of garden decoration—storybook creatures of white rabbits, frogs, Wendy from *Peter Pan*, and assorted pixies created from cement art stone. The Stumpp & Walter pedestal for the gazing globe become the focus of greater ingenuity in the postwar period, when the company departed from earlier designs of classical columns to create a "rustic" pedestal made of steel-reinforced cement. Its faux bark surface matched their designs for a charcoal grill and backyard incinerator. The uniqueness and durability of these rustic designs were lauded in the text, along with their ability to blend into the surroundings for the suburban home. The rustic pedestal sold for fifteen dollars, and a 14-inch globe for just thirteen. The falling prices indicate that people with lower incomes could purchase these items. By 1960, a 10-inch gazing globe from Artcrete was only $9.50.[11] By then, the gazing globe was primarily marketed to the broad segment of middle- and working-class Americans, residing in postwar suburbs and barbequing on backyard grills. Whether displayed on rustic cement or on the increasingly favored plastic pedestal, the gazing globe was still a sign of prosperity and disposable income, but it now spoke of middle-class domesticity rather than of upper-crust cultivation.

Despite its decline in status over the course of the century, the gazing globe is beginning to make a comeback in the 1990s, when it is more frequently seen displayed with other merchandise at garden stores and more frequently found in American yards than in past years. Its rediscovery and revaluation may be due to the growing interest in historical garden styles, as Americans grow to appreciate the beauty of flowers and garden designs from earlier eras along with their antique garden statuary.[12] Unlike the cast-iron animals and urns from the Victorian era, gazing globes were far too fragile to earn the status of antiques. Not to worry—the silvery orbs currently manufactured resemble the originals almost exactly, even though they usually come in only one size, and their ceramic pedestals, made from copies of earlier molds, echo the 1920s styles of Galloway Pottery and of the gazing globe at Mrs. Frederick Taylor's Boxly.

IMAGES OF CHILDHOOD AND THE BLACK JOCKEY

Imaginary children were popular subjects in classical European garden sculpture, from cherubs and *putti* to youngsters representing virtues or ideas. This imagery found enthusiastic buyers on American soil, when European copies of such subjects were imported in the late nineteenth and early twentieth centuries. In 1915, for instance, Mary Clark Thompson's summer estate in Canandagua, New York, featured several cherubs as the focal point for her garden. Children frolicking with each other or with animals were popular commissions for the gardens of wealthy patrons, while the same pieces were often reproduced in less costly materials for a middle-class market. Middle-class homeowners, for instance, enjoyed the sentimental fountain sculpture, "Out in the Rain," which featured two ragamuffins at its center, standing under an umbrella. These images of children in nature merged the innocence qualities associated with both subjects at the turn of the century.[13]

By the late nineteenth century, garden statuary began to represent American experiences more directly. The figure of a barefoot boy with a fishing pole, waiting lazily for a bite, was such a piece, fashioned to sit beside a pool. By the time its sculptural version appeared, the image had become widely popular in American art and literature, in popular prints, and in the imagination of urban businessmen, many of whom were taking up sport fishing in the post–Civil War era and writing about it for the sporting press. Sport fishing itself offered upper- and middle-class men a respite from work pressures and city life by immersing them in a soothing natural setting, where they could re-enact boyish fun. The barefoot boy with a fishing pole expressed that longing for boyhood and release from adult responsibilities. In visual sources, the image was circulated in the Currier & Ives print by Frances F. Palmer, *The Barefoot Boy*, of 1872 and in the many works by Winslow Homer picturing straw-hatted boys languishing near streams and ponds, such as his engraving, *Waiting for a Bite*, of 1874. Mark Twain provided lively and popular literary counterparts in the characters of Huck Finn and Tom Sawyer. Many writers for sporting magazines employed the image when waxing poetic on their own boyhoods. In "A Fisherman's Reverie" published in *Western Field and Stream*, attorney Grace Lincoln Hall wrote, "Fishing has always been a favorite pastime of mine ever since my days of barefoot boyhood when a bent pin served as a successful hook." He went on to lament that he could not take his fishing daydreams back to "the hurry and struggle" of his business world. The barefoot boy was an appropriate image for the suburban yard of the day, when the suburban setting itself functioned as a similar antidote to city problems and business pressures, as did sports fishing.[14]

Variations on the barefoot boy sculpture include a barefoot black boy holding a fishing pole. But the most common African-American image in the yard has undoubtedly been the statue of the black jockey. We find it, for instance, in 1959 at Eleutherian Mills, the ancestral home of the du Pont family of Wilmington, Delware, where a cast-iron statue of a black boy holding a lantern stood outside the front door at a house. Next to the sprawling gardens at Eleutherian Mills, this was an object too neglible to be well-documented except through a photograph, now in the slide collection at the Archives of American Gardens at the Smithsonian Institution. The statue nonetheless was a very visible expression of power relations at the home of a wealthy landowner. E.I. du Pont had established his estate at the site in 1803. Over many years, du Pont and his descendants built the large grounds into working and ornamental gardens. The statue was left from the nineteenth century, when most of the gardens were built, though they had been reconstructed in the 1970s, becoming a tourist attraction as part of the Hagley Museum and Libary complex in Wilmington.[15]

Like other garden imagery that refers to idealized places, the black jockey suggests the southern plantation as an ideal site of aristocratic ease and power, even when transferred to other regions. The black jockey placed in the front yard or next to the front door asserts the power of the white homeowner at the expense of the African-American, pictured as a servant or slave. The image participates in the common images of black servants in American popular culture, appearing in advertising and popular drama from the stage and radio to television and film.[16] The black jockey also forms part of garden statuary traditions, mostly of European origins, which picture peasants, shepherds, shepherdesses, and other servants in the landscape. Like their counterparts in European painting, peasants working the land, gathering crops, and tending to animals suggested an appealing pastoral world where people and nature worked in harmony.

Though by and large considered a derogatory image of African-Americans today, the statue has a fascinating history that is little known among African-Americans and virtually unknown by most other Americans. Evidence exists that African-Americans have intervened in the interpretation of the black jockey statue. African-American oral traditions include a legend that George Washington was the originator of the black jockey lawn statue. According to the story, "Jocko," the reputed subject of the statue, was the son of a free black man, Tom Graves, who fought with the Continental Army in the American Revolution. One night, after Graves had visited his family on furlough, Jocko tried to follow him back to the troops. Finding army troops but not his father, Jocko helped the men by holding and quieting General Washington's stallion during a winter storm on the very night before

Washington crossed the Delaware. Jocko was so dedicated to his task that he froze to death holding the reins of the General's stallion, (ironically, in the very pose adopted by the statue, with one arm out raised). Upon discovering the tragedy, Washington and his men were deeply moved. In homage to the boy, Washington promised to commission a statue of Jocko for his home at Mount Vernon.[17]

As with many legends whose origins are speculative, the story of Jocko is not corroborated by historical facts. According to the Mount Vernon Ladies' Association, which maintains George Washington's estate as a historical site, there is no evidence that Washington ever had such a statue. Curator Christine Meadows states:

> As you might imagine there are literally hundreds of views of Mount Vernon, painting, prints, photographs, etc., dating from the 18th century. Not one, to my knowledge, shows anykind of hitching post near the Mansion. Neither is there any documentation supporting Koger's assertion that George Washington ordered a statue of a small black boy for this home. Whatever the origins and evolution of these hitching posts...I do not believe that George Washington had any part of it.

Nor do Sidney and Emma Kaplan detail the story of Jocko or document Thomas Graves in their study, *The Black Presence in the Era of the American Revolution*. Yet, as folklore scholars assert, the real importance of a narrative lies in its existence and its telling, not in whether it is "true."[18]

Regardless of the precise origins of the statue, we do know that cast-iron statues of a black boy wearing bedraggled clothes were manufactured in antebellum days, often referred to in trade catalogs as "the faithful groomsman." The statue was functional as well as ornamental. Some figures served as hitching posts; others held lanterns to light driveways and doorways. We also know that the statue was sometimes used during abolitionist days to indicate a "safe house" on the underground railroad. Abolitionists would light the lantern, post an American flag in the jockey's hand, or tie a kerchief around its neck to signal those fleeing slavery that it was safe to seek shelter there. Historian Wilbur Henry Siebert, who conducted interviews in the late nineteenth and early twentieth centuries with people who had escaped slavery, documented this practice. His research identifies the home of federal judge Benjamin Piatt in West Liberty, Illinois, as a safe house.

Piatt's (unnamed) wife was an abolitionist, though the judge himself was not (the federal government supported laws that fined and imprisoned American citizens for aiding fugitive slaves). Mrs. Piatt would place a flag in the hand of the statue at their home as a means to signal that runaways were welcome. If there was no flag, it meant that the judge was home and the travelers would have to pass by.[19]

By the late nineteenth century, two major variations of the statue developed: one, the bedraggled little boy, and the other, a polished black jockey in riding clothes, both cast at miniature size. These versions were still offered in cast iron by J.W. Fiske Iron Works of New York in 1920 and have appeared in private yards and in public places, often as hitching posts in front of stores and other commercial sites. Homeowners today can buy them cast in cement, though most often now they are painted white, not black. This color change became common in the 1960s, when the black jockey statue caught the wrath of the civil rights movement, along with other disparaging images of blacks, and white Americans became more aware of racist imagery. Since then, African-Americans have inverted the imagery by buying white jockeys for their lawns or painting black jockeys white.[20]

Historian George Lipsitz has written about the notion of "countermemory," meaning the stories told among disempowered groups that validate their experiences and perceptions of history, which are often left out of dominant historical narratives.[21] The legend of Jocko, George Washington, and the black jockey statue may have arisen in that way, countering an image of subservience with an image of honor.

THE FARM MINIATURIZED AND RECREATED

The rural life of the southern plantation alluded to by the black groomsman intersects with other rural associations with the yard. In European traditions, the *ferme ornée* served as a playground for European aristocrats who could play at the simple life of peasants. Marie Antoinette, for instsance, could imagine herself a shepherdess at Versailles's Petit Trianon, where one section of the garden was designed as a miniature farm. Farm imagery in American yards, rather than arising from an attraction to playing the rube, refers to an honorable and usable American past.[22]

It is difficult to document the precise moment when farm artifacts and imagery became decorative ornaments for the American yard. But the 1930s were a critical time for the transformation of elements of the farm landscape into visual icons, ready to find symbolic roles in urban and suburban front yards.[23] American Regionalist artists of the period, in whose work the physical elements of the farm became symbolically charged with representing the whole way of rural life, were vehicles for this iconization. John Steuart Curry, Thomas Hart Benton, and Grant Wood pictured the farm of the American Midwest in prints, paintings, and murals. At a time when the future of farm life was most in doubt, when the plains became dust bowls, driving many farmers from the land, and when the Depression caused an epidemic of farm foreclosures, images of the farmer and of life on the farm took on highly charged meaning. Farms of the past, where hand plows rather than the contemporary engine-driven tractors turned the rich earth, were depicted as idyllic landscapes where nature is the Garden of the World: fertile, orderly, and predictable—unlike the unpredictable nature of the 1930s, when rain wouldn't fall and crops wouldn't grow.

Of the major regionalist artists, it was Grant Wood who did most to make the midwestern farm into a visual icon, identifying features that would later appear in suburban yards: the windmill, the well, the pump, and the barn. In his manicured farmscapes, crops grow in precise rows like miniature sculptures in landscapes patterned by human hands, more like suburban yards than real farm fields. In *Fall Plowing* (1931), haystacks have become a kind of topiary art in a field covered with plant stalks that look like embroidery stitches. In the foreground, a new hand plow, blade gleaming, turns up the fresh earth. Wood's plow is an ornamental object, on display as though on stage in front of a backdrop of field and farmstead. Its work associations are referred to rather than put into action: no horse is hitched up and no farmer stands behind it. Antique plows like the one in *Fall Plowing* and brand new copies have since become popular garden centerpieces. Homeowners pose them in yards much as Wood posed his in the farm field, ready to do service. Placed in front of urban and suburban homes, the plow symbolically transforms those sites into the fields and farmsteads like those in *Fall Plowing*.

Wood's paintings document an iconography of the midwestern farm that was later translated into sculptural forms in American urban and suburban yards. Functional water pumps like those standing in front of the rural schoolhouse in *Arbor Day* (1932) or in the yard in *The Birthplace of Herbert Hoover* (1931) would become purely decorative centerpieces. Real water wells became decorative flower pots. Grant

Wood's ubiquitous windmill (an image used so often it became the artist's trademark, appearing behind him in one self-portrait) would shrink from functional size into a decorative accent for the yard. Miniature barns became children's playhouses, tool sheds, or purely ornamental structures, surrounded by an appropriately stocked barnyard of plastic chickens, Holstein cutouts, cement pigs, and fleecy sheep. As they appear in Wood's paintings, these objects from the rural landscape of the past serve as signs of the virtuous life of the farm, where hard work and rootedness to nature still hold sway.[24]

Farm objects in the domestic landscape present the farmscape in miniature, with lilliputian barns and windmills. Joan and Gordon Tolleson of Los Angeles, for instance, call their yard their "barnyard," with the house painted barn red and a windmill and well surrounded by barnyard animals. Joan grew up on a farm, but she prefers the city now. She says, "I like the sidewalk under my feet when I step out." As a hobby, the Tollesons build dollhouses and other miniatures for children's charities and for sale. Landscapes of the past are popular subjects for miniatures in general. Like the farm, the railroad, the mill, and some other industrial sites become idealized, benign, and memorialized at small scale. In 1930s Michigan, for instance, out-of-work cabinet makers created a miniature version of Traverse City under the auspices of Public Works Administration, filling a 200-by-30 foot area near the local sawmill with 200 city structures, built to scale.[25]

DISNEY'S WOODLAND CREATURES

Farm livestock are not the only animals to populate American yards. Quasiwild animals and magical creatures inhabit some of them. In many American yards, friendly woodland creatures—rabbits, frogs, deer, owls, and squirrels—frolic beside giant polka-dotted mushrooms and wizened gnomes, creating scenes straight out of an enchanted forest. Much of this imagery draws on European sources—folk tales and legends—filtered through American popular culture, most notably Walt Disney's animated films. Two of his first feature-length animated films, *Snow White and the Seven Dwarfs* and *Bambi*, in particular, have influenced popular garden sculpture. For the 1937 *Snow White*, Disney transformed the Grimms' fairy tale into a highly dramatic but reassuring vision. He employed Gustaf Tenggren, a Swedish artist who had illustrated folktales of gnomes and trolls in his native country, to provide inspirational drawings for the animators. Tenggren's original drawings of Dopey, Doc, Grumpy and the gang were too rough for Disney. The final versions smoothed and softened the dwarfs' knobby knees and knuckles to make them look more amiable. The birds and small forest animals that populate the dwarfs' forest were similarly altered from real animals to cuddly playthings.[26]

Nonetheless, Disney artists took great pains to model their figures after real animals. For *Bambi*, they used live deer as models and live-action footage to achieve realistic movement. Later they adapted the anatomy they studied to sweeten the characters' appearances and to accommodate their speaking parts. Bambi's endearing little friends, Thumper and Flower, were added to Felix Saten's original story to inject humor into what was a soberly heroic depiction of survival in nature. Today, garden ornament manufacturers such as Artline in Chicago market little deer that look just like Bambi and friendly skunks that look just like Flower. Lawnware of Morton Grove, Illinois, creates squirrels, bunnies, owls and raccoons that look as though they could start talking any moment. Other cute frogs come straight out of cartoonland, anthropomorphized like animated characters, playing guitars or courting each other on a miniature park bench. Given the widespread affection for and popularity of Disney cartoons, these animals and magical gnomes make the yard into an enchanted place. This is culture celebrating an artificial nature. Just as the yard and garden embody an idealized floral world, cartoonlike animal statuary refers to an idealized nature, one where garden pests—real rabbits and deer—don't eat the plants in the garden.[27]

AMERICAN EXOTIC: THE FLAMINGO FROM FLORIDA TO FRONT YARDS

In this magical and idealized space of the yard, the pink flamingo merits a place of honor as a particularly American artifact. The history of flamingo imagery demonstrates that the bird represents the exotic, an imaginary and desired place set off from the ordinary world. The American flamingo was first depicted as part of the unusual flora and fauna of the New World in some of the earliest imagery from these shores, and its subsequent appearances have alluded to its early exoticism. Englishman Mark Catesby included an American flamingo in his compendium of New World wonders and exotica, *The Natural History of Carolina, Florida, and the Bahama Islands*, published in England from 1730 to 1747. Commissioned by the Royal Society of

London to collect and document the biological wonders of the New
World, Catesby traveled through the Carolinas and along the Florida
coast, collecting specimens and painting watercolor sketches during the
1720s. Upon returning to England, he spent the rest of his life
engraving and coloring prints for *The Natural History.* The work
contributed greatly to the subsequent development of taxonomic
systems and earned Catesby entrance into the Royal Society.[28]

Catesby's *Natural History* documented animal and plant life, but
he was most fascinated by American birds, finding them significantly
different from British and European varieties. Birds became the center
of his study "as there is a greater variety of the feather'd kind than of
any other animals . . . and as they excel in Beauty of their colours."[29]
Departing from earlier styles, Catesby portrayed American birds in
natural habitats as much as possible and attempted more lifelike poses
than the stiff profiles of other naturalists. Drawn during sightings in
Florida and the Bahamas, Catesby's flamingo is a stout bird, but larger,
more unusual, and more vibrantly colored than any flamingo he had
seen in southern Europe.

One of the first visual records of New World wildlife, Catesby's
History was widely circulated in Britain, Europe, and America—and
not only in the scientific community. Booksellers on both continents
sold the books; sections were published in the British *Gentleman's
Magazine*, and prints of lesser quality than Catesby's originals were
sold and circulated. In the American colonies, Catesby's work was
popular among both naturalists and a wider public until Audubon's
work in the nineteenth century. Thomas Jefferson owned two copies of
The Natural History, one of which he donated to the College of
William and Mary. Catesby subsequently earned the distinction as "the
father of American ornithology."[30]

A century later, John J. Audubon masterfully documented the
continent's exotic and varied birdlife in his famous *Birds of America*,
first published between 1824 and 1838. Audubon knew Catesby's
work. He adopted Catesby's technique of sketching birds in their
natural habitat, but rendered them with far more skill and grace. If
Catesby was the founder of American ornithology, Audubon became its
legendary hero. Affectionately called "the American Woodsman," he
traveled the wilderness, hunting bear with Daniel Boone and tirelessly
chronicling natural wonders. Like Catesby, he took considerable pains
to travel to Florida to document the American flamingo. Writing in
1831, upon first sighting the birds, Audubon wrote, "I thought I had

now reached the height of my expectations, for my voyage to the Floridas was undertaken in a great measure for the purpose of studying those lovely birds."[31] Audubon's rose-colored flamingo adopts an animated pose, drooping its neck to the sand. This view was not only natural but necessary, since Audubon drew all birds at life-size for his elephant folio edition of *Birds of America*, a technique that required larger birds to curve their necks toward their feet. Audubon's flamingo became one of his most famous bird portraits, reproduced in numerous editions, from the original prints engraved by British artist Robert Havell to inexpensive copies reproduced by unknown publishers. As part of the ever-popular *Birds of America*, the flamingo has never been far from the public eye. The book itself has gone through numerous expensive and popular editions, while reproductions of single images have been made in "an endless proliferation" of "copies of copies." Audubon's flamingo and several other birds were, for instance, available in the 1950s as attractive decorator prints to hang on living room walls. The flamingo probably reached its largest audience in 1951, when used for a U.S. postage stamp commemorating the centennial of Audubon's death.[32]

In the hands of Catesby and Audubon, the flamingo became an emblem of America: wondrous and exotic. The association of the flamingo with the exotic was a notion later reenforced by their presence in American zoos. The naturalist-artists had spotted the flamingo in southern Florida, a place that remained a remote outpost until the late nineteenth century. Nonetheless, flamingo displays at zoos familiarized the American public with the real bird. Like the work of Catesby and Audubon, "zoological gardens" (abbreviated to "zoo" in 1847 in Britain, a colloquialism that soon spread to America) combined interests in the scientific and the exotic. The appeal of rare and unusual animals from distant places of trade and conquest extends from ancient Rome to northern Europe. Royal menageries of lions, tigers, elephants, and birds—including flamingos—were collected for display on royal estates, becoming the precursor to public zoological gardens of the nineteenth century.

ZOOS AND PUBLIC DISPLAY OF FLAMINGOS

Public zoos in the United States followed rapidly on the heels of those established in Europe. The first opened at Fairmount Park in Philadelphia in 1874, serving as a key attraction at the Centennial

Exposition held in the park two years later. As an element in urban planning of the late nineteenth century, zoos were regarded like public parks. These were places designed for the urban masses, where families from all socioeconomic groups could enjoy nature in an edifying setting, momentarily escaping the congestion and industrial grime of the city. American zoos also borrowed some of the carnival-like atmosphere of P.T. Barnum's circus and Buffalo Bill's Wild West Show (both Barnum and Cody contributed animals to the nation's first zoos). The establishment of American zoos also coincided with increasing concern with species extinction, an issue brought to public attention by the threatened future of the buffalo, the loss of the passenger pigeon, and the passing of flamingos from southern Florida, all developments that prompted the formation at century's end of the National Audubon Society, dedicated to protection of remaining bird populations.[33]

Flamingo exhibits became a hallmark of American zoos early in their history. Along with bear and bison, exotic animals from the American West, zoos displayed strange creatures from other lands. An elephant and a rhinoceros were included in the first displays at Fairmount Park. No records document the inclusion of flamingos at the Fairmount Park aviary, but they did become a central exhibit at the New York Zoological Park or "Bronx Zoo," opened in 1899 with the backing of the famed conservationist, Theodore Roosevelt. Just after the turn of the century, the zoo added a colony of flamingos to its aquatic exhibit. The birds also were an early addition to the National Zoological Park in Washington, D.C., a park landscaped by Frederick Law Olmsted, and they were common in zoos developed from world's fairs of the era.[34]

At the turn of the century, world's fairs displayed animals along with the latest technological wonders, works of art, and exotic humans from other lands ("Little Egypt" on the Chicago World's Fair Midway Plaisance in 1893; Phillipinos at the St. Louis Fair in 1904). Quite often, animal exhibits became the core of a city zoo at the fair's conclusion. This happened in St. Louis shortly after the 1904 fair and in San Diego after the Panama-California Exposition of 1916. Flamingo displays formed key attractions at these zoos. A well-known example is the San Diego Zoo, where its flamingo colony appeared as the opening exhibit, the first sight visitors saw to mark the transition from city life to the idealized world of the zoo. The flamingos have since become the zoo's identifying logo, reproduced on zoo souvenirs and in the city's tourist literature.

Public zoos have multiplied across the United States during this century. Nearly every metropolitan area of more than 250,000 must have its own zoo as a requisite urban amenity, something that marks a city's status as much as its precursor, the menagerie, did for the aristocracy. Flocks of flamingos have kept pace with the growth of zoos. In fact, the birds have become synonymous with these sites of leisure. Gregory S. Toffic, curator of birds at the Dallas Zoo, host to the nation's largest flamingo colony, noted that flamingos are "the most photographed animals in the Dallas Zoo, both as subject and as background for family snapshots." Many American zoos, he points out, display flamingos prominently at their main entrances in environments "not unlike lawn ornamentation, being more formally landscaped than all other exhibits throughout the park."[35] As Toffic's comments suggest, real flamingos in zoo exhibits have influenced the bird's representation in garden statuary through their association with well-tended natural settings and through their displacement from natural habitats in the Caribbean to other regions.

Many flamingos for the earliest American zoos came from southern Florida and, after human settlements grew at Florida's tip at the end of the nineteenth century, from the Bahamas. The concern with wildlife protection that prompted the creation of zoos coincided with worries over the flamingo's disappearance from Florida. Despite its migration to Caribbean islands, the bird became a prominent Florida symbol. As an emblem of the exotic established by naturalist-artists and by its zoological settings, the flamingo now signified the out-of-the-ordinary experience of vacation and tourism. Its associations with Florida have contributed mightily to its meanings in American culture as an image of the exotic, the idyllic, the daring, and the modern. Its connections to Florida are worth examining in some detail for they provides clues to the intricate relationships between actual things and their representations.

FLORIDA MADNESS AND FLAMINGOS

It is somewhat ironic that the flamingo would become a sign of Florida, since nineteenth-century accounts confirmed that the elusive bird had not nested in Florida for several generations. By the 1890s, even casual visits by flamingo flocks to southern Florida ceased with a building boom there, when railroad construction spurred human migration to the area. The tip of the peninsula had once been a vast tropical swamp, accessible only by boat. In 1894, Henry M. Flagler and Henry Plant built a railroad to a point along the southern Atlantic coast and named it "Palm Beach." They built the luxurious Breakers Hotel, immediately attracting a smart set of tourists. Then, in 1896, Flagler and Plant pushed the railroad further south to Miami, which at that time consisted of about sixty people and a post office, and the city blossomed overnight.[36]

If the railroad was responsible for Miami's growth, Indiana businessman Carl Fisher must be credited with making the city into the nation's premier winter resort. Will Rogers aptly called Fisher "the midwife of Miami Beach," for when Fisher visited the area in 1913, the peninsula across Biscayne Bay from Miami was a dense mangrove swamp. Determined that such prime land along the Atlantic Ocean not go unused, Fisher set out to transform it into a winter playground. With characteristic grandeur, he said, "I'm going to build a city here! A city like magic, like romantic places you read and dream about, but never see." His vision meant, of course, complete transformation of the land. He hired cheap labor to tear down the jungle (completed with stunts like using elephants to pull trees and carts) and pumped sand from the bay for landfill. Fisher then began building hotels and villas along the beach that would become wildly popular in the 1920s.[37]

After World War I, Miami became the favorite destination point of American tourists and of land speculators, attracting people from all parts of the country. The area was called "The American Riviera" and "The Gold Coast," and Miami, at its center, was the "Pleasure Dome" and "The Wonder City." Appealing to the spirit of the twenties, Miami offered glamor, gaiety, sunshine, bootlegged liquor, and sometimes a chance to get rich. And all this was available to middle-class Americans, not just the wealthy of Palm Beach. Novelist Ring Lardner captured the appeal of 1920s Florida in several stories set in Miami and surrounding areas. Florida, he believed, showed "Americans still pursuing their elusive dreams, still looking for that Eden that would make their fondest wishes come true . . . in the 1920s Florida still held out a promise of fulfilling one's dream of restored health or hedonistic pleasure."[38]

Historian Frederick Lewis Allen offers similar explanations for the Florida Fever of the 1920s in *Only Yesterday*. He notes that Florida offered the climate that had just become "healthy"—lots of sunshine and fresh air. It also was a convenient vacation spot for tourists from Eastern cities, who could now drive there in the new automobile, essential to middle-class tourism. The "Coolidge Prosperity" and urban growth also brought a renewed emphasis on homeownership and a building boom. Ironically, Lewis argues, the very ethic of hard work (increasingly in bureaucratic, white-collar jobs) that undergirded the new prosperity was countered by a revolt against routine and standardization, making Miami's carefree climate, sensuous beaches, and fantastic hotels attractive getaways.[39]

The Florida boom brought breathtaking growth—Miami's population grew 400 percent from 1920 to 1930 while Florida's entire population increased only 50 percent. Besides drawing large numbers of land speculators, Florida attracted middle-class investors. Some were interested in settling; many were interested in a quick windfall through a turnaround sale at high profit, prompted by stories of lots being bought for $25 and selling soon after for $150,000. The facts and the stories are dizzying: in 1925, Miami was a town of 75,000 with an estimated 25,000 real estate agents. Land speculation was rampant, causing political leaders to outlaw the sale of real estate—or even the opening of a map—on the street to prevent traffic jams. Miami newspapers carried more advertising than any other publication in the world, most devoted to real estate sales. The *Miami Daily News* produced a record-sized newspaper on July 26, 1925, its 504 pages weighing in at over seven pounds. Building was going up so fast and furiously that construction materials bumped the transport of other essentials (e.g., food), reaching a crisis situation in 1925, when shipments of building materials had to be suspended for thirty days.[40]

Much of the real estate speculation proved to be based on hype, since most sales were made from blueprints, sight unseen. When buyers did see their newly purchased property, they often found a swamp, or they discovered that eight other mortgages were held on the same spot. By 1926, land sales failed to generate the expected profits and the market slowed. That winter, a terrific hurricane killed 400 people and left 50,000 homeless. Tourists were scared away, resulting in more damage to an already sagging economy. The boom bubble had burst.[41]

Tourists accompanied those coming to settle or invest in Florida. Cars brought a new class of tourist from across the nation, and the newly expanded highway system made southern Florida accessible. To accommodate visitors, 480 hotels and apartments were built in Miami Beach alone in 1925. Florida's climate now attracted vacationers with changing attitudes about the outdoors and sunshine and with renewed concerns about health. Prompted by recent research on vitamin D and the benefits of sunshine, ideas about sun exposure were changing. In earlier times, a tan had been a sign of the working classes, but now it became a status symbol, a display of having the means to travel. In this regard, Americans were influenced by European trends. European tourists had begun to visit the Riviera year-round, not only during winter months. Americans also knew of bohemian artists like F. Scott Fitzgerald and Isadora Duncan, who vacationed at the Riviera, giving the ocean beach an aura of excitement, freedom, and sensuality. American moral and social standards were changing, too, as women cut their hair, donned short dresses, and tossed out their corsets. New fashions reflected social changes in women's roles as they gained new status in politics and employment. Altered gender relations, including increased sexual activities outside of marriage, scandalized some with news of "petting parties" and of sex in the new covered automobiles. Prohibition had curtailed drinking for many, but it also made drinking attractively forbidden, ushering in the era of speakeasies.[42]

As the "land of eternal youth," Florida became a key site for enacting the decade's liberation, even if just during a short vacation. There, women could wear daring bathing suits. Visitors could imagine themselves Hollywood stars in movie-set hotel lobbies, a scenario watered profusely with easily-had bootlegged liquor from the Caribbean. Combined with the excitement of race tracks and gambling casinos, Florida became the place where you could do what you couldn't—or wouldn't—do at home. It offered an aura of liberation and escape from everyday taboos.[43]

The flamingo began to proliferate in Florida during these boom years. All live flamingos to be found in the area had to be imported from the Bahamas, as was the famous flock established in the center of Hialeah Race Track. Nonetheless, flamingo imagery dominated Florida architectural ornament and Florida souvenirs. Its association with exotica fit the sensibility of this vacation land, and it soon became a symbol of the state. A mural in one Miami hotel from the era clearly shows the explicit connection between Florida and flamingos. Depicting a scene from Florida legend, it shows a flock of flamingos greeting explorer Ponce de Leon as he steps upon New World shores in 1513. According to folklore, he took the birds to be a flowering bush and thus named the land "Florida," the isle of flowers. Carl Fisher employed the bird's associations with Florida in naming his first lavish

Miami Beach hotel "The Flamingo," which opened in grand style on New Year's Eve, 1920. Everything about the hotel was grand, from its terraces and courtyards to its tropical landscaping, which "seemed to affirm, in architectural terms, that Miami was indeed a tropical paradise—an American Garden of Eden."[44]

If the bird's name alone could conjure visions of paradise, the bird's form did, too. During a building boom in south Miami Beach from 1936 to 1941, flamingos made popular accents in hotel architecture. In these structures, the formerly dominant Mediterranean style of the Flamingo Hotel was eclipsed by the streamlined style of art moderne (a style later termed "art deco"). Miami Beach soon earned the distinction of hosting the largest area of such art deco buildings in the United States. There, the inherently streamlined flamingo appears in numerous architectural details including murals, iron work, and bas relief. The bird's color is matched by the use of pink stucco in many structures, a common feature in architecture throughout Miami. One author stated that the new architectural style had created "the most stylish resort in North America, an exotic escapist fantasy filled by the wealth of free-spending vacationers."[45]

Florida souvenirs were one thing that free-spenders bought as reminders of their trip. Along with a tan, souvenirs showed friends and neighbors that one had been to Florida, and they reminded their purchasers of the city's exciting aura. Florida souvenirs spread flamingo imagery throughout the nation, from Miami Beach to small northern towns, where flamingos had never been seen before. On postcards, on trays, on silk scarves, and as ceramic statues and salt and pepper shakers, the flamingo quickly signaled one vacation spot: Florida. As a regional mascot for a vacation land *par excellente*, the flamingo stood for all that Florida had to offer. Florida itself represented an inversion of the everyday for visiting tourists, offering a carefree life, where one could sip rum drinks and ogle nearly-naked people. On a Florida vacation, tourists' routine differed from the common world back home, and the casual atmosphere of the beach loosened constraints of conventional behavior.[46]

Laden with associations to Florida, freedom, unconventionality, and leisure, the flamingo could express an inversion of everyday life in other settings, too, one reason for its widespread adoption in hotels and motels across the United States. Another vacation mecca on the other side of the country, Las Vegas adopted the tradition of fantasy hotel architecture that would immerse tourists in an altered reality.

Figure 3. Miami Beach souvenir, wooden plate with incised and painted image, c. 1930.

Appropriately enough, the Flamingo Hotel led the transformation of Las Vegas into a gambling capital after World War II. Designed as a desert oasis, the hotel exterior features a dramatic neon display that dominates the strip: a row of flamingos and a four-story-high flamingo tail. Inside the hotel, the eponymous motif continues. Even the hotel's floor show dancers look like flamingos, wearing flamboyant pink-feather headdresses and costumes. On a smaller scale, neon flamingos hail the highway traveler to numerous Flamingo Motels throughout the United States. Their locations show no qualms about regional accuracy: even Des Moines, Iowa, has its own Flamingo Motel.[47]

THE DOMESTICATED FLAMINGO

The flamingo also became associated with architecture outside of hotels and motels. Its use as garden statuary has connected it with the single family home, causing it to evoke images of suburbia as much as of Florida. But given the flamingo's inversion of the ordinary associated with Florida, how did it alight in the American yard? Evidence points to the likelihood that the flamingo first appeared in lawn statuary in the 1920s, when Florida fever was at its height and when tourists could drive north with cement flamingos made in Florida stashed in the trunks of Model T's. This was also the time when cement became a favored material for garden ornaments and domestic building materials. The first flamingo ornaments had steel-reenforced necks, like the skyscrapers of the day. The concrete flamingos are a *rare avis* today, since many garden ornament makers discontinued the species because their necks often broke, despite reenforcements.[48]

At the same time that Florida was booming and zoos were multiplying, meteoric suburban growth was taking place across the United States. Housing starts had slowed during World War I, causing a housing shortage that spurred dramatic new construction in the 1920s. Early in that decade, *Building Magazine* predicted that at least 500,000 new homes would be needed. Most growth in new housing occurred in the suburbs. Over the course of this decade, suburbs gobbled up farmland around cities and grew in population at twice the rate of city centers. In Minneapolis alone, suburban housing tripled from 1920 to 1922, a significant rise even though starting from a low population base.[49]

Increased interest in garden and lawn care accompanied the growth of new suburbs. Home magazines called it a "gardening boom" and offered numerous how-to articles on the subject, arguing that home gardens were a matter of civic and community pride. New gardening clubs sprang up, giving suburban women a chance to make friends while learning about roses and hollyhocks. Even President Harding recognized the renewed interest in gardening and responded by declaring the first National Garden Week in April 1923. Department stores followed suit by staging elaborate flower shows, where customers could admire lavish flower displays and learn of new garden products.[50]

Along with up-to-date strains of hybrid roses, garden shows and garden magazines promoted the latest in garden statuary. Garden accents for middle-class yards were promoted in ads and articles. Writing about the garden, one author noted that "there is dawning in our garden consciousness a recognition of the vitality which a well-chosen statue lends to a scene"[51] Cast iron, the molding material of the nineteenth century, was still used in marking garden decor but now more ornaments were made from cement. In the 1910s and 1920s, cement was *the* modern molding material. Less expensive than iron, cement products were more accessible to a wider public than cast iron had been. And Americans found countless uses for the new material, from large scale projects like the Panama Canal to domestic architecture and decorative objects. Commenting on the many uses of cement during this time, art historian Russell Lynes says, "Americans took to cement with glee. . . . " In 1908 *House Beautiful* declared that Americans were living in "the Age of Concrete."[52]

Given the exuberant uses of cement, it is not surprising that a cement flamingo was first fashioned in the 1920s. Birds had been standard garden fare as live specimens and in sculptural versions. European aristocrats kept live exotic birds on their estates—peacocks, cranes, and flamingos—and encouraged indigenous birds to roost there. Bird statuary in diverse materials had also adorned gardens of the wealthy. By the 1920s, garden accents in the forms of eagles, chickens, cranes, and other bird species were widely available for middle-class homeowners too. Wooden cutouts of birds, then called "decoys," also appeared in the 1920s. They had the practical function to attract wild birds to the yard, a function shared by other popular yard accents like bird baths and bird houses. The live peacocks that had roamed estate and upper-middle class grounds at the turn of the century had moved inside the house, where they were stuffed and set next to the fireplace.[53] Flamingos statuary took their places outside the home near bird baths or next to garden ponds, where they recreated Floridian environments. Associated with the Florida craze of the day and with the streamlined look of art moderne, the flamingo served as a more fitting garden sculpture for the times.

The American home offered a hospitable place for the flamingo, inside and outside. Its placement in the garden was echoed in decorative arts in domestic interiors from the 1930s to the 1950s, when mass-produced items in art deco designs proliferated. The bird's sensuous curves and attentuated lines matched the streamlined shapes of art moderne, which contrasted with the earlier, intricate designs of Art Nouveau, the province of the peacock. Flamingos became elements in modern decorating schemes, appearing as ceramic statuettes or on kitchen canisters. The ceramic pieces probably originated as Florida souvenirs. The earliest ones from the 1920s and 1930s were finely made, with soft glazes and clearly defined legs. Artists' initials often were engraved on the base. By the 1940s, the flamingo appeared even more widely in interior design. Along with other popular motifs like tropical fish, cockatoos, parrots, and cranes, its imagery adorned numerous household items: drinking glasses, serving trays, metal boxes, and ashtrays. During the same period, a series of inexpensive prints in art deco styles featured flamingos (and in others, swans and cranes) wading in a tropical paradise. Produced by the Turner Company of Chicago, the prints sometimes were sold in mirrored frames or were printed directly onto a mirror. These items now comprise "Florida Deco" antiques, sought after by contemporary antiquers.

FLAMINGOS IN PINK AND POSTWAR PLASTIC

In the post–World War II era, flamingo imagery multiplied in new products for the home, so much so that many current associations with that period connect the pink flamingo with life in the suburban ranch-house subdivisions of the fifties. The flamingo did appear in American homes of the period more often than ever before. The plastic version of the ornament made its debut on American lawns during this decade, making plastic pink flamingos one of the constellation of popular memories of the era along with fin-tailed cars, poodle skirts, and "I Love Lucy." Many factors converged during that decade to contribute to these popular associations.

Don Featherstone created the first pink plastic flamingo lawn ornament in 1957. Just out of art school, Featherstone was hired by

Union Products, Inc. of Leominster, Massachusetts to design three-dimensional molds for plastic yard sculpture. This was, after all, an era in which the use of plastics skyrocketed, drawing on new technology that developed from wartime research. After designing a duck mold, Featherstone spent a month on flamingo research before executing the mold for the bird. Unlike the company's other plastic experiments with three-dimensional cats, toadstools, and fire hydrants, the flamingo met with great success, and pink flamingos soon adorned thousands of small plots around fifties suburban homes. Union Product's flamingo employed the latest in plastics technology in its use of polyethylene and of blow-mold construction. Like Melmac dishes and Tupperware, this was an object that was easy to use and did not break. Unlike its cement predecessor, it could be moved easily for lawn mowing.[54]

The flamingo was a common decorative image inside the fifties home, too. The bathroom of the postwar ranch house was one popular spot for flamingos. The bird adorned bathroom tiles, bent its necks on shower curtains, and disguised toilets on chenille covers of the day. Bathrooms filled with images of fish, swans, and flamingos suggested fantasies of tranquil garden ponds. In 1957, Russell Lynes noted the new extravagance in bathroom decor, commenting that the smaller size of the bathroom in postwar housing was compensated for by the "desire for nonsense, luxury, and sensuousness."[55]

The pink flamingo's popularity in and outside the American home coincided with an explosion of pink throughout the house as kitchens, bathrooms, bedrooms, and family rooms were painted and decorated in the color. For the first time, Americans could buy pink toilets and tubs, pink stoves and refrigerators, pink cupboards and pink dinette sets, and pink plastic dishes. The color was so popular that *Life* magazine declared 1955 "The Peak Year for Pink." The magazine's photograph of household goods from Macy's Department Store featured a pile of pink products, among them mops, pots, towels, clocks, and lamps.[56]

Americans were not only decorating with pink, they were wearing it—both men and women. According to *Life*, New York's Brook Brothers had introduced a pink shirt back in 1900 that met with lukewarm response. In 1949, when the company changed their advertising strategy to appeal to college women, the shirt suddenly caught on with both sexes. Pink and gray clothing became part of the Ivy League style.[57] Another fashion first was the introduction of pink lipstick in the 1950s. And to top it all off, Americans could leave their pink houses wearing pink clothes and whiz off in pink cars, another first time use of the color.

If pink found a place in the Ivy League set, it also was used by those outside elite circles, who wore the color with an edge to it. In 1954, early in his career, Elvis Presley adopted pink and black as his personal colors, although his pink was hot, not the pastel shades of the Ivy League. At that time he was likely to wear wild color combinations—a hot pink shirt, red slacks, and a green jacket. When Presley first started touring, he bought a used Cadillac that he painted pink and black. When he started making money, Presley's first major purchase was a brand new pink Cadillac, his "supreme symbol of hipness," one that he would make the subject of a song. Rebellious in his adoption of African-American musical styles and in his erotic musical delivery, Elvis still aimed for mainstream signs of success. Nonetheless, his use of pink demonstrates that the color meant more than conformity to values of the Ivy League.[58]

The reasons for the popularity of a color at a particular historical moment are difficult to explain, especially if one goes beyond simple, though necessary, technological explanations. In the 1950s, the development of new dyes and new materials had made it possible for many new products to adopt pink hues. Yet social and cultural factors generated their popular appeal. As happened after World War I, pink and other bright colors became popular fashions in these postwar years. While men donned gray flannel suits for white collar jobs, they also wore bright sports clothes at home, including the era's popular Hawaiian shirt, which featured wild flower compositions and lively color combinations. As with other bright color for clothing, pink may have expressed a desire for happier sentiments after the war and the Depression. At the same time, the suburban home in all its pink glory became a female-segregated setting. Women quit their wartime jobs, sometimes involuntarily, to become full-time homemakers and new mothers, the only socially sanctioned female roles during that decade. As an innocent color associated with little girls, pink may have both expressed and enforced women's childlike dependency. More vibrant shades of pink closer to red, however, are aggressive and sexual: the hot pinks of Marilyn Monroe's strapless gown in *Gentlemen Prefer Blondes* compared to the tame pastels of Doris Day in her modest "Peter Pan" blouses. During the fifties, the term "pink-o" came into common use to refer to communists, who had previously been called "reds," a change suggesting an attempt to minimize their perceived threat by emasculating them with a label associated with femininity.[59] Pink in its many guises during the fifties expresses paradoxical impulses: femininity and masculinity; mainstream identification and anti-mainstream sentiments. Its many uses suggest a desire to break through, or at least to confuse, the rigid political and gender codes of the time. Contemporary uses of the pink plastic flamingo often pick up on these conflicts and ambiguities over color as an important part of its current meanings.

Little direct commentary on the pink plastic flamingo existed until more recent times. One thing that we do know is that the object became considered evidence of bad taste and kitsch by upper-middle-class groups, even though sales figures document that the ornament steadily sold hundreds of thousands each year. By the 1980s, when the plastic flamingo craze generated many articles in major newspapers throughout the United States wondering about its cause, many considered them "tacky" and "offensive." For example, Allen Lacy, garden writer for *The New York Times*, writes, "One of the most profoundly embarrassing experiences that anyone can have—especially someone like me, who's not very good at concealing his thoughts with a polite fib or a discreet silence—is to have someone else proudly show off something that's in flamboyant bad taste. Something, for example, like pink flamingos as garden ornaments."[60]

A variety of factors seems to have prompted the devaluation of the garden ornament, at least among the cultural cognoscenti, a group that most likely never was counted among its fans or buyers. One reason may have been the flamingo's association with 1950s suburban subdivisions. These subdivisions provided good housing for millions of first-time homeowners after the war, but culture critics soon castigated postwar suburbs for their poor-quality housing and architectural conformity. During the same period mass culture also became subject to increasing criticism from intellectuals and art critics, in part brought on by the rise of television. Critics feared that anything other than elite arts or folk culture posed serious dangers for the American public. Mass culture, in their view, was imposed on audiences, making them intellectually, morally, and politically susceptible to manipulation. Other opprobrium directed at the flamingo lawn sculpture arose from its plasticity. By the late 1960s, when the film *The Graduate* made "plastics" a byword of an older generation with skewed values and goals, Americans had expressed mixed reactions to the plastics explosion of the fifties and sixties. On one hand, plastic had been hailed as miracle material, able to be molded into nearly anything from furniture to clothing. Yet it also evoked ambivalence about the changing feel of everyday life. Not only was the flamingo plastic, it was pink. The bright colors of op art, pop art, and psychedelic styles that had infiltrated popular fashion and interior design in the 1960s gave way to natural earth tones by decade's end.[61]

FLAMINGO REVIVALS

The flamingo's fall from favor was short-lived. By the mid-1970s, a variety of groups were discovering the flamingo for a variety of reasons. Many folks continued to buy the ornaments as attractive accents to adorn their lawns, setting them in pairs next to bird baths or front steps, with little care or thought to their significance. Others more self-consciously manipulated the bird's risky connotations as a taboo object of bad taste. These more recent uses benefit from ethnographic data and from more plentiful and accessible sources of data than earlier practices. Recent uses reveal the complexities of interpreting this common object, which Americans use to express commentary on social status and on relationships to dominant cultural values.

A resurgent interest in art moderne styles in the 1970s contributed one strand to the revival of flamingo imagery. In the late sixties Pop artists Frank Stella and Roy Lichtenstein had incorporated art deco motifs into their paintings. At the same time, American art museums mounted exhibitions on decorative arts of the 1920s and 1930s. For the first time the streamlined styles were termed "art deco," previously known simply as "art moderne." A number of museum exhibitions such as *The World of Art Deco*, organized by Bevis Hillier for the Minneapolis Institute of Arts in 1971, caused collectors and general audiences to revalue this varied group of mass-produced objects that included furniture, household appliances, ceramics, and architecture. The style was more widely popularized by several Hollywood film made in the 1970s and early 1980s but set in the 1920s: *The Great Gatsby* and *Reds*, for example. By 1979 art deco had achieved historic status, as reflected by the designation of Miami Beach's deco district for the National Register of Historic Places, the first time an entire area of twentieth-century structures was marked for preservation.[62]

Associated with the roaring twenties and with Florida, the art deco style in architecture and decorative arts referred to a world of glamor and leisure. Cashing in on these associations, a number of new

Figure 4. Typical pink flamingo display with flamingos on either side of bird bath.

buildings constructed in the 1980s adopted the deco style, especially those devoted to leisure pursuits: restaurants, hotels, and nightclubs. In some cases, interiors were designed in deco to create a glamorous setting for dining, drinking, and dancing, even when the building itself was designed in a completely different style. The Embassy Suites Hotel in downtown Minneapolis, for example, a nondescript structure built on top of a six-floor parking ramp, went crazy on art deco for interior decor. Stylish lighting fixtures, pink and turquoise colors, leaping antelope motifs, and flamingo prints all contributed to its deco delirium inside.

The art deco fad prompted collectors to scour antique stores for flamingo items, which they could find sitting next to Saturn lamps and decorative chrome airplanes, other hallmarks of the deco age. Enterprising businesses began cranking out new art deco lines. In the early eighties, Sasspirilla Company of California began manufacturing copies of flamingo pieces in their Deco Design line. Using earlier molds for flamingo salt and pepper shakers, sugar and creamers, and ash trays, their revival flamingo products filled the shelves of novelty gift stores. Across the continent in New Jersey, Cat's Pajamas made the flamingo their favored motif in dozens of products, the more outrageous the better. The handle of a toilet plunger could easily be fashioned into a flamingo neck and head; a towel rack could be made from the same motif. In fact, nearly any domestic object, whether for the kitchen table or the bathroom, could be improved by adding flamingos. The company's repertoire included flamingo-decorated toilet tissue, drinking glasses, shower curtains, light fixtures, and clocks, along with sartorial fashions of flamingo ties, watches, and earrings. In its ads and catalogues, the company playfully admonished buyers to "ruin the neighborhood" by buying a plastic flamingo for their lawn.[63]

By the early 1980s, the flamingo had acquired paradoxical connotations. On one hand, the image was associated with elegant art deco, and at the same time, the plastic ornament was associated with bad taste, a connection that some groups exploited and promoted. The notoriety of the film *Pink Flamingos*, directed by the self-professed King of Bad Taste, John Waters, made the bird a popular image in gay culture. *Pink Flamingos*, which opens with a shot of two plastic flamingos in front of the lead character's trailer home, features the drag queen Divine playing him/herself as the film's protagonist. Having just achieved the accolade of "Filthiest Person in the World," Divine is attacked by her rivals, a couple who think they deserve the "filthiest" distinction. The film follows her battle to retain the title, a challenge at which she does succeed. Throughout the adventure, the film presents startling scenes and images that present inversions of many cultural norms, evoking mixed reactions ranging from laughter to shock to disgust to disbelief.

The underlying logic of the film works through inversion and paradox. Divine, the most holy, is the filthiest; a man is a woman, portrayed in exaggerated dress, make-up, and manner in drag-queen style; Divine's house is a trailer; her mother is a baby in a playpen. Cultural order is further overturned by the violation of conventional taboos in matters of cleanliness and sexual behavior, especially when these are presented as everyday reality. The film's inverted order is most graphically portrayed in the closing shot, when Divine follows a poodle down the street and literally "eats shit." In this context, the opening shot of pink plastic flamingos in front of Divine's trailer provides the overarching emblem of inversion also pointed to by the film's title.

Released at the beginning of the Gay Pride Movement, *Pink Flamingos* gained a cult following in gay circles. Considered a camp masterpiece, the film has influenced an ironic use of the plastic pink flamingo in reference to the film. At some film screenings, audience members bring pink flamingo ornaments to the theater, waving them around before the film starts. Philip Core has written about camp as a "lingua franca" that groups who live double lives use to communicate their differences from the dominant culture and their alliances with others. In a highly stylized, self-conscious display, camp involves the rearrangement of a sign system so that an object's meaning is changed, sometimes in a way that is understood only by cultural insiders. By the late 1970s, the flamingo had become "the American eagle" of gay culture, according to one San Francisco antique store owner. By appropriating a sign of suburban, heterosexual family life, gays asserted the homosexual as the ideal, while also highlighting the hedonism suggested by the bird's vacation land connections. In the late 1970s, when serious earth colors still dominated mainstream fashion and design, the flamingo's bright fuschia was more closely tied to gay men; one gay flamingo collector bluntly stated, "Pink's kind of a fag color."[64]

Other subcultures in the late 1970s employed the color pink and pink flamingos to mark themselves off from the dominant culture.

Youth in the punk and new wave music scenes in Britain and the United States wore shocking pink with their predominantly black clothes. Hot pink clothing stridently asserted their alliance with codes of bad taste just as their musical style—lyrics shouted at high volume and instruments played as a barrage of sound—violated musical expectations, even for rock and roll. Rejecting the subdued natural colors and the navy blue and gray promoted by the popularly earnest "dress for success" look of the late 1970s, bright pink and black clothing marked their separation from the conventional working world. Their introduction of "shocking" pink in clothing marked for many the first glimpse of the color since op art clothing of the mid-sixties. Punks and new wavers also adopted fashion styles from an earlier era, often a bedraggled version of the white t-shirt and straight-legged jeans of Brando and Dean or "retro" outfits put together from fifties clothing bought at second-hand stores and rummage sales.

Though American punk attracted predominantly middle-class youth, in contrast to the working-class composition of British punk, the movement and its related musical developments, grouped under the umbrella of "new wave music," nonetheless expressed similar disenchantment with and critiques of existing mainstream culture.[65] In American new wave music created by such popular groups as the Talking Heads, the Ramones, and the B-52's, cultural critiques balanced a thin line between embracing mass culture as the cultural heritage of American youth and rebelling against its inanities. Musicians often made use of the very popular styles they were critiquing, such as surf music or b-movie images, to express an ironic critique.

The irony expressed in new wave music and in its sartorial and behavioral practices constitutes a popular level of "postmodern" culture.[66] One of the major characteristics associated with postmodernism among elite culture producers is the propensity to utilize and mix elements from historical styles into new formations. These combinations are often executed with an ironic distance that calls into question the meaning of cultural images and forms. On the popular level, musical producers utilized elements from American popular culture to create a postmodern melange of punk and new wave styles. After the increasing complexity of rock composition in the 1970s, these new composers, often proud members of "garage bands," resurrected the simplified rock styles of the fifties and early sixties by using simple chords and few chord changes, though they intensified their speed and volume to humorous levels, as in many songs by The Ramones. The music represented a democratization of rock. This was music anyone could play or sing without being a virtuoso: style was more important than musical talent. Live performances by hundreds of new bands filled new music clubs across the United States with an insistence on live music in reaction to the canned music of the seventies disco scene. While interest in fifties rock music also spurred a resurgence of rockabilly, a blend of rhythm and blues and country music that was most notably connected with Elvis Presley, punk and new wave usually alluded to fifties popular music without reproducing it note for note. Rather than borrowing the exact melodies, punk adopted the rebellious spirit of fifties rock and roll.

For some members of these youth subcultures, the pink flamingo formed just one part of an elaborate sign system constructed of music, fashion, political attitudes, and social values responding to their contemporary concerns. In its activation of these elements, punk and new wave differed from and in fact opposed strictly nostalgic appropriations of 1950s culture a la Ronald Reagan, who resurrected a reassuring version of that decade, when mom was home baking in her apron and dad was undisputed patriarch. As a symbol of middle-class suburbia, the flamingo could express problematic relationship with youths' "home" culture. Its associations with bad taste paralleled other outrageous stylistic elements: fuschia and orange hair, mohawk hair cuts, safety-pinned clothing and ears, and bright make-up applied in unconventional ways. As part of American pop culture, the flamingo also corresponded to the absurd and "fun" ethos of some of this music, similar to the B-52's reference to inane beach party movies and music given a surrealistic, nonsensical slant in their popular 1979 song "Rock Lobster." Like other elements from popular culture that were disassembled and put together in new ways and in new juxtapositions, the pink plastic flamingo took on new meanings when displayed in urban environments, in store windows, on stage for performances, and in other unconventional manners.

SAY IT WITH FLAMINGOS

The paradoxical attitudes represented by the pink flamingo—its ability to represent mainstream American culture associated with the suburban home, the nuclear family, and the work ethic, and an inversion of mainstream values for those with problematic and oppositional relationships to them—is evident from observing where flamingo imagery appeared commercially. Flamingo lawn ornaments can be bought at mainstream stores: K-Mart, Target, garden and hardware stores. At these sites, flamingos are treated as merchandise, not art, in contrast to the prominent treatment they receive at other commercial sites, usually small stores representing countervailing values of the erotic, the sensual, the noncorporate, the idiosyncratic, the ironic and humorous. In the Minneapolis area of Cedar-Riverside, near the University of Minnesota, a long-standing counterculture enclave since the 1960s, many shops prominently display flamingo imagery and sell flamingo artifacts. A neon flamingo stands in the window of "Come to Your Senses," a store selling hot tubs, massage books, exotic lotions and soaps, and electric massagers. Around the corner, a cooperatively owned hardware store regularly fills their window with pink flamingos, next to wood stoves and bicycles. A gift store down the block decorates their front window with flamingo neon sculptures to advertise an array of flamingo merchandise: cards, ceramics, lamps, t-shirts, and ties. Similarly, in Little Five Points, a section of Atlanta known for its punk/counterculture population, a store called "Pink Flamingos," just two doors down from the punk clothing store, "The Junkman's Daughter," sells "modern clothing" (according to its business card) along with flamingo artifacts.

Postmodern expressions utilizing the pink flamingo are also created by those not necessarily part of more coherent subcultures to express resistance to or discontent with American culture and with structures of authority. The flamingo allows them to express ambivalence about their social roles and about their relationship to mainstream culture. In doing this, they often distinguish their use of the pink plastic lawn ornament from conventional displays. They may draw attention to the contrived quality of lawn displays and to the plastic flamingo as an object itself rather than to its allusion to paradise. Flamingo-swiping serves as one example of this phenomena. In this common prank, a group of teenagers (usually) steal all the plastic flamingos in their neighborhood and move them to one front yard, causing the homeowner surprise and embarrassment, and sometimes, a laugh. This guerrilla raid reverses the usual power relationship between young people and adults and draws vivid attention to the contrived, toylike quality of adults' flamingo practices.

In 1980 a similar stunt generated intense discussion and self-examination among residents of Quincy, Illinois, when "flamingo thieves" stole twenty ornaments around town, and left ransom notes complaining about the lack of activities for young people in that town. Before two teenage girls admitted to the thefts, Quincy residents exchanged thoughtful letters in the town press that responded to the thieves's claims and argued about the appropriateness of their tactics. The newspaper discussion drew wider press coverage to the incident, prompting one Chicago artist, Lloyd Legrane, to create a public art piece for Quincy. As a homage to the town's "flamingo consciousness," Legrane set 500 plastic flamingos in precise rows in the town's public park, like stalks in a corn field. Surprised by the display, which appeared without warning one Saturday morning, Quincy residents showed up to have family pictures taken in front of the plentiful flamingos. Many commented that "it was the most exciting thing that happened in Quincy in over twenty years." Suddenly, the very problem identified by the teenagers' prank had been momentarily suspended.[67]

Even yuppies, those young urban professionals who pursued success and money during the 1980s, employed the pink plastic flamingo as a means to rebel, however meekly, against the rigid demands of Reagon economics. Attorney Jeffrey Jacobs, for instance, continually moved his pair of flamingos around his front yard in a Minneapolis suburb, simulating what he called "the mating dance of the pink flamingos." On other occasions he and his friends played football with them. Having bought his first house in a ranch-house-style fifties suburb, he decided to buy flamingos because he thought people would have displayed them there in the fifties. While his flamingos expressed a connection to the neighborhood, his unconventional manipulations of them expressed his alienation from the neighborhood and his ambivalence about his new role as homeowner.[68]

As Jacobs' antics point out, the pink plastic flamingo has been widely used to comment on homeownership. The birds became a popular housewarming present as humorous gifts exchanged among young urban professionals. The joke arises from the tacit recognition that these urban sophisticates would never display something as tasteless as the pink flamingo. Its humor helps to dispel the seriousness of mortgage obligations and the anxiety of the transition to a more settled stage of life, yet the joke also acknowledges that domestic reality is always more complex than—and often contradicts—the ideals that symbols embody. One flamingo collector commented on the artificiality of the flamingo ornament and on its ability to represent domestic life by saying, "It's so fakey—like Ozzie and Harriet."[69]

Figure 5. Ironic display of flamingos by Jeffrey Jacobs, Minneapolis, Minnesota.

As flamingo imagery became increasingly popular during the 1980s, it was used more widely by mainstream groups and media to signal an inversion of ordinary life. These practices alluded to its vacation associations in Florida but also borrowed from its dangerous connotations as a taboo image. To this end flamingo imagery was used to promote all manner of leisure events: pink parties, flamingo balls, festivals, and picnics, often with the implication that these would be extraordinarily wild and crazy. An ad in a Minneapolis newspaper by the local department store, for instance, demonstrates the connection between leisure, fun, and pink flamingos. The ad presents the store's cache of flamingo merchandise—sweatshirts, barbecue aprons and mitts, glasses, plates, cups and decorative objects—complete with pink ink for the flamingo images. The text ponders why the flamingo has become so popular, not bothering to answer the question but stating: "Now he's showing up at the cocktail parties, picnics, and poolside barbecues of the 1980s."[70] Soon after this ad appeared, the usually lofty Twin Cites Opera Guild jazzed up its annual fundraiser by using a flamingo motif on its invitation to attract potential donors to the "exotic tropics" at the Minnesota Zoo. At about the same time, a Flamingo Ball was held as another benefit for a local theatre group. In these examples, flamingo imagery suggests that one reject the rigors of discipline, long work hours, and the drive for monetary success, so promoted during the Reagan years, to escape, relax, and have fun. Some turned to cocaine, another popular means of escape at the time, but for many, the flamingo was a safer means to resist, overturn, or ignore those pressures. By the end of the decade, when "Miami Vice" puttered out in its last season, the popularity of flamingo imagery was abating, too. Many collectors had declared the flamingo passé because it had become too mainstream. Even film director John Waters had abandoned the bird.

The eighties were an appropriate time for the flamingo to have reached its zenith, given the intensified drive for financial success and homeownership, conditions similar to the 1920s and the 1950s, when the flamingo was also popular. In the age of Reagan, when the dominant culture was increasingly uneasy with forthright dissent and opposition, material culture became an even more important means to express one's opinions and identities. Because the flamingo is a complex sign, able to express alignment with, resistance to, and rejection of mainstream American values associated with family life, hard work, taste, and propriety, its specific contexts need to be examined to understand its specific meanings. Flamingo uses demonstrate that a continual popular commentary occurs with consumer objects which utilizes their historical associations but asserts, extends, revises, and inverts previous meanings.

The flamingo in the garden reveals that the American yard is a place where arguments over culture and nature, taste and class, mainstream culture and subcultures are played out in public for neighbors, passersby, strangers, and other community residents. In spite of the efforts by Americans to express idyllic and lofty sentiments in the yard, the space in fact acts as a more contested cultural ground. The middle landscape envisioned by Jefferson sometimes recalls the landscape of the farm. But it also refers to the classical idylls of Arcadia, or to the exotic tropics where flamingos wade, or to the humorous cartoons of Walt Disney. The popular imagery in American yards—no longer in the bronze, lead, and marble of aristocratic gardens but in wood, cement, and plastic—has made culture more democratic and has given voices to those who might otherwise be silent.

NOTES

1. The connection between "Miami Vice" and pink flamingos is mentioned in Aaron Kahn, "Splendor in the Grass," *St. Paul Pioneer Press,* August 21, 1987, 1C, 2C; Kay Melchisedech Olson, "Lawn Ornaments," *Garden Supply Retailer,* January 1990, 10-13; and Elizabeth Sporkin, "Those Tacky Birds are Taking Wing," *USA Today,* September 30, 1985, D1, D2. In the latter article, Don Featherstone of Union Products reported that their firm sold 250,000 pairs of flamingos already that year, 38 percent more than the previous year and the most in any year in the bird's thirty-year history.

2. Slides and slide file information from the GCA/Pennsylvania slide collection, Office of Horticulture Library, Smithsonian Institution, Washington, D.C. See also Helen Van Pelt Wilson, "Philadelphia Gardens," *House Beautiful,* May 1936, 62, 150.

3. Galloway Terra-Cotta Company, *Terra-Cotta and Pottery for Garden and Interior.* Catalogue No. 14 (Philadelphia: Galloway Pottery, 1904), back cover. Vertical Files, Horticulture Library, Office of Horticulture, Smithsonian Institution, Washington D.C.

4. Ibid., p. 2.

5. The average annual earnings for all U.S. employees in 1904 was $490, cited in *Historical Statistics of the United States from Colonial Times to 1970* (Washington, D.C.: U.S. Department of Commerce), 168. Slides of gardens

from Archives of American Gardens, McFarland Collection, Horticultural Services Division, Smithsonian Institution.

6. Phillip V. Snyder, *The Christmas Tree Book* (New York: Viking Press, 1976), 36, 86-91.

7. *Galloway Pottery* (Philadelphia: Galloway Terra-Cotta Company, 1920), catalogue no. 29. Hagley Museum and Library, Wilmington, Del.

8. See cover illustration of *Journal of Garden History*, 9, 4(October-December 1989), slide in collection of William and Carol Menke, landscape architects, Swarthmore, Penn.

9. *The Book of Lawn Furniture* (Kansas City, Mo.: Long-Bell Lumber Co., 1925), 10; see no. 1048 in E. Richard McKinstry, *Trade Catalogues at Winterthur: A Guide to the Literature of Merchandising, 1750 to 1980* (New York: Garland Publishing 1984), 180.

10. "Hershey Rose Gardens and Arboretum" in *Great Gardens of America*. Carroll C. Calkins, general editor (New York: Coward-McCann, Inc. and Waukesha Wisconsin: Country Beautiful, 1969), 162-67. Slide of Hershey Rose Garden with gazing globe in the McFarland slide collection at the Horticulture Library, Smithsonian Institution, Washington, D.C.

11. *Gifts for Outdoor Living* (New York: Stumpp & Walter, 1948), 22. *Artcrete for the Garden and Interior Decoration* (Havertown, Penn.: Artcrete, 1960) cat. no. 150. Both catalogues in vertical files, Office of Horticulture, Horticulture Library, Smithsonian Institution, Washington, D.C.

12. Rita Reif, "Heavy Metal Invades the Garden," *New York Times*, April 8, 1990, 40H.

13. On children as popular subjects in garden statuary, see Bogart, *Fauns and Fountains*, n.p.; Doell, 62; on "Out in the Rain" fountain, see Tice, 66. Children were also popular subjects in Victorian cemetery sculpture; see Ellen Marie Snyder, "Innocents in a Worldly World: Victorian Children's Gravemarkers," in *Cemeteries and Grave Markers: Voices of American Culture,* edited by Richard E. Meyer (Ann Arbor: UMI, 1989), 11-29.

14. For lengthier discussion of the development of sport fishing and connections to the image of the barefoot boy, see Colleen Sheehy, "American Angling: The Rise of Urbanism and the Romance of the Rod and Reel" in *American Play 1840-1914,* edited by Catherine Grier (Amherst: University of Massachusetts Press, 1992), 77-92. For Palmer print, see *Currier and Ives: A Catalogue Raissone* (Detroit: Gale Research, 1984), 41, 52; Winslow Homer's engraving was first published in *Harper's Weekly*, August 22, 1874. Grace Lincoln Hall, "A Fisherman's Reverie," *Western Field and Stream*, June 1986, 58. On the related topic of imagery of the mischievous boy, see Jadviga M. Da

Costa Nunes, "The Naughty Child in Nineteenth-Century American Art," *Journal of American Studies* 21(August 1987): 225-47.

15. Images of black jockey statue in slide collection, Archives of American Gardens, McFarland Collection, Horticultural Services Division, Smithsonian Institution, Washington, D.C. Information on Eleutherian Mills from "Gardens & Countrysides" *Journal of Pictureesque Travels*, May 1990; and *E.I. du Pont's Garden at Eleutherian Mills* (Wilmington, Del.: Hagley Museum and Library). Both are in the research files for this site at the Archives of American Gardens.

16. See Patricia Turner, *Ceramic Mammies and Celluloid Uncles: Black Images and Their Influence on Culture* (New York: Anchor Books, 1994). Turner discusses the black groomsman briefly, placing it in the context of black servants in artifactual form as well as in film, advertising, and folklore.

17. Earl Kroger, Sr., a Baltimore insurance agent, published the brochure, "The Legend of Jocko: The Boy Who Inspired George Washington" in 1963, and he also published a book for children: *Jocko: A Legend of the American Revolution* (Englewood Cliffs, N.J.: Prentice-Hall, 1976).

18. Letter to author from Christine Meadows, curator of the Mount Vernon Ladies' Association, November 14, 1990. Sidney Kaplan and Emma Nogrady Kaplan, *The Black Presence in the Era of the American Revolution* (Amherst: University of Massachusetts Press, 1989). On legends, see Gary Alan Fine, "The Goliath Effect: Corporate Dominance and Mercantile Legends, *Journal of American Folklore* 98, no. 387 (January-March 1985), 63-85; Jan Van Bruvand, *The Vanishing Hitchhiker: American Urban Legends and Their Meanings* (New York: W.W. Norton, 1981), esp. 1-2.

19. Wilbur Henry Siebert's earlier study of the underground railroad documents the use of the statue by abolitionists in *The Mysteries of Ohio's Underground Railroads* (Columbus, Ohio: Long's College Book Co., 1951),143-46. Information on the origins of the black jockey statue from interview with Charles L. Blockson, curator, Charles L. Blockson Afro-American Collection, Temple University Press, October 19, 1989; and Charles L. Blockson, "Escape from Slavery: The Underground Railroad," *National Geographic* July 1984, 3-39. See also Chester M. Hampton, "Jocko: Symbol of Pride," *Washington Post,* September 7, 1970, B1, B5.

20. For controversies about the statue see, for instance, "Carriage Boy Statues Offend Visitors, Cause Town Furor," *Minneapolis Star Tribune*, August 4, 1984, 4S. For example of statue, see hitching post c. 1875 from collection of Greenfield Village and Henry Ford Museum, included in Robert Bishop, *American Folk Sculpture* (New York: Bonanza Books, 1985), 159.

21. George Lipsitz, "History, Myth, and Counter-Memory: Narrative and Desire in Popular Novels" in his collection *Time Passages: Collective Memory and American Popular Culture* (Minneapolis: University of Minnesota Press, 1990), 211-31.

22. On the *ferme ornée*, see Thacker, 15, 199, 234; Tuan, *Dominance and Affection*, 31.

23. On imagery of the farm in American art prior to the 1930s, see *Farm Life in America: Prints from 1843-1948* (New York: Wunderlich & Company, 1986).

24. On Grant Wood, see Wanda Corn, *Grant Wood: The Regionalist Vision* (New Haven: Yale University Press, 1983) throughout; on *Fall Plowing*, 90; on windmill as his signature image, 126. On the mural art of regionalist artists, major and minor, and use of farm imagery as a means to weather the trials of the Depression, see Karal Ann Marling, *Wall to Wall America: A Cultural History of Post-Office Murals in the Great Depression* (Minneapolis: University of Minnesota Press, 1982).

25. Interview with Joan Tolleson, Los Angeles, California, November 10, 1988. On the Traverse City miniature, other outdoor sites, and miniatures in general, see Georgene O'Donnell, *Miniaturia: The World of Tiny Things* (Chicago: Lightner Publishing, 1943), 191-203 and throughout.

26. On Gustaf Tenggren's contributions to *Snow White*, see Mary T. Swanson, *From Swedish Fairy Tales to American Fantasy: Gustaf Tenggren's Illustrations, 1920-1980* (Minneapolis: University of Minnesota Art Museum, 1986), 6-14, and "The Tenggren Gallery" in *Walt Disney's Snow White and the Seven Dwarfs Golden Anniversary* (Prescott, Ariz.: Gladstone Publishing, 1987), 5-10.

27. On creation of Walt Disney films, see Richard Holliss and Brian Sibley, *The Disney Studio Story* (New York: Crown Publishers, 1988), 28-31, 35-36. Contemporary yard statuary in Art Line's *Decorative Lawn and Garden* catalogue, (Chicago, 1984) and Lawnware's *Lawn, Garden and Patio Accessories* catalogue (Morton Grove, Ill.: n.d.), 3. The home garden as an appropriate place for magical creatures and spirits is related to the belief that gnomes lived in rookeries. In the 1880s, rookeries became popular garden additions in England. Grottoes and rookeries were common features of gardens since ancient times. On gnomes and rookeries, see Helena Barrett and John Philips, *Suburban Style: The British Home, 1840-1960* (London: MacDonald & Company, 1987), 177.

28. George Frick, introduction to Mark Catesby's *Natural History of Carolina, Florida, and the Bahama Islands* (Savannah, Ga.: Beehive Press,

1974), xiii; George Frick and Raymond P. Stearns, *Mark Catesby: The Colonial Audubon* (Urbana, Ill.: University of Illinois Press,:1961), 58.

29. Mark Catesby, *Natural History*, 6.

30. Frick and Stearns, 99-106.

31. Quoted in "Audubon Centennial Stamps," *Audubon Magazine*, May/June 1951, 170-71.

32. Roger Tory Peterson and Virginia Marie Peterson, editors. *Audubon's Birds of America*, facsimile edition of the baby elephant folio(New York: Abbeville Press, 1981), n.p.; "Birds of America," *Time*, November 22, 1937: 57-58; Marshall B. Davidson, "A New Look at Audubon," *Horizon*, Spring 1966: 41.

33. Lord Zuckerman, ed., *Great Zoos of the World: Their Origins and Significance* (Boulder, Col.o.: Westview Press, 1980), 3; *A Zoo for All Seasons: The Smithsonian Animal World* (New York: W.W. Norton for Smithsonian Exposition Press, 1979), 30-33.

34. On the animal displays at the Centennial Exposition, see J.S. Ingram, *The Centennial Exposition Described and Illustrated* (Philadelphia: Hubbard Brothers, 1876), 106. On the New York Zoo, see "In the Pink," *Reader's Digest*, July 1943, 38. On the National Zoo, see James Toovey, "Washington: The National Zoological Park and the Smithsonian" in *Great Zoos of the World*, cited above. Today a large flamingo flock is established at Disneyworld's EPCOT Center, a place with connections to world fairs and their pleasure palaces and to idealized zoo landscapes.

35. Letter to author from Gregory S. Toffic, Curator of Birds, Dallas Zoo, February 11, 1985.

36. *Florida, Insight Guide Series* (Hong Kong: Apa Productions, 1982), 50.

37. Jeffrey Limerick, et al., *America's Grand Resort Hotels* (New York: Pantheon Books, 1979), 187; Kenneth L. Roberts, "Tropical Growth," *Saturday Evening Post*, 29 April 1922, 78-79; "Pleasure Dome," *Time*, 19 February 1940, 20.

38. Lardner quoted in Anne Rowe, *The Idea of Florida in the American Literary Imagination* (Baton Rouge, La.: Louisiana State University Press), 91.

39. *Only Yesterday* (New York: Bantam Books, 1931; rpt. 1946), 304; 315.

40. Felix Isman, "Florida's Land Boom," *Saturday Evening Post*, 20 August 1925: 14; Allen, 302-08; Federal Writer's Project, *Florida: A Guide to the Southernmost State* (New York: Oxford University Press, 1939), 125-26; Gertrude Mathew Shelby, "Florida Frenzy," *Harper's Monthly*, January 1926: 175.

41. Allen, 313.

42. On changing attitudes about sunshine and relation to use of sun motif in art deco, see Hillier Bevis, *The World of Art Deco* (New York: E.P. Dutton with the Minneapolis Institute of Arts, 1971), 42-44. *Florida: A Guide*, 56; on changing morals and manners, see Allen, 106-43.

43. James Roe discusses a related idea in a paper entitled "A Skyline Becomes Las Vegas: 1946-1972," presented at the California American Studies Association Meetings, San Luis Obispo, May 9,1990. He identifies the allure of "safe dangers" of gambling and drinking associated with Las Vegas vacations, which he also connects to the nuclear testing in the area after World War II. I am grateful to Mr. Roe for sharing his work with me.

44. The Ponce de Leon legend was printed on the back of a Florida postcard (c. 1950) that pictured flamingos at the tourist attraction Parrot Jungle in Miami. The mural depicting the flamingos greeting Ponce de Leon is in the Tiffany Hotel; see Laura Cerwinske, *Tropical Deco: The Architecture and Design of Old Miami Beach* (New York: Rizzoli, 1981), 92.

45. Michael O'Connor, "A Moderne Dilemma: Contrasts and Conflicts in Miami Beach's Deco District," *Art & Antiques*, May 1984: 43-44; see also Cerwinske, *Tropical Deco*.

46. Anthropologist Nelson Graburn has argued that modern-day vacations function in similar ways to the festive rituals of primitive cultures. Both are marked by heightened experiences that are set off from ordinary life. Events take place in a differentiated time and space that prompt unconventional kinds of behavior. See Graburn, "Tourism and the Sacred Journey," in *Hosts and Guests: The Anthropology of Tourism*, Valene Smith, ed. (Philadelphia: University of Pennsylvania Press, 1977), 20-21. Florida was different enough from "back home" of most Americans that it offered an easy separation from the everyday.

47. Limerick, et al., 247m 259-64. Henry End, *Interiors Book of Hotels and Motor Hotels* (New York: Whitney Library of Design, 1966), 44.

48. Phone conversation with Lorraine Borka, owner of Borka's Garden Store in Prior Lake, Minn., March 1, 1985.

49. Gwendolyn Wright, *Building the Dream: A Social History of Housing in America* (Cambridge, Mass.: MIT, 1981), 195.

50. Frances Duncan, "Gardening Unashamed," *Garden Magazine*, February 1919: 22-23; Frances Duncan, "The Boom in Organized Gardening," *Garden Magazine*, March 1919: 77; "Triumphs of National Garden Week," *Garden Magazine*, March 1923: 45; and Leonard Barron, "Meet Me at the Flower Show," *Garden Magazine*, May 1923: 194, 201.

51. "Apollo in Southampton, Long Island," *Garden Magazine*, September 1919: 45.

52. Russell Lynes, *The Tastemakers: The Shaping of American Popular Taste* (New York: Dover Publications, 1949; rprt., 1980), 193-94.

53. Lynes, 165.

54. "Lawn A-Mercy! Don Featherstone Rules the Roost in Plastic Flamingos," *People*, May 19, 1986: 125-27. Union Products, where Featherstone is now a vice president, still uses his original design for the flamingo. They added his signature to the mold in 1986. Lawnware Products of Morton Grove, Illinois, produces another style of lawn flamingo, originating their version at about the same time as Union Products. These two companies, along with Tucker Plastics, Inc. ,of Toronto, are the only manufacturers of pink flamingos in North America. See Janet Cawley, "Plastic Flamingos are Something to Crow About," *San Diego Union*, 1 January 1986: D3.

55. Russell Lynes, *The Domesticated Americans* (New York: Harper and Row, 1957), 299.

56. "The Peak Year for Pink, *Life*, 2 May 1955: 74-76.

57. Ellen Melinkoff, *What We Wore: An Offbeat Social History of Women's Clothing, 1950-1980* (New York: William Morrow, 1981), 34.

58. Albert Goldman, *Elvis* (New York: McGraw Hill, 1981), 155, 129; see also Greil Marcus, "Elvis: Presliad" in *Mystery Train: Images of America in Rock and Roll Music* (New York: E.P. Dutton, 1975; rpt. 1980), 187-91.

59. On the Hawaiian shirt, see H. Thomas Steele, *The Hawaiian Shirt: Its Art and History* (New York: Abbeville, 1984) 15; Professor Lary May of the Program in American Studies at the University of Minnesota pointed out the adoption of "pinko" in the 1950s as a substitute for the previous use of "red" to label a communist.

60. Allen Lacy, "Flamingos!" in his collection *Farther Afield: Gardener's Excursions* (New York: Farrar Straus Giroux, 1986), 218.

61. On the critique of suburban design, see, for instance, Kenneth T. Jackson, *Crabgrass Frontier* (New York: Oxford University Press, 1985), 236-37; Herbert Gans, *The Levittowners* (London: Penguin Press, 1967), xv-xvi; and William H. Whyte, Jr., *The Organization Man* (New York: Simon and Schuster, 1956). On mass culture critique, see Bernard Rosenberg and David Manning White, eds., *Mass Culture: The Popular Arts in America* (Glencoe, Ill.: The Free Press, 1967) and Gillo Dorfles, editor, *Kitsch: The World of Bad Taste* (New York:Universe Books, 1969). Jeffrey Miekle discussed Americans' ambivalence about plastic in the postwar era in a paper entitled "Plastics and Plasticity," presented at the American Studies Association in Toronto, Canada, November 4, 1989.

62. Hillier Bevis, *The World of Art Deco;* Michael O'Connor, "A Moderne Dilemma, 43-44.

63. See *The Cat's Pajamas Swell Stuff Catalog*, Montclair, New Jersey, 1987.

64. Information about people taking plastic flamingos to showings of *Pink Flamingos* from letter from Rob Niemiec to the vice president of Lawnware, Inc., one of the manufacturers of flamingo ornaments. Letter is undated, probably circa 1981. Letter shared with author by company vice president Jeff Niemiec (no relation to letter writer). Philip Core, *Camp: The Lie that Tells The Truth* (New York: Delilah Books, 1984), 9; on camp, see also Susan Sontag, "Notes on Camp," *Partisan Review,* Fall 1964: 515-30. Phone conversation with Alex McMath, owner of "Sugar Tit Gifts" in San Francisco, March 1985. Interview with David Kasparsak, Minneapolis, February 17, 1985. The use of the pink flamingo by gays and other groups in contemporary American culture can be viewed as acts of inversion. On the importance of cultural inversion, see Barbara A. Babcock, *The Reversible World: Symbolic Inversion in Art and Society* (Ithaca: Cornell University Press, 1978).

65. On British punk, see Dick Hebdige, *Subculture: The Meaning of Style* (London: Mutheun, 1979); on punk in England and in the United States and its historical precedents, see Griel Marcus, *Lipstick Traces: A Secret History of the Twentieth Century* (Cambridge: Harvard University Press, 1989).

66. See Frederic Jameson, "Postmoderism and Consumer Society" in *The Anti-Aesthetic: Essays on Postmodern Culture* Hal Foster, ed., (Port Townsend, Wash.: Bay Press, 1983), 112.

67. On the flamingo thefts in Quincy, Ill., see Winston Williams, "500 Plastic Pink Flamingos Offer a Flight of Fancy," *New York Times*, July 25, 1985, 16. Another well-known and memorialized large flamingo display was created by students at the University of Wisconsin-Madison in the late 1970s, where 1,000 flamingos were placed in front of the administration building one night. A postcard of the display was made and continues to sell throughout the United States. Flamingo swiping and other excessive displays are examples of what scholar John Fiske identifies as the small acts of rebellion or "guerrilla raids," rather than outright revolt, common in popular culture. See John Fiske, "Commodities and Culture" in his *Understanding Popular Culture* (Boston: Unwin Hyamn, 1989), 32-34.

68. Interview with Jeffrey Jacobs, Minneapolis, March 1985.

69. Numerous people have told me of their pink flamingo housewarming presents. Interview with David Kasparsak, February 17, 1985.

70. Dayton's ad, *Twin Cities Star and Tribune*, 26 February 1986: 2A.

IV

Creating the Domestic Landscape
The Home Handyman and Craftswoman Respond to Consumer Culture

A cartoon appearing in a 1961 issue of *Popular Mechanics*, a magazine featuring a "how-to" approach to home living, shows two women talking over the fence between their yards. In the background, one woman's husband happily lays brick for a fantasy structure that may be an overblown child's playhouse or a free-form sculpture. His wife complains to her friend, "It all started out as an outdoor fireplace." The fireplace sits completed in the foreground, overshadowed by the construction behind it.[1] The cartoon exaggerates the practices of the home handyman, a self-sufficient do-it-yourselfer, who at times gets carried away with his home projects, crossing the border between sober, practical work and exuberant aesthetic expression. It also points to the importance of manual labor to the domestic environment, whether it be handcrafting objects that decorate home exteriors and interiors, landscaping yards and gardens, or repairing, expanding, or restructuring the house.

The cartoon man's humorous example of home craft and do-it-yourself projects represents practices that have continued at signficant levels in an industrialized, consumer America, particularly among the working class and the middle-class, particularly those at the lower to middle range of the latter class. Many Americans who create yards studded with statuary make these objects themselves as just part of recreational work in the home. They may also adapt or personalize storebought items, reuse old objects for new purposes, or create entire assemblage environments from both manufactured and self-generated artifacts. These practices in the realm of garden decor and home projects represent responses to consumer culture that have been largely overlooked by scholars of consumerism, perhaps because they fall outside of boundaries of folk art and decorative arts, the material culture subjects that have received most attention. A consideration of these popular handcrafts challenges conceptions about the complete transformation of American society into a consumer culture and the related notion that the home has become a palace for the display of consumer goods. By figuring home handcraft and design projects into our model of consumer culture, even those practiced at small scales and involving simple skills, a more finely tuned model of material culture production and use emerges. In this model, the home continues to be an important site for the production of artifacts, especially of decorative classes of domestic objects and is reconceptualized as a place where consumer culture is actively mediated rather than simply displayed or celebrated.[2]

A study of domestic objects needs to be viewed within the larger context of the home itself. The creation, adaptation, or arrangement of artifacts such as yard statuary in the domestic environment highlights the malleability of the American home and its locus as a site of individual and family power. Part of this power arises from the literal mastery over space, landscape, and materials of the home—the homeowner's freedom to change his and her domain through renovation, decoration, and landscaping. These material manipulations provide expressive power to communicate individual experiences and allegiances, whether at the scale of the house as a structure itself or at the smaller scale of domestic artifacts.

DEMOCRATIC POWER AND THE HOME AS PLASTIC SPACE

Eileen Szewczak, who lives with her family in the old mill town of Manayunk, Pennsylvania, just outside Philadelphia, provides a good example of how one person's yard participates in broader activities that create and manipulate the domestic environment.[3] She and her husband have dramatically renovated their row house and its yards since moving there from an apartment three blocks away in the mid-1970s. At that time, the place needed urgent repairs, since, as Szewczak describes the home, "it looked like a haunted house." An elderly woman had owned the home and had not been able to keep it in good condition before her death. Szewczak says, "A couch in here was growing to the wall." Over their years of ownership, the Szewczaks renovated it inside and outside.

In this working-class town, where many row houses do not even have front yards, the Szewczaks' place stands out as a particularly well-kept and welcoming home. The modest, eight-by-fifteen-foot front yard reflects their reclamation efforts in its bushy flower borders, patch of grass, and garden statuary. Even when it had been full of weeds, the yard was a selling point for the Szewcazks because they had never before had one. "Just to have a little bit in front meant a lot to me," Eileen Szewczak says. She tried planting flowers, adding more over the years until "I got something I liked." Along with her natural plantings, she put in statuary to create "some sort of diversion other than just the flowers." She made some yard ornaments and bought others or received as them as gifts, then arranged them all carefully in the small space.

Now, a plaster rabbit peeks out from a flower bed; a Madonna stands near the porch; a ceramic duck (wearing a bonnet) and her duckling waddle along nearby, while a plastic cardinal sits on the fence overlooking a little Dutch girl, and a cement turtle surveys the scene near the sidewalk. Besides this visual evidence of her dedication to the yard, Szewczak's seriousness is reflected by her participation in the city garden contest sponsored by the Philadelphia Horticultural Society. She entered for the first time in 1988, when she placed as a finalist out of six hundred entrants.

Eileen Szewczak's yard is an important part of her home decorating efforts in general. An active craftswoman, she macrames plant hangers, makes dried flower wreaths, creates ceramic statuary, cuts and paints wooden wall plaques (like the welcome sign that hangs outside their front door), and sews soft sculpture figures of scarecrows, horror figures, and Santa Claus for her yard at Halloween and Christmas.

The material adaptibility of the domestic landscape can be especially important in the context of social change. Szewczak views her renovation work as a contribution to the rebirth of Manayunk, bringing new residents to the neighborhood and new businesses to Main Street, a change that she sees as positive. A different attitude toward social change is expressed by Tony and Emily Bushinski, elderly residents of "Frogtown," an inner city neighborhood of St. Paul, Minnesota. They take meticulous care of their home and yard in an area often threatened by crime and poverty.[4] Like Eileen Szewczak, the Bushinskis have dramatically changed their home landscape, where they have lived for over fifty years. Their well-kept yard, surrounding a modest two-story house, has become a community landmark of sorts, with neighbors and strangers often commenting on its appearance during neighborhood strolls. Covered with a thick carpet of Kentucky blue grass, clipped sharply at the borders, the yard is flanked by forty rose bushes and adorned with yard sculpture. A statute of the Blessed Virgin serves as a focal point for a rose garden on one side of the house, where two cement flamingos add to the paradisical effect. Giant monarch butterflies rest on the side of the house, while a cement bird bath welcomes feathery friends to the yard.

Despite the considerable labor required for their yard and the substantial annual investment for flowers, grass seed, and other items, the Bushinskis consider it essential to create a beautiful yard each year. "It's better than having a slum," Emily Bushinski says. It took considerable efforts to achieve the notable yard, as Mrs. Bushinski explains: "When we moved here in the late 1920s, there was nothing here, just water and ashes. It was a big coal dump. There was no yard, not even dirt, just coal ash." Just to start the project, they had to dig up ash and fill the property with dirt. Now, after decades of cultivation, they have been recognized for their contributions to the neighborhood, and won an award for the most beautiful yard in the early 1980s from the Frogtown Neighborhood Association. Speaking of her husband's dedication to the yard, Emily says: "That's what you call his pride and joy." In the face of increased crime and other neighborhood changes, the Bushinskis find their yardwork a source of empowerment: this is a place where they are in control, right down to the straight edge of the lawn's border. The experiences of the Szewczaks and the Bushinskis in transforming their homes into pleasing environments match those of many other homeowners in this study, whose well-crafted yards and gardens often have been dramatically relandscaped and designed with statuary.

The belief that property invests individuals with power has been a cornerstone of American democratic philosophy, notions embodied in the contemporary experiences of the Szewczaks and the Bushinskis. The American home inherited qualities associated with ideas about "property" from eighteenth-century thought. The connection between property and power was articulated with increasing conviction by political leaders and social commentators during the early years of the republic. Thus, Thomas Jefferson argued that a society of landowners would ensure stability in a democracy, helping Americans to avoid the class conflicts of European societies. Property provided individuals with equal standing and with a place to exercise individual rights, where the powers of a ruling class or of the state could not hold sway. From these premises, Jefferson developed his vision of a nation of "yeoman farmers," who would serve as a strong base for democracy, stemming the rise of inequality and aggrandisement of wealth by a minority in a growing industrial order. Writing to James Madison in 1785, Jefferson commented that "the small land holders are the most precious part of the state."[5]

His views were widely shared by other influential writers and philosophers of his day. Hector St. John Crevecoeur recognized that agriculture and domestic architecture were public, material expressions of a democratic nation:

> We are all tillers of the earth . . . we are a people of cultivators . . . We are all animated with the spirit of industry which is unfettered and unrestrained because each person works for himself. If he travels through our rural districts he views not the hostile castle, and the haughty mansion, contrasted with the clay-built hut and miserable cabbin [sic] . . . A pleasing uniformity of decent competence appears throughout our habitations.[6]

These ideas provided the basis for an agrarian social policy that led to the promotion of free land for settlement and, eventually, to the Homestead Act of 1862.[7]

By the turn of the present century, similar beliefs shaped public policy that made ownership of houses, not only of farmsteads, essential to the national interest. As the nation increasingly changed from a rural to an urban and suburban populace, values formerly applied to the farm were transferred to the home. Widespread homeownership became the means to a stable society. In the housing boom years of the 1920s, a decade that found more Americans living in urban than in rural areas for the first time, President Calvin Coolidge argued for the value of homeowning in similar terms to Jefferson's earlier promotion of the yeoman farmer: "No greater contribution could be made to the stability of the Nation, and the advancement of its ideals, than to make it a Nation of Homeowning families." These convictions later were re-enforced by the federal government through tax credits to homeowners, planning and support for public highways for suburban expansion, and housing financing programs. Homeownership was good for the nation's economic growth, spurring the housing and automobile industries. The single family home, it was thought, embodied an individualistic society and nurtured democracy, giving each homeowner a stake in a stable society.[8]

Homeownership became an important sign of power and success in American culture, a subject that scholars from a number of disciplines have studied. Analyzing the impact of these values on the built environment of the United States, historian Kenneth Jackson notes that the single family home is "the paragon of middle-class housing, the most visible symbol of having arrived at a fixed place in society, the goal to which every decent family aspired." Anthropologist Constance Perin corroborates Jackson in her study of American beliefs about homeownership and renting. She confirms that Americans expect themselves—and others—to move along a predictable path, or "ladder," in the life cycle from renting to homeownership. Comments by those Perin interviewed reveal that a significant attraction of homeowning is the freedom and power owners gain over their domestic environment, in contrast to renters, who remain subject to landlords' rules and have little incentive to improve the material quality of a residence, even if it is home. The single family home, whether an urban row house or a suburban ranch house, offers independence, a place where a person can do what he or she wishes to adapt, decorate, and modify the home and its surrounding real estate.[9]

The power to create one's own domestic scene—to build the home one wishes, or to change and modify an existing home and yard—is a powerful component of the American dream of homeownership. Landscape historian John Stilgoe identifies the national attraction to built environments that can be modified and manipulated: "Plastic space and structure," he writes, "enjoy tremendous favor among most Americans," adding that the widespread preference for wood as a home building material arose from the relative ease with which wood structures could be renovated and modified as much as from its easy availability. The use of architectural plan books in building American homes from the mid-nineteenth century to today's "pattern language" architecture is due, in part, to the ease with which plans could be individualized by home builders. Much attention in customizing plans focuses on small features and architectural ornaments to personalize basic designs that were used by numerous others across the country or in the same neighborhood.[10]

From the Queen Anne houses of the Victorian suburbs to the mass-produced housing of the post–World War II era, plan books and advice literature recommended that homeowners personalize their home, making it an expression of the individual family. And homeowners did take this advice. In his study of Levittown, New Jersey, in the late 1950s, sociologist Herbert Gans found that new owners were eager to distinguish their prefabricated house in that suburban subdivision by adding bay windows, painting interiors and exteriors, landscaping gardens, and modifying other ornamental features. More recently, folklorist Michael Owen Jones's study of "add-ons and re-dos" in Los Angeles homes and fellow folklorist Simon Bronner's examination of one man's changes to the exterior of his home in Harrisburg, Pennsylvania, both document the continued importance of manipulating and changing the domestic environment today, when most Americans move into pre-existing housing stock.[11]

Americans also view the yard as a plastic space where power can be exercised through landscaping, gardening, and adornment.[12] In the 1840s, landscape architect Andrew Jackson Downing urged Americans to landscape and beautify the grounds around their home to express their character and their cultivated tastes. His many publications provided lengthy verbal instructions and visual examples of just how to do that. Downing's advice led the way into a gardening boom in post–Civil War decades, as the growth of suburbs with requisite green spaces offered homeowners a landscape that they could beautify. The scale of the Victorian yard was not as important as the fact that it was individualized: "The window box, the flower or vegetable garden, the landscape—all satisfied the need for an environment visually responsive to one's personal efforts."[13] Homeowners' efforts created a cultivated space around the home: the yard as parlor rather than as wild nature. Prefigured by Downing's advice to add embellishments to the homegrounds, Victorians adorned yards with vases, pots, statuary, and garden furniture, items that had become available in mass-produced forms, although some of them continued to be made by hand.[14]

As consumer culture developed hand in hand with industrialization in the post–Civil War era, the role of the American home as a locus of power, control, and self-expression became even more important. In a corporate America, the public worlds of work and politics became more bureaucratized and less responsive to individual action.[15] But the domestic scene remained strongly tied to the notion that there homeowners have power over their environment. Homeowners could alter the structure of the house or redesign the outdoor landscape. Like larger scale efforts to remodel the house and yard, home handcrafts expressed a similar sense of power over the material world. So while artisan occupations decreased with industrialization, amateur craft activities in the home continued, shifting from being mandatory to survival to serving as hobbies enjoyed during leisure hours.[16]

HOME HANDCRAFT AND THE POPULAR PRESS

One place we find evidence of this shift is in home magazines. A staple of the popular press from the mid-nineteenth century through the present, home magazines have offered reams of advice on decorating, garden design, handcrafts, and practical fix-it projects.[17] Such nineteenth-century publications as *Godeys' Lady's Book* and *Women's Home Companion* featured home handcrafts as regular offerings to their readers. This content continued in later magazines like *Good Housekeeping* and *Better Homes and Gardens*. Magazines consistently presented the home as a space to be altered and adapted to the needs and desires of its occupants, often through handcraft projects practiced in the home as well as through manufactured artifacts. Home-centered activities ranged from large-scale projects to landscape the yard or build garden architecture to small-scale projects to build or refinish furniture, to create household textiles and clothing, or to make holiday decorations and gifts.

Most analyses of the popular press have emphasized its role in creating new consumer identities, promoting new products and new styles in its advertising and editorial content.[18] By overlooking the persistent inclusion of handcraft articles and ads for materials and instruction books, this perspective has failed to take account of publication content as a whole. In addition to promoting new products in their advertising and modern sensibilities in their articles, these magazines retained regular sections on do-it-yourself projects and handcraft. This content implies that readers' notions of home retained values of thrift and self-sufficiency. In this way, home magazines offered some cultural ballast by balancing new notions of consumer-oriented identity with earlier production and thrift-centered values.

Magazines aimed primarily at the homeowning middle class reveal a consistent trend of informing and instructing readers about do-it-yourself projects for men, women, and children. Many articles were addressed to the woman of the home as the chief shaper of the domestic environment. *Good Housekeeping,* for instance, promoted the latest styles in women's fashions, but offered a "pattern service" for those wanting to make the clothes themselves. The magazine carried many "how-to" articles instructing readers on a wide range of projects. In one piece from 1920, the author advised readers on "How to Refinish Old Furniture":

> Under present conditions,when the practise [sic] of self-help is at a premium and the do-it-yourself formula is finding hundreds of exponents, specific directions for furniture renovation will doubtless find more ready acceptance than ever before among interested householders.[19]

Another article in the same issue instructed readers on painting furniture and observed that this kind of home project helped to save money and " . . . to achieve individuality of self-expression, using your personal resources for work and artistry."[20]

Although women's handcrafts were highlighted, home magazines did not ignore handiwork projects for men. A publication such as *Better Homes and Gardens* aimed at male as well as female readership with articles on "the home workshop" and regular features on "tips for the handyman." In the late 1920s, the editors made a special pitch to the "handyman," saying, "We shall have more space than ever, and shall print many articles telling how to do the many simple and practical things inside and outside the house which make for solid comfort and more beauty." Articles enthusiastically exhorted the ambitious homeowner who wanted to save money and use leisure time productively to "build these closets yourself!" "Now *you* can tile your walls!" Or "make yourself a flower carrier and garden tool kit!"[21]

A magazine aimed exclusively at male readership, *Popular Mechanics* also recognized its readers' domestic roles by devoting entire sections and numerous articles to home repairs and do-it-yourself projects, even while its major editorial content focused on technological advances, machine inventions, and engineering feats. Along with instructions for making such "homemade" gadgets as a photographic copy stand or x-ray equipment, projects of greater aesthetic dimensions were presented, often drawn from creations submitted by readers. In 1910, for instance, Frank H. Miller of Woronoco, Nevada, sent instructions for making a concrete fountain for the yard, decorated with embedded rocks. Other articles offered readers suggestions on ornamenting homes with rustic window boxes made from branches (harking back to popular rustic work of the 19th century) or on building a "sunlight flasher" as a garden accent (similar to the reflective gazing balls that were popular at the time). *Popular Mechanics* encouraged readers to make home repairs themselves, instructing them in plumbing and electrical work. The happy homeowner envisioned by these magazines was a person satisfied when busily improving his home, a person much like "Mr. Do-It," from a 1960s comic strip in the magazine, who always appeared as an intelligent, capable, and self-sufficient homeowner, ready to repair a screen door or fix a toilet, and foiled off against "Bungle," his incompetent and lazy neighbor.[22]

The popular handcraft and do-it-yourself practices promoted by periodicals aimed at the middle class have been largely overlooked in artifactual studies of the twentieth century, perhaps because these crafts fall outside of the confines of folk arts, elite decorative arts, and organized craft movements. Yet they constitute a significant level of handwork that has continued despite industrialization. These popular activities intersect with organized efforts at promoting handcrafts, some of which were more self-consiously oppositional to industrialization and mass production.

The Arts and Crafts movement, which developed first in England under William Morris and his followers, reacted strongly against industrialization by promoting the revival of craft traditions. Factory work, according to Morris, dehumanized workers and produced shoddy merchandise. The revival of handcraft—making furniture, paper, books, and other decorative arts—had a moral dimension in that it could provide workers with meaningful work and create beautiful objects with which to surround themselves at home. Gustav Stickley, a furniture maker and home designer based in Syracuse, New York, served as the chief proponent of the Arts and Crafts philosophy in the United States. From 1901 to 1916 his publication, *The Craftsman*, shared his furniture, garden, and architectural designs along with his aesthetic philosophy with homeowners throughout the nation. Stickley's designs reached even larger audiences in mainstream home magazines, many of which carried "how-to" articles on building Craftsman furniture or stenciling Craftsman-styled motifs on bedroom walls.[23]

Allen Eaton's efforts in supporting the continued practice of immigrant and rural crafts during the 1920s and 1930s comprises another organized effort to preserve the manual arts. Eaton believed that an appreciation of immigrant folk arts, showcased in locally based festivals, could help ease tensions between immigrants and native-born Americans. He helped to organize several "Americans in the Making Expositions" in the 1920s and provided advice for others on how to do the same. His parallel efforts with rural communities in the southern highlands of Kentucky and Tennessee strove to make local handcraft traditions an important source of income in an otherwise bleak economic situation.[24]

Alongside of these efforts at promoting contemporary handcraft, modern artists and art collectors began collecting and exhibiting American folk art in the 1920s and 1930s, a trend that was part of a broader "antiques craze" and an increased interest in colonial Americana among the general populace, professional collectors, and museums. Collectors focused primarily on folk arts of the eighteenth and early nineteenth centuries, but their interest in handwork prompted a revaluation of contemporary handcraft, too. This was reflected in the the *Index of American Design*, a pictorial survey of American crafts begun during the Depression under the New Deal. Holger Cahill, an originator of museum exhibitions of folk arts, served as the director.[25] These movements, combined with the popular level of handcraft and do-it-yourselfism among working- and middle-class groups constitute a significant amount of handwork in the twentieth century, even if these practices have remained subordinate to consumerism.

Organized craft movements and home magazines provide historical evidence of the continued importance of craft production in the twentieth century, practices also confirmed through contemporary ethnographic study. In the domestic outdoor landscape, a range of handcrafted items are found today. Homeowners make original creations as well as pieces made from craft patterns. They also adapt and alter manufactured objects, reuse and transform consumer items, and construct designed environments from mass-produced things. Plywood Scotty dogs, wooden geese, old farm machinery, and assemblage sculpture make up some of the diverse objects in American yards. This class of domestic objects provides a useful case study for general theorizing about contemporary use and creation of material culture.

MAKING YARD ART: POWER, PERSONALIZATION, AND BRICOLAGE

Handmade objects for outdoor display vary greatly in material, form, and degree of originality. Though handmade, they are relatively simple crafts, not artisan objects such as the silverware or furniture made in the eighteenth and nineteenth centuries.

Some homeowners create original sculptures for their yards. Mike Schack's five-foot-high mosquito is just such an object. With its cedar pole body, sheet metal wings, and wire conduit antennae and legs, Schack's mosquito is the only one of its kind. In making his sculptures, which also include a tyrannosaurus rex, an alligator, and Popeye, Schack engages in a common artistic process. After his initial inspiration—for the mosquito piece, the moment came during an evening battling the pesky bugs—he searches for materials that will put his idea into form. The materials often come from salvaged scraps of metal and wood, as did the mosquito's wings and body. Other times, Schack literally stumbles upon a "goofy" log or piece of wood on walks in nearby forests, which sparks his imagination. This process led to his pipe-toting Popeye, whose pudgy cheeks and mouth are made from the natural forms of a swollen tree branch. In talking about his artistic process, Schack says: "It's through your own creation, you might say. Doing something, using your hands and your mind and your imagination, that's what makes your mind work. It makes you wonder what it's going to look like."[26] While proud of his original creations, Schack is not a handcraft purist. His yard includes plywood cut outs made by himself and by others, given to him by friends and family.

Schack's cutouts of Snow White and the Seven Dwarfs are examples of another group of widely popular handmade pieces for the yard. Cutout forms do not involve a great deal of skill to make other than the basic techniques of sawing and painting required by every handyman in his home workshop. They nonetheless provide a creative and fanciful outlet for use of practical skills. Made simply by drawing a shape on plywood, cutting it out with a jigsaw, and painting it, these pieces—sheep, bears, cows, geese, and Santa Claus, to name a few—highlight imagery more than technical skills or innovative materials. They sometimes offer a way to convey the homeowner's sense of humor, as happened with the "granny fannies" or "yard butts" that suddenly appeared on many domestic scenes in the 1980s. This image of a man or woman, but most often a women, bending over as though working on his or her garden, offered a visual joke to passersby, who, at first glance, thought they were getting an eyeful of someone's rear end. The yard butt matches other humorous, and sometimes whimsical, handmade yard sculptures. Whirligigs, fanciful wind-driven pieces, feature animated scenes of goats kicking unsuspecting owners or of farmers frantically milking cows as the wind blows. Cutouts and whirligigs offer options for a craftsman's original ideas, or they can simply offer a chance to apply basic skills, since mass produced patterns for both items are commonly available at craft stores or in popular magazines.[27]

While men are more likely to create objects drawn from their skills, tools, and materials as home handyman, women create outdoor items that resemble decorative touches inside the home. One popular item for the craftswoman is the front door wreath, an all-season variation on the Christmas wreath. To create these, women buy dried flowers, straw, ribbons, reeds, and a branch or metal frame, then interweave the materials to create individual designs. Everyday wreaths or holiday wreaths are hung inside the home as well as on the front door. Eileen Szewczak in Manayunk, Pennsylvania, for example, makes wreaths along with ceramics, wall plaques, macrame plant hangers, and holiday fabric sculptures, decorative objects that transform her porch and yard into an extension of the home interior.[28]

Eileen Szewczk's soft sculptures of horror figures at Halloween and Santa Claus at Christmastime highlight the fact that holidays serve as temporal foci for home handcraft, just as they are times of more intensive traditional activities in general. Many craftspeople turn their talents and energy to creating prominent indoor and outdoor displays, especially for Christmas and Halloween. Frederika Goldstein of Mar Vista, California, and her three daughters create Halloween displays that are visited by a growing number of people each year. In 1988, they built a harvest figure and graveyard scene for their front yard. A scarecrow, made from old clothes stuffed with straw, sported a pumpkin head and stood imposingly on bales of hay. Pumpkins, both natural and plastic, surrounded him, next to a plastic skull and a cardboard gravestone with hand lettering: "How about you?" This display was rather tame compared to years past when Goldstein has, for instance, created a coffin for their front window for her to lay in. Her daughter dressed as Dracula and lurked nearby on the porch, as horror-movie music played.[29]

The Goldstein's Halloween displays form part of an annual cycle of holiday craft activities, as is true for many active craftspeople. At Christmas, they decorate inside the house and make a gingerbread house; at Thanksgiving they make a cornucopia and Indian corn displays; at Easter they make and give away Ukrainian Easter eggs, a connection to Goldstein's Slavic background. As a Campfire group leader for the past ten years, Frederika structures the girls' activities around holiday crafts, which they give as gifts or use to decorate their own homes. When not working as a professional caterer and cake decorator, Goldstein makes numerous other craft items: painted china and ceramics. It is an understatement when she says, "I tend to be kind of an artsy-craftsy person."[30]

Holiday displays like Frederika Goldstein's usually involve mixing natural elements—pumpkins and straw—with mass-produced and handcrafted objects. Natural objects become cultural expressions when "worked" or changed in some way: pumpkins carved into jack o'lanterns for Halloween; an evergreen tree decorated with ornaments, lights, and tinsel for Christmas. Holiday displays also typically combine handcrafted and mass-producd objects with little regard to valuing one over the other. Christmas displays might feature a plywood cutout of Santa alongside storebought plastic creche figures. Consumers sometimes "work" mass-produced items to create a handcrafted or natural appearance. Polyester green garlands, bought at local drug or discount stores, are wrapped around porch pillars or lamp posts to create the appearance of natural evergreens at Christmas.[31] Holiday decorating traditions reveal that a close, often reciprocal relationship exists between handcrafted and manufactured artifacts for the yard.

Even when yard ornaments are storebought, creative alterations or additions by consumers personalize manufactured items, a practice that has received increasing notice from folklorists, as some have studied ways in which such objects as Detroit-manufactured cars are painted, decorated, and jacked up in the rear by urban youth to create highly individualized vehicles from assembly-line products. These practices show a willingness to take advantage of the easy availability of mass-produced items but an insistence on individualizing them. Anthropologist Grant McCracken regards this phenomenon as an important ritual by which people in consumer societies take possession of mass-produced goods and endow them with meaning.[32]

Some methods of personalization in yard art take modest expressions. Pink plastic flamingos might sport red bows at Christmastime or wooden geese might be dressed in handmade bonnets and vests. In other cases, such as the work of Werner Muense of northeast Minneapolis, mass-produced objects are consistently altered.[33] Muense's small corner yard bordering a plain three-story house is filled with miniature scenes of animals, architecture, painted rocks, and fantastic creatures. When asked about his creative process, Muense insists that he makes all the objects in his yard himself, when he has, in fact, incorporated numerous pieces of mass produced statuary into his tableaux, usually cement animals and children. He changes these pieces by painting them bright colors to match his handmade deer, snakes, frogs, and painted rocks. This technique "makes them look more lifelike—people like that," Muense states. After painting the figures, he cements them into a base to create a tableau (and to prevent theft), as he has done with a small fawn, identified by a plaque underneath it as "Bambi." Muense freely mixes mass-produced pieces with his handmade creations. In the Bambi tableau, red and white polka-dot toadstools, made from tin cans, shelter the baby deer. Like the rocks he paints with animals, cartoon figures, and other popular images, the cement pieces function as raw materials for the final execution of his ideas. Muense's telling claim that *he* creates all the things for his yard reveals a belief that adapting mass-produced items functions in a similar way to creating entirely original pieces.

Werner Muense's use of the storebought for raw materials is a common practice in yard art and environments. Reused objects may retain their original integrity or be disassembled and converted into new forms. Tractor tires, painted and unpainted, make sturdy flower bed borders or children's sandboxes, and similarly, old car tires are turned inside out, cut open, and serrated into flower shapes to make inexpensive planters. Colorful glass bottles (7-Up, milk of magnesia) and other glass objects are broken and embedded in cement in a tile-like technique used to make fences, to decorate cement yard figures, and to adorn large-scale structures and building. The Watts Tower built by Simon Rodia in Los Angeles is probably the most well-known and monumental structure that uses a technique common in many smaller scale versions. Variations occur in the use of entire ceramic dishes or glass figurines as embedded decorations, as found in homemade patio barbeques constructed by African-Americans in Los Angeles, or in the use of whole bottles as basic building blocks, most prominently seen in

Figure 6. Werner Muense's "Bambi" tableau in Minneapolis, Minnesota.

the well-known "Bottle Village" built by Tressa "Grandma" Prisbrey in Simi Valley, California.[34]

A homeowner might select an object to be transformed based on his or her occupation. This is the case with Harold Kaplan, a retired farmer who lives just outside the central Minnesota town of Onamia. Having moved to the area from a farm in southern Minnesota, Kaplan retains references to his past working life by transforming his old farm machinery into yard sculpture.[35] He has taken apart pieces from old farm equipment, painted them blue and white to match the house, and adorned them with flowering plants and handmade pop-bottle whirligigs. One wire sculpture comes from a hay baler that is mounted on a pole and painted white. A cream separator is painted blue to become a flower pot; another piece from the cream separator is painted blue and turned into a whirligig; a blue tractor tire now holds a garden of flowers, and a blue milk can serves as a base for another flower pot. Interspersed in careful arrangements throughout the yard, the Kaplans' sculptures form dramatic accents to his lavish flower gardens. Harold and Ethel Kaplan still engage in small-scale farming in their substantial vegetable garden, but this is leisure rather than work, and the sculpture made from manufactured equipment has transformed objects of toil into objects of beauty.

The transformation of materials and objects into new forms for aesthetic displays in the home and yard is a widespread practice not confined to farmers and farm wives, from whom one would expect facility in fixing and adapting objects. This practice speaks of a persistent cultural trait of thrift and ingenuity, a holdover from frontier living when materials were hard to come by. Today it remains common among poor and working-class groups, who reuse materials when unable to afford to purchase soemthing new. Yet this is a practice also participated in by American middle-class groups, especially the lower- to mid-middle class.

Its middle-class dimensions are reflected in many popular home magazines, which promote new uses of old objects as a mark of creativity and as a way to save money on domestic expenses. An article in *Good Housekeeping* in 1955, during the height of one consumer boom, nonetheless recommended that women make their own dressing tables rather than buying them:

> . . . on these pages we demonstrate the trick with six examples of attractive little dressing tables that started life as something else . . .

Of course one way to acquire a dressing table is to go to the store, choose one, charge it, and send it. But there's another way, which requires less cash but just a bit more ingenuity. . . . [36]

Some analysts have identified reuse of materials as a characteristic of women's arts and crafts, and certainly women's folk arts such as quilts and rag rugs have relied on salvaged materials. But the practice is not limited to women's work. *Popular Mechanics* strongly encouraged male homeowners to concoct ingenious uses of mass-produced objects for decorative purposes. A "novel stand" for an outdoor flower pot could be made from a discarded washing machine agitator, an object that would create a "modern appearance" in the yard, or a windmill could be made from old bicycle wheels. Outside and inside the home, new uses could be found for objects that otherwise would be tossed out as trash. In "Making Useful and Attractive Novelties from Odds and Ends with Glue," readers learned "how a humble coffee can may be transformed into an attractive wastebasket" or how to make a "novel and attractive doorstop" from a pint bottle filled with sand then decorated with sateen and embroidery.[37]

Thrifty and creative practices find ample expression in the yard, where, besides novel stands made from washing machine parts and car tires made into flower pots, one finds cast-iron pots, hand plows, or wooden wheel barrels as garden centerpieces and old bathtubs converted into religious grottoes. Folklorist W.F.H. Nicholaison interprets the practice of creating new uses for old objects, something he names "distorted function."[38] Many of these objects, he notes, have rural associations—the wheelbarrow, the plow, the wagon wheel, the milk can—and argues that the values associated with them of the simple life and the close community are referred to and wished for by placing them in urban or suburban settings. In this way, material culture can assert values that may be most threatened by modern life.

This certainly is the case with Bonnie Flurschutz of College Park, Georgia, a suburb of Atlanta.[39] Owner of Bonnie's Trading Post, a small antique store, Flurschutz created a tableau in her front yard from objects found at flea markets and garage sales. A hand plow, a wooden barrel, a wagon wheel, and a claw foot bathtub sit there carefully arranged. Originally from the Georgia hills, where she grew up in poverty on a farm, Flurschutz comments that these objects remind her of the country. Although country folk would use these things for practical purposes, whether old or new (she mentions that an old

Figure 7. Bonnie Flurschutz's tableau of antiques in College Park, Georgia.

bathtub would become a drinking trough for cattle), Flurschutz displays them as decorative pieces that remind her of the country: "I guess it's just because I'm from the country. You like to think about the past and kind of wish you were back there." For someone who expresses fear of social change and of rising crime in her suburb, Flurschutz's antiques connect her to a simpler rural life while also representing her separation from that life—utilitarian objects are now showpieces. Her antiques help her negotiate relationships within her neighborhood, expressing her desires for neighborliness and trust in her current home. She comments that she was afraid her neighbors might not like her display but has been pleased with their compliments since she set things out. The fact that nothing has been stolen, another source of apprehension, confirms her hopes that the neighborhood will remain a safe place.

Antiques like Bonnie Flurschutz's plow and wagon wheel are common in yard displays. Many antique objects were originally handcrafted or were used for manual work, thereby representing the world of handcraft and honest labor even when not constructed by the person creating the display.[40] Their associations with the olden days of handcraft are emphasized by leaving wooden objects unpainted, giving them a weathered appearance. Other pieces that were actually mass produced—bathtubs or milk cans, for instance—nonetheless convey an "old-timey" feeling, even when they are not salvaged from actual houses or farms. Milk cans in decorator colors or with rosemalled designs can be purchased at many garden stores. The use of antiques in the yard, usually objects that at one time were considered cast-offs, items that would be laying around the barnyard as junk, now displayed in designed domestic settings, points to the shifting division between cultural categories: "junk," something without value that needs getting rid of, and "antiques," something old and valuable that can be set out for display.[41]

In some cases, materials for yard displays literally come from the garbage. Throughout the United States, some homeowners create complex yard environments made from salvaged objects and materials. Many sites have been studied by a variety of researchers—art historians and artists, folklorists and freelancers.[42] In *Making Do or Making Art,* folklorist Verni Greenfield analyzes the recycling of consumer objects by folk and fine artists, comparing the practices of artist Edward Keinholtz in his creation of surrealistic tableaux with those of folk artists Grandma Prisbrey, who built "Bottle Village," and Leo Dante, who creates assemblage pictures from found objects. Greenfield rightfully argues that reusing consumer materials is a common aesthetic practice of both twentieth-century folk and fine artists, rather than an original aesthetic on the part of fine artists or an eccentric one by lesser-known creators.

Two creators from Los Angeles add to the repertoire of yard environments constructed from salvaged items. One uses materials found in dumpsters to decorate his home, and another makes use of industrial garbage to create original sculptures for his yard. Chester Nachtwey in the Mar Vista section of Los Angeles collects a multitude of discarded materials from local dumpsters outside of apartment buildings and stores, where he finds items that are slightly damaged, worn, or just unwanted.[43] He takes some materials for his own use and gives much of the loot to local charities. Now retired, he spends part of nearly every day rummaging for suitable castoffs, from toys to clothing to furniture and tools. Some of his finds contribute to a lively outdoor environment: a well-furnished patio in his front yard and a colorful display alongside his house. On the side that borders a busy street, Nachtwey has set children's plastic stools on a low brick wall. On the house above these, he has stuck dimestore bows in symmetrical designs and, on one section, spray painted silver polka dots next to the garage door that bears a mural-sized sunset painting by one of his sons. Constantly changing his outdoor environment depending on just what articles he finds to spark his imagination, Nachtwey says, "I'm artistically inclined . . . I keep arranging things all the time." His comment indicates that the act of rummaging and then rearranging found objects constitutes an aesthetic act, something with which many fine artists would agree.

African-American Lew Harris, a garbage collector, salvages and transforms industrial castoffs into intriguing sculptures for his yard in southeast Los Angeles. He works on weekends, often with his sister, Diane, and brother, Marvin, to create an industrial-looking environment of dramatic steel towers and turbines combined with plastic shapes and figures, all of which completely obstruct the house. "We got involved with garbage because it was something to make things out of and we can get the latest materials," Lew Harris says, noting that lucite, a material he finds at industrial sites and businesses, was also used in the space shuttle. Located in an economically depressed area not far from the Watts Towers, the Harris home has become a focal point for neighborhood kids, who stop by to talk, to view the sculptures, and to eat donuts that Harris gives away. Neighbors for the most part

Figure 8. Side of garage decorated with salvaged materials at Chester Nachtwey's home, Los Angeles, California.

appreciate the Harrises work and become curious about any additions or changes. One neighbor commissioned Lew to construct a sculpture in his yard down the block. Recognition for their work extends beyond the neighborhood, since the Harrises have sold sculptures to several art collections and wealthy collectors.[44]

The use of salvaged consumer objects to create aesthetic pieces and environments enjoys widespread participation throughout the United States among tinkerers, handymen, crafts enthusiasts, and fine artists. The yards of Bonnie Flurschutz, Harold Kaplan, Chester Nachtwey, and Lew Harris reveal a *bricolage* process of selecting and mixing divergent sources of objects to construct sculpture, small tableaux, and entire environments. While still subordinate to consumer buying, salvaging objects for new uses is not as marginal and eccentric as it is sometimes regarded but reveals a practice of thrift that resists dominant practices of a throw-away consumer culture. It also goes beyond principles of thrift to demonstrate a common process by which consumers reconceptualize consumer objects. It is an aesthetic practice of twentieth-century consumer culture with roots in earlier cultural values and economic necessities. In new compositions, an object can be freshly seen for its formal properties alone, divorced from its utilitarian associations: a child's stool as a plant stand; a car tire as a flower pot. Whether intended by the creators or not, viewers inevitably make cultural associations with these objects in a process that vacillates between seeing them in formal terms of shape, color, and materials and seeing them in associational terms as signifiers.[45]

This kind of aesthetic interplay is characteristic of several twentieth-century art movements, from cubist collages and dada compositions to pop art pieces and assemblage sculpture. The very material surfeit of this century has prompted artists to utilize new materials beyond the traditional media of paint, bronze, and marble. The use of real objects that had independent lives before being used in collage or assemblage encourages a closer assocation between art and life. Sculptor Edward Keinholz began using actual objects to construct his tableaux in the 1950s and 1960s, saying, "I think a picture is more like the real world when it's made out of the real world." Fittingly, his early works were inspired by vernacular scenes remembered from the churches and Grange halls of his youth in Fairfield, Washington.[46]

Like mixed-media and assemblage sculpture, yard displays present familiar consumer objects not originally meant for the yard in new ways and in new configurations. Out of their original context, dimestore dolls clustered in groups, toilets with ferns growing from the bowls, or children's toys set in designed compositions may appear humorous or surrreal. Yet these displays reveal a poetic use of objects in similar ways to work by fine artists in which familiar objects are disengaged from their original context and reassembled in new relationships. There is a growing attempt to reconceptualize the arts and crafts of a consumer culture to include the manipulation of consumer objects, not only those altered, salvaged, or transformed. Scholars from different disciplines are increasingly recognizing that the selection and arrangement of mass-produced objects functions as an act of production, producing meanings as well as aesthetic compositions, and functioning as an art form in a consumer society, a concept pioneered seventy years ago by Marcel Duchamp with his "readymades."[47]

This study of yard art practices among Americans from various regions and groups demonstrates general responses to consumer culture by working- and middle-class individuals. Their varied practices complicate our notions of how people create and use objects and revise strict distinctions between the handcrafted and the mass produced. Handcraft continues in the production of domestic objects, despite the fact that similar items are readily available as mass-produced commodities. These activities straddle divisions between folk and popular traditions, at times deriving from folk practices among ethnic, regional, and economic groups and at times deriving from popular avenues such as magazines, craft classes, and mass-produced craft patterns. Even when not starting from scratch, consumers show remarkable ingenuity with mass-produced objects, altering and personalizing them, reusing them in creative ways, arranging them in complex assemblages, and transforming "junk" into aesthetic displays. The home, as site of these creative productions, must be regarded as a place where Americans wield power over their material and their expressive environment. Perhaps one reason that yard art shows such wide-ranging creativity in the use of material culture is related to the yard itself, which requires manual labor to shape the landscape, to build and cultivate gardens, to plant trees, and simply to mow the lawn. That may be why the yard evokes a desire for handiwork, becoming a landscape where Americans can reenact in miniature the labor of a preindustrial past, where handymen can build brick barbeques or fanciful sculptures.

NOTES

1. *Popular Mechanics*, May 1961, 241.

2. For discussion of consumer culture of the late nineteenth and twentieth centuries, see Richard Wightman Fox and T.J. Jackson Lears, *The Culture of Consumption* (New York: Pantheon Books, 1983); Simon Bronner, ed., *Consuming Visions: Accumulation and Display of Goods in America, 1880-1920* (New York: W.W. Norton & Co.). Daniel Horowitz analyzes the transformation to consumer culture and moralistic rhetoric about those changes in *The Morality of Spending: Attitudes Toward Consumer Society, 1875-1940* (Baltimore: The Johns Hopkins Univeristy Press, 1985). Analysis of the home as an object itself as well as a site of conspicuous consumption was originally and forcefully presented by Thorstein Veblen in his classic work, *The Theory of the Leisure Class* (New York: MacMillan Company, 1899; repr., New York: New American Library, 1953); see discussion of property, 34-36; dwelling as consumption, 60, and women as domestic consumers, 62-63;

3. Interview with Eileen Szweczak, Manayunk, Penn., September 23, 1988.

4. Interview with Tony and Emily Bushinski, St. Paul, Minn., January 20 and June 9,1 983; interview with Emily in August 1991. Tony died in 1987. See also Tom Rogers, "ITA Gardeners Digging It," *Frogtown Forum*, May 1982, 10. For another example of changes to home exterior as significant in context of social change, see Simon Bronner's account of Cal in Harrisburg, Penn. in *Grasping Things: Folk Material Culture and Mass Society in America* (Lexington: University Press of Kentucky, 1986), 63-86.

5. *The Writings of Thomas Jefferson*, ed. Paul L. Ford (New York, 1892-1899), VII, 36, as quoted in Henry Nash Smith, *Virgin Land* (Cambridge: Harvard University Press, 1950), 128; see also David Handlin, *The American Home: Architecture and Society 1815-1915* (Boston: Little, Brown and Co., 1979), 62-3.

6. *Letters from an American Farmer* (London: 1782), 46-48.

7. Smith, *Virgin Land,* 124-28; 134-35.

8. Handlin, 68-69; Constance Perin, *Everything In Its Place: Social Order and Land Use in America* (Princeton: Princeton University Press, 1977), 72, quoting from John P. Dean, *Homeownership: Is It Sound?* (New York: Harper & Row, 1945), 40-41; *Good Housekeeping*, February 1920, 4; Kenneth T. Jackson, *Crabgrass Frontier: The Suburbanization of the United States* (New York: Oxford University Press, 1985), 290-96; Gwendolyn Wright, *Building the Dream: A Social History of Housing in America* (Cambridge: MIT, 1981), 240-49. In 1920, housing advocate Chesla Sherlock, editor of *Good*

Housekeeping, added a more urgent tone to Coolidge's sentiments by tying homeownership to protecting democracy from communism. In one editorial he argued: "It (Bolshevism) will never come to this country while there are in every community a majority of home-owners; no man sets a fire that may reach a house he owns. . . . " See *Good Housekeeping*, February 1920, 4.

9. As early as the 1850s, architect Andrew Jackson Downing argued that a "good house" was an "echo" of the character of its owners. See *The Architecture of Country Houses* (D. Appleton & Co, 1850; repr. Toronto: Dover Pub., 1969), ixx-xx; Kenneth T. Jackson, *Crabgrass Frontier,* 50; Perin, 32-80. Robert and Helen Lynd's classic study of Muncie, Ill., in the 1920s also confirms the association of homeownership with independence and respectability, *Middletown: A Study in Contemporary American Culture* (New York; Harcourt, Brace,1929), 103; see also a remarkable editorial in *Better Homes and Gardens*, "What A Difference It Makes!", May 1926, 3. On the relationship between the home and personal identity in American culture, see David Hummon, "House, Home, and Identity in America" in *Housing, Culture, and Design: A Comparative Perspective* edited by Setha M. Low and Erve Chambers, (Phil.adelphia: University of Pennsylvania Press, 1989), 207-28.

10. *Common Landscape of America, 1580 to 1845* (New Haven: Yale, 1982), 342-45; Alan Gowans examines mail-order architecture in *The Comfortable House: North American Suburban Architecture, 1890-1930* (Cambridge: MIT, 1986); Clifford E. Clark, Jr., *The American Family Home, 1800-1960 (*Chapel Hill: University of North Carolina Press, 1986), 52-54. For discussion of farm families' vernacular interpretation of plan book architecture, see Fred W. Peterson, "Vernacular Building and Victorian Architecture: Midwestern American Farm Homes" in *Common Places: Readings in American Vernacular Architecture,* Dell Upton and John Michael Vlach, eds., (Athens: University of Georgia Press, 1986), 433-46.

11. Wright, 112-13; Wright notes the dichotomy between asserting both individual and community values in domestic architecture, 193-94; Herbert Gans, *The Levittowners: Ways of Life and Politics in a New Suburban Community* (London: Allen Lane The Penguin Press, 1967), 277-78; Historian Clifford Clark confirms that these practices were widespread in postwar subdivisions in his historical study of domestic architecture, 229-31. Jones, "L.A. Add Ons and Re-dos" in *Perspectives on American Folk Art*, edited by Ian M.G. Quimby and Scott Swank (New York: Norton with the Henry Francis du Pont Winterthur Museum, 1980), 325-63; Bronner, *Grasping Things,* 63-86; see also Hummon, 210-13 and Amos Rapoport on importance of manipulating nonfixed or semifixed features of the American home in *The Meaning of the Built Environment* (Beverly Hills, Sage, 1982), 92-96.

12. For discussion of power exercised in creating in gardens, see Yi-Fu Tuan, *Dominance and Affection: The Making of Pets* (Princeton: Yale University Press, 1984), especially chapters "Gardens of Power and of Caprice," 18-36, and "Fountains and Plants," 37-68. Tuan's examples are drawn primarily from aristocratic gardens, but his analysis could also be applied to the small-scale domestic landscape.

13. Christine Klim Doell, *Gardens of the Gilded Age* (Syracuse: Syracuse University Press, 1986), 5-7.

14. Patricia Tice, *Gardening in America, 1830-1910* (Rochester, N.Y.: The Strong Museum, 1984), 64-69; Ellen Marie Snyder, "Victory Over Nature: Victorian Cast-Iron Seating Furniture," *Winterthur Portfolio* 20 (Winter 1985): 221-22.

15. On these changes, see, for instance, Alan Trachtenberg, *The Incorporation of America: Culture & Society in the Gilded Age* (New York: Hill and Wang, 1982), and T.J. Jackson Lears, *No Place of Grace*, cited above.

16. In the preindustrial era in the United States, the home was the center of hand manufacture of many family necessities, especially in rural areas. On this subject, see Warren Roberts, "Folk Crafts" in *Folklore and Folklife*, edited by Richard Dorson (Chicago: University of Chicago Press, 1972), 233-252; and Ian M.G. Quimby, ed., *The Craftsman in Early America* (New York: W.W. Norton with the Winterthur Museum, 1984). Catherine Beecher argued that the home should retain values connected to manual labor, and she provided women with instructions on sewing, embroidery, and gardening in *Treatise on Domestic Economy* (1848). In *The American Woman's Home* (1869), written by Beecher with her sister, Harriet Beecher Stowe, the authors urged women to practice crafts and other manual labor in the home as one means to maintaining a Christian home and family: " . . . hand-labor is most important to health, comfort, and beauty. . . . " Nineteenth-century middle-class women created a wide array of "fancywork" to ornament the home, particulary the parlor. Utilizing needlework, crochet, knitting, and assemblage of moss, leather, shells, wax, and pinecones, women made fanciful ornaments for the home. Beverly Gordon argues that this work offered evidence of a woman's personal skills and her attention to the home, while it provided imaginative release from what was otherwise a constricted and sober role as upholder of the family's moral values. See her article, "Victorian Fancywork in the American Home: Fantasy and Accomodation" in *Making the American Home* , edited by Marilyn Ferris Motz and Pat Browne (Bowling Green, Ohio: Bowling Green University Press, 1988), 46-68. See also Harvey Green, *The Light of the Home: An Intimate View of the Lives of Women in Victorian America* (New York: Pantheon, 1983), 147-48. In emphasizing persistent handcraft practices among American women, I do

not mean to minimize the pressure placed on them to "modernize," especially at the turn of the century, when social workers and the new home economists denigrated craft traditions among both native-born and immigrant women. On this subject, see Glenna Matthews, *"Just A Housewife": The Rise and Fall of Domesticity in America* (New York: Oxford University Press, 1987), 145-46, 150.

17. For a discussion of early home magazines and their influence on interior decorating, see Jean Gordon and Jan McArthur, "Interior Decorating Advice as Popular Culture: Women's Views Concerning Wall and Window Treatments, 1870-1920" in *Making the American Home*, 105-20.

18. For instance, Stuart Ewen, *Captains of Consciousness: Advertising and the Social Roots of Consumer Culture* (New York: McGraw-Hill, 1976); Roland Marchand, *Advertising the American Dream: Making Way for Modernity, 1920-1940* (Berkeley: University of California Press, 1985); and Christopher P. Wilson, "The Rhetoric of Consumption: Mass-Market Magazines and the Demise of the Gentle Reader, 1880-1920" in *The Culture of Consumption*, 39-64.

19. Harold Donaldson Eberlein, "How To Refinish Old Furniture," *Good Housekeeping*, February 1920, 22-23.

20. Ralph Erskine, "Painting Furniture for Your Own Home," *Good Housekeeping*, March 1925, 45.

21. On the overlooked topic of men's domestic roles at the turn of the century, see Margaret Marsh's fascinating article, "Suburban Men and Masculine Domesticity, 1870-1915," *American Quarterly* 4 (June 1988), 165-86; Marsh does not mention the handyman's role specifically, but refers to male involvement in home maintenance and decoration on p. 185. "Across the Editor's Desk," *Better Homes & Gardens*, December 1929, 86.

22. All following citations from *Popular Mechanics*: "Rustic Window Boxes," November 1906; for examples of "home-made" gadgets, see December 1908, 882, 884, 886; "How to Make A Rustic Seat," May 1908, 348; "A Concrete Fountain," April 1910, 577; "Sunlight Flasher for the Garden," September 1913, 449-50; for "Mr Do-It and Bungle" comic strip, see June 1961, 176-77.

23. On Stickley, see Mary Ann Smith, *Gustav Stickley: The Craftsman* (Syracuse: Syracuse University Press, 1983); T.J. Jackson Lears has interpreted the antimodern strain of the Arts and Crafts movement in the United States, aruging that it was ultimately compromised to the very economic system it originally opposed as Stickley adopted mass-production techniques. Lears also notes that it was the first of periodic craft revivals in twentieth century American culture; see *No Place of Grace: AntiModernism and the*

Transformation of American Culture, 1880-1920 (New York: Pantheon Books, 1981), 59-91. For popular interpretations of Arts and Crafts styles, see "The Making of Arts-Crafts Lamps," *Popular Mechanics*, November 1910, 708-09 and *The Good Housekeeping Manual of Home Handicraft* (Phelps Pub., 1908), esp. 1-7 and 34-39.

24. Allen H. Eaton, *Immigrant Gifts to American Life* (New York: Russell Sage Foundation, 1932); *and Handicrafts of the Southern Highlands* (New York: Russell Sage Foundation, 1937).

25. For history of folk arts collecting, see Beatrix Rumford, "Uncommon Art of the Common People: A Review of Trends in the Collecting and Exhibiting of American Folk Art" in *Perspectives on American Folk Art*, 13-53; also Eugene Metcalf, "The Politics of the Past in American Folk Art History" in *Folk Art and Art Worlds: Essays Drawn from the Washington Meeting on Folk Art*, edited by John M. Vlach and Simon J. Bronner (Ann Arbor:UMI, 1986), 27-50. On the antiques craze, see Elizabeth Stillger, *The Antiquers* (New York: Knopf, 1980). She documents the rising interest in collecting antiques during the last quarter of the nineteeth century through the 1920s, noting that the 1920s was the time of the most popular involvements in "antiquing," greatly spurred by public exhibitions of decorative arts of colonial America, especially by the opening of the American Wing at the Metropolitan Museum of Art in 1924. Interest in collecting American antiques was intertwined with interest in colonial America and the early republic; on colonial revivals, see Karal Ann Marling, *George Washington Slept Here: Colonial Revivals and American Culture, 1876-1986* (Cambridge: Harvard University Press, 1988); Alex Axelrod, ed., *The Colonial Revival in America* (New York: W.W. Norton, 1985). See Holger Cahill, *American Folk Art: The Art of the Common Man in America, 1750-1900* (New York: The Museum of Modern Art, 1932), and Holger Cahill, Introduction in *Index of American Design*, edited by Erwin O Chistensen (New York: MacMillan, 1950).

26. Interview with Mike Schack, August 18, 1988. Chain saw sculpture is a regional form of original sculpture that occurs in Minnesota, Wisconsin, Michigan (as well as in Oregon and Washington, and perhaps, in other forested regions of the nation). Chain-saw-toting homeowners transform dead or downed trees in their yards into statuary of local animals and mascots. In northern Minnesota, bears, fish, eagles, pelicans, and trolls are common. On chainsaw sculpture, see Willard B. Moore, "Circles of Tradition: Toward an Interpretation of Minnesota Folk Art" in *Circles of Tradition: Folk Arts in Minnesota* (St. Paul: Minnesota Historical Society with the University of Minnesota Art Museum, 1989), 18-19.

27. For examples of craft patterns advertised in mass periodicals, see "Craft Patterns" in the *Twin Cities Star Tribune*, which runs every Sunday with examples of yard architecture and statuary that enterprising craftspeople can make along with information on ordering instructions. The home craftsperson sometimes makes several copies of the same piece, giving them away or selling them to relatives and neighbors, resulting in a localized concentration of certain patterns of whirligigs, cut-out sheep, or yard fannies. These ornaments can be copied easily by neighbors or passersby, causing wider dissemination of certain patterns. Other handmade items include pieces made from cement, stone, bricks, or wood. Decorative cement projects might occur as a purely aesthetic afterthought of building the home patio or repairing the sidewalk. See, for instance, reader Dick Hutchinson's instructions for making cement toadstools in *Popular Mechanics,* April 1946, 201.

28. Not all wreaths are made by the woman of the house. Many are purchased today at craft fairs, touristy "country" boutiques, upscale florist shops, mainstream department stores, and even discount stores. Even when not constructed by the homeowner herself, the aura of handcraft is important in outdoor decor, making handcrafted pieces popular purchases at art fairs, festival craft stands, and tourist shops along the highway, and as gifts from creative friends.

29. Interview with Frederika Goldstein, Los Angles, Calif., November 10, 1988. There is a large body of popular literature on holiday crafts, both in monographs and in popular magazines, most of which include projects for interior and exterior decoration. See, for instance, *Holiday Decorations You Can Make* (New York: Better Homes & Gardens Books, 1974); John Burton Brimer, *Christmas All Through Out the House* (New York: Funk & Wagnalls, 1968); *The Time-Life Book of Christmas* (New York: Prentice-Hall, 1987).

30. Fredrika's homecrafts are small-scale activities compared to the complete home renovation that she and her husband were currently engaged in.

31. Folklorist Jack Santino notes the bricolage combination of natural, handmade, and manufactured elements in Halloween harvest displays in an essay that provides an excellent analysis of this folk expression: "The Folk Assemblage of Autumn: Tradition and Creativity in Halloween Folk Art" in *Folk Art and Art Worlds,* 151-69; see also his related essay, "Halloween in America: Contemporary Customs and Performances," *Western Folklore*, XLII (January 1983), 1-20.

32. On personalization or customizing of mass-produced objects, see Barbara Kirschenblatt-Gimblett, "The Future for Folklore Studies in America: The Urban Frontier" in *Folklore Forum*, 16, 2 (1983): 214-20; on "low rider" cars see William Gradante, "Low and Slow, Mean and Clean," *Natural History,*

91, 2 (1982): 28-39. For "possession rituals," see Grant McCracken, "Meaning Manufacture and Movement in the World of Goods" in his *Culture and Consumption: New Approaches to the Symbolic Character of Consumer Goods and Activities* (Bloomington: Indiana University Press, 1988), 85-87.

33. Interview with Werner and Thekla Muense, Minneapolis, Minn, January 6 and June 14, 1983; August 5, 1986, and August 20, 1990.

34. For examples of practices with discarded glass or whole glass, see *Naives and Visionaries* (New York: E.P. Dutton & Co. with the Walker Art Center, 1974), especially essays on Simon Rodia by Calvin Trillin, 21-32; Fred Smith's Concrete Park by Judith Hoos and Gregg Blasdel, 53-60; Herman Rusch's Prairie Moon Museum and Garden by Judith Hoos, 71-76; and Grandma Prisbrey by Esther McCoy, 77-86; see also Verni Greenfield, "Silk Purses from Sow's Ears: An Aesthetic Approach to Recycling" in *Personal Places: Perspectives on Informal Art Environments*, edited by Daniel Franklin Ward (Bowling Green, Ohio: Bowling Green State University Popular Press, 1984), 133-47. On African-American practices, see *Home and Yard: Black Folk Life Expressions in Los Angeles* (Los Angeles: California Afro-American Museum, 1988).

35. Interview with Harold and Ethel Kaplan, Onamia, Minn., August 6, 1987. Geographer John Fraser Hart noted that many farm families in his studies transform either outdated or worn-out farm machinery into garden sculpture in his lecture "The Look of the Land," Duluth, Minn., January 14, 1986; offered in conjunction with the exhibition *Shaping the Land: Minnesota Landscapes 1840s to the Present* at the Duluth Public School District's Central Administration Building. Aesthetic recycling of materials in folk arts often relates to a person's occupation; see, for instance, Steven Ohrn, "Tinkering With Iron: Recycling Skills and Materials" in *Passing Time and Tradition: Contemporary Iowa Folk Artists* (Ames: Iowa State University with the Iowa Arts Council: 1984), 142-48; also noted in Alan E. Mays, "The Welded Chain Mailbox Support: A Study in Material Culture," unpublished paper from course at Pennsylvania State University, Harrisburg, November 25, 1985; graciously shared with author by Mr. Mays.

36. *Good Housekeeping*, February 1955, 75.

37. On the salvage aesthetic of women's arts and crafts, see Lucy Lippard, "Making Something from Nothing (Toward a Definition of Women's Hobby Art), *Heresies*, 1, 4(1978): 62-65, and Melissa Meyer and Miriam Shapiro, "Waste Not, Want Not: An Inquiry into What Women Saved and Assembled, *Heresies*, 1, 4(1978): 66-69; On the novel flower stand from washing machine, see *Popular Mechanics*, May 1964, 147; for glue projects, see *Popular Mechanics,* April 1925, 653-55.

38. "'Distorted Function' in Material Aspects of Culture," *Folklore Forum* 12, nos. 2&3 (1979): 223-35. On reuse of objects in the yard, see also Fred Schroeder, "The Democratic Yard and Garden" in his *Outlaw Aesthetics* (Bowling Green, Ohio: Bowling Green University Press, 1977), 118-19.

39. Information from fieldwork with Bonnie Flurschutz, College Park, GA, October 23, 1988.

40. Elizabeth Stillinger comments that antique collecting in the late nineteenth century was informed by a conviction about the moral superiority of handcraft and the hard-working artisan of colonial America, see *The Antiquers*, xii-xiii.

41. For example of milk cans transformed by rosemaling to make "beautiful dry flower vases," see James S. Baird, *Hoard's Dairyman Dairy Collectibles* (Fort Atkinson, WI: W.D. Hoard & Sons 1987), 30; he features a cream separator as an outdoor flower pot on page 45. For discussion of shifting cultural categories of objects, see Michael Thompson, *Rubbish Theory: The Creation and Destruction of Value* (Oxford Unviersity, 1979), esp. 1-12.

42. The literature on environmental folk art is growing. Some key sources are *Naives and Visionaries*; *Personal Places*; Greenfield, *Making Do and Making Art;* also architect Jan Wampler's *All Their Own: People and the Places They Build* (New York: Oxford University Press 1977), J.F. Tuner, *Howard Finster: Man of Visions* (New York: Alfred A. Knopf, 1989), Seymour Rosen, *In Celebration of Ourselves* (San Francisco: California Living Book with the San Francisco Museum of Modern Art, 1979), as well as newsletters by SPACES, based in Los Angeles and the Kansas Grassroots Art Association, based in Lawrence. Both of these groups document environmental folk art throughout the nation.

43. Interview with Chester Nachtwey, Los Angeles, Calif, November 8 &10, 1988.

44. Information from phone interview with Lew Harris, November 10, 1988; from correspondence, December 27, 1988; Lizzetta LeFalle-Collins, *Home and Yard: Black Folk Life Expressions in Los Angeles* (Los Angeles: California Afro-American Cultural Museum, 1988), 17; Charles Hillinger, "Family Takes Pride in Turning Trash into Art," *Los Angeles Times*, August 7, 1988, Part VI, 1, 9.

45. The concept of *bricolage* comes from anthropologist Claude Levi-Strauss, who used the term to refer to the creative intellectual processes of "primitive" peoples; interestingly, he notes that in French culture the term "bricoleur" refers to an odd-job kind of "handyman." See *The Savage Mind* (Chicago: University of Chicago Press, 1966), 16-17; for use of bricolage in home exterior, see Bronner, *Grasping Things,* 75-86; for aesthetic reaction to

and perception of assemblage pieces and environments, see Greenfield, *Making Do*, 95-108, and William C. Seitz, *The Art of Assemblage* (New York: Museum of Modern Art, 1961), 81-86.

46. Robert L. Pincus, *On A Scale That Competes with The World: The Art of Edward and Nancy Redden Keinholz* (Berkeley: University of California Press, 1990), 1. On assemblage, see also *40 Years of California Assemblage* (Los Angles: University of California with the Wight Art Gallery, 1989). Anne Ayres's essay in this volume, "Directions in California Assemblage," makes the point that fine artists were directly influenced by the assemblage work of many California folk artists, see page 60.

47. On Duchamp's readymades, see Seitz, 44-47. Scholarship that has pointed the way in this endeavor includes work by folklorist Michael Owen Jone, who has argued that the way people in a Los Angeles neighborhood arranged their garbage cans in certain formations could be considered a folk art expression. See his "Modern Arts and Arcane Concepts: Expanding Folk Art Study" in *Exploring Folk Art: Twenty Years of Thought on Craft, Work, and Aesthetics* (Ann Arbor: UMI, 1987), 81-95. Similarly, art historian Marion Nelson suggests that arrrangements of such mass-produced articles as clothing constitute a form of contemporary folk art. Marion Nelson, "Traditional Art in the Museum Context," lecture at Symposium on Minnesota Folk Arts, May 6, 1989, University of Minnesota-Minneapolis, in conjunction with the exhibition *Circles of Tradition: Folk Arts in Minnesota,* organized by the University of Minnesota Art Museum. In the past fifteen years, British Cultural Studies have contributed to understandings of popular culture by analyzing the meanings that disempowered groups produce with consumer objects by using and manipulating them in distinctive ways, an approach that John Fiske has applied to popular commodities in the United States. Numerous works have been published in British Cultural Studies, most notably by authors Stuart Hall, Tony Bennet, and Dick Hebdige. See, for example, Stuart Hall and Tony Jefferson, eds., *Resistance Through Rituals* (London: Hutchinson, 1976); Tony Bennett, Colin Mercer, and Janet Woollacott, eds., *Popular Culture and Social Relations* (Philadelphia: Open University Press, 1986), Dick Hebdige, *Subculture: The Meaning of Style* (London: Methuen, 1979). See John Fiske, "Commodities and Culture" in his *Understanding Popular Culture* (Boston: Unwin Hyman,1989), 23-49 as well as other essays in that work and in his *Reading the Popular* (Boston: Unwin Hyman, 1989). For instance, in "Shopping for Pleasure" in that volume, Fiske states: "The point is that the meanings of commodities do not lie in themselves as objects, and are not determined by their conditions of production or distribution but are produced by the way they are consumed. The ways and the whys of consumption are where cultural meanings are made and

circulated; the system of production and distribution provides the signifiers only." And sociologists have analyzed the meanings people ascribe to personal objects and the ways they are assembled within the home to express individual and family beliefs, desires, and relationships. For an excellent sociological work on domestic artifacts and self-conceptions, see Mihaly Csikszentmihalyi and Eugene Rochberg-Halton, *The Meaning of Things: Domestic Symbols and the Self* (Cambridge: Cambridge University Press, 1981).

V

Neighborhood and Nation
Shared and Distinctive Practices in American Yard Art

Several American films offer telling commentary on the uses of garden sculpture as means of communicating ideas about their characters. In the opening scenes of *The Magnificent Ambersons,* Orson Welles's voice-over narration describes the wealth and standing of the film's family namesake, as Eugene Morgan, suitor to Isabel Amberson, opens the cast-iron gates to the family mansion, where an iron deer and a classical statue flank the front walk. The garden statuary quickly conveys the aristocratic pretentions of this nouveau riche family, whose ancestors were nineteenth-century industrialists, aspirations confirmed by the narrator's comments: "the magnificence of the Ambersons' was as conspicuous as a brass band at a funeral."[1] Their magnificence is a thin veneer. George Amberson, the family scion, already a spoiled child as the film opens, grows into a man of little discipline or moral character who cannot maintain the family fortune. The iron deer and classical figure glimpsed in an opening shot make the Amberson's conspicuous attempts to mimic the landed aristocracy of Europe explicit, just as their mansion adopts the style of a French chateau, in the tradition of the Vanderbilt mansion on New York's 5th Avenue.

Yard statuary appears as a signal of lower class taste and, even worse, of boorishness in a more recent film, *Back to the Future Part II.* Marty McFly, played by Michael J. Fox, travels back to the 1950s from 1985, when he confronts his teenaged father's enemy, Biff.[2] Trying to rectify one version of the future in which Biff kills Marty's father, marries his mother, and becomes his stepfather, Marty goes to Biff's childhood home to change the course of future events. The first shot of

Biff's house shows the yard filled with cement yard statuary—a black jockey, deer, ducks, and a seahorse bird bath—amid hand-lettered signs stating, "No Trespassing." These objects act as an explanation of the bad taste that Biff carries into the future, when his 21st-century high-rise pleasure hotel is decorated in Las Vegas style, complete with leopard skin patterns throughout. The statues even suggest the childhood origins of his stupidity and sadism.

Another recent film offers a more celebratory commentary on popular artifacts. In *Pee-Wee's Big Adventure*, Pee-Wee Herman, the man-child played by Paul Reubens, lives by himself without parents or other adults in a fantasy home full of American pop culture. When Pee-Wee leaves his house, viewers see a yard filled with statues of horses, deer, cows, an Indian on horseback, windmills, and all kinds of Christmas ornaments, even though it's summertime. With his characteristic chuckle, Pee-Wee gives his deer an affectionate pat as he passes by, as if it were a real pet.[3] Pee-Wee's deer is cement—not the iron deer of the Amberson's. His is a middle-class object, part decoration and part toy, equivalent to the colorful and crazy American pop artifacts inside the house (e.g., his lava lamp) and to his prized possession, a 1950s-style hot rod bike. In his tongue-in-cheek manner, Pee-Wee Herman celebrates yard art as playful, slightly wacky, and quintessentially American.

These movies demonstrate that yard art is a means by which people in various groups read and assess others who display these objects. That these objects have figured in self-conscious ways in numerous Hollywood films reveals that yard statuary participates in a widely recognized national culture which conveys meaning about people, groups, and places. Hollywood directors know that audiences will see these objects, even in a quick shot, and read them as clues to the film's characters.

The purchase, creation, and display of American yard sculpture is indeed a nationwide practice. This is not to say that it appears uniformly in every neighborhood, city, suburb, or small town. Yet it does constitute a shared element in American culture. Similarities in the choice and placement of popular statuary can be found throughout the United States, with varied inflections from place to place. Region, neighborhood, class, ethnicity, religion, and age all influence the appearance of yard art. An examination of some of the similarities and differences found in contemporary fieldwork provides evidence that material culture comprises a complex system of use and meanings that Americans utilize, manipulate, and read.

Different uses, valuation, and judgments about objects often fall under the rubric of "taste." Taste is a rather slippery term, however, often used in a judgmental manner to set one individual or group off from another. Despite the common sayings, "there's no accounting for . . . " or "to each his own . . . ," taste is not merely the realm of personal aesthetics but is an aesthetic shaped by social factors of ethnicity, class, education, and income. Discussions and judgments about taste, often thought of as neutral, are really masks for conflicts between groups of different age, ethnicity, region, education, or income. French sociologist Pierre Bourdieu utilizes the concept of "distinctions" to discuss differences in the consumption and use of objects by class groups. In his study of French society in the 1960s, Bourdieu shows that these distinctions are clusters of preferences and attitudes that align themselves according to class backgrounds, education, economics and aspirations. Using his survey data, he thus can chart the correspondences among choices in food, films, furniture, music and visual arts for such groups as craftsmen, manual laborers, teachers, and business executives.

Bourdieu's analysis is more pertinent to French society, where class is an overt and recognized category of social and cultural difference compared to the United States. Americans generally refuse to acknowledge class differences despite overwhelming evidence to the contrary, since consciousness of class violates American notions about democracy, equality, and opportunity. Yet Bourdieu's basic argument that "art and cultural consumption are predisposed, consciously and deliberately or not, to fulfil a social function of legitimating social differences" also pertains to American judgments about taste.[4]

The American films discussed above demonstrate the system of valuation with which yard art tacitly functions as a means to evaluate others through their choices of imagery and materials on display. Bourdieu associates taste distinctions primarily with class groups, but the use of and preference for certain artifacts also reflects and maintains distinctions between ethnic, religious, age, and other kinds of groups. In American culture with its resistance to class recognition, objects, in fact, become even more highly charged with the function of distinguishing groups, on one hand, and at the same time, of erasing, blurring, or obfuscating those distinctions.

REGION, ETHNICITY, CLASS, AND NEIGHBORHOOD

Region remains a relevant category of cultural analysis of objects, despite fears that mass media and mass culture would homogenize the nation, erasing differences between one part of the country and another. As documented by geographers and folklorists, regional differences in language, customs, folklore, and other cultural expressions continue to thrive in the United States. Scholars in those disciplines have utilized the concept of a region as a basis for cultural analysis for decades.[5] Regional analysis of yard art practices, therefore, offers a useful mode for comparative study that reveals nationwide similarities as well as differences. Yard art includes mass produced objects that are marketed nationwide, items made by locally based, family-owned businesses, and handmade artifacts whose patterns derive from varied sources, ethnic, local, and national. Regional differences in the choice of imagery, materials, placement, and frequency are useful to understand reasons and motivations for material culture use.[6]

I found significant similarities and differences in regional areas in which fieldwork was undertaken: the Midwest focusing on Minneapolis, the Eastern seaboard focusing on Philadelphia, the South focusing on Atlanta, and the West focusing on Los Angeles. Local domestic architectural traditions, climate, vegetation, ethnic populations, and regional culture in general influenced the appearance of yard art, the choices of objects for display, and the placement of these in the yard and on the house. Variations most often meant different emphases, frequency of display, and choice of imagery. Some imagery was exclusive to one or two regions. With the national market for garden statuary and with rapid diffusion of new items through tourism and craft marketing, new images and objects travel quickly from one area to another.

Although similarities exist among all areas, residents of Philadelphia and of the Twin Cities display yard art more frequently than those living in Atlanta or Los Angeles. I have speculated about why this might be so. Major factors seem to be climate and related local vegetation. With Minnesota's harsh, long winters and short growing season, Minnesotans have to cultivate yards and gardens more diligently and more intensively than residents of other regions. The cold northern climate also leaves yards brown and bare or snow-covered for half the year. Lacking year-round natural adornment, culture makes up for nature's color and beauty. Several Minnesotans mentioned that they like to leave their yard art up all year (with some changes for holidays) because the statuary provides lively color during bleak winter months. In a state where many urban residents have family on farms or have themselves moved to the city from farms, and where there are ongoing exchanges between rural agricultural and forested areas and the metropolitan region, popular sculpture related to the farm and forest is also abundant in miniature barn outbuildings, cows, ducks, deer, and bears.

In ethnic and religious population, Philadelphia and Minnesota have higher percentages of Catholics compared to Atlanta and Los Angeles. Catholic homeowners were found to use statuary—religious and secular—more often than other religious groups. While Pennsylvania's climate is more moderate than Minnesota's, the area is not as warm year-round or as lush as Atlanta or Los Angeles (even though L.A.'s lushness is artificially maintained). Philadelphia is home to strong ethnic neighborhoods that continue to practice craft traditions which, in turn, influence other groups living nearby. In Los Angeles, too, ethnic neighborhoods were places where yard art was found with more consistency.

It is on the level of neighborhoods that the realities of class and ethnicity intersect and find forms in cultural expressions. Most American neighborhoods are firmly class-based. Housing stock is built to be generally uniform in a given area, requiring a certain level of income to purchase. American communities have shown great resistance to neighborhoods of mixed income or race as reflected, for instance, in frequent rejection of new housing codes to allow for multiple family dwellings in an area dominated by single family homes. Ethnicity also works as a factor in neighborhood formation. In the historical past and still today, immigrant groups often settle in one area of a city or a state, sometimes maintaining ethnic neighborhoods and businesses for several generations. Folk art scholars have extensively documented the relationship between ethnicity and the creation of folk arts, and material culture scholars have begun to document relationships between class and choices of consumer goods and styles.[7] It is in neighborhoods that patterns of material culture use related to class and ethnicity were discovered and examined.

Like many eastern cities, Philadelphia proper is filled with block upon block of brick row houses. Small front yards are squeezed next to the front steps or in front of a porch of these attached homes. In some neighborhoods row houses are built flush with the sidewalk, and in many of the city's suburbs row houses and attached "doubles" are the norm in domestic architecture. Even here, where the architecture and surrounding yard varies from the American suburban ideal of a detached single family home in the midst of green space, yard art and outside decoration find their place in many Philadelphia neighborhoods. When yards are absent altogether or only postage-stamp size, the front space of the homes—windows, doors, stoops and small gardens—are adorned, designed, and decorated with popular sculpture and other artifacts.

The south side of the city, known locally as "South Philly," has been a strong Italian neighborhood since immigrants first settled there in the late nineteenth century. Continued interchange with relatives in Italy and continued small-scale immigration has maintained the ethnic character and population of the neighborhood, even with recent migration to adjacent areas by upwardly mobile Philadelphians returning to colonial row houses from the suburbs and by African-Americans. Italian culture is bolstered by the local churches, numerous Italian businesses, and an outdoor Italian market in this long-established working-class community.

Row houses are the dominant domestic architecture found throughout the district. Some are made from brick. Many are covered with tile siding. Most row houses in the neighborhood do not have yards at all—front stoops lead directly to the public sidewalk. Italian residents have adapted their material culture displays to the architecture by adorning the fronts of home, especially doors and windows, with decorative objects.[8] "Dressed windows," as they are called here, form a strong aesthetic tradition in the neighborhood. The window is the place to display decorative objects and ornamental sculpture. Window displays function in an analogous way to the front yard. Many objects placed in windows in this neighborhood are found at a slightly larger scale in yards or gardens in other neighborhoods. Here, objects in windows signal changes in the annual cycle of seasons and holidays. Because the window offers protection and because displays are also physically part of the indoor culture of the living room, objects made of ceramic, china, or glass displayed there are smaller and more delicate than those appearing in yards. Like yard sculpture, these figures make idyllic references through images of the Blessed Virgin, angels, classical figures, and animals. Many refer to the Italian classical tradition in the arts, and local shops do a brisk business in imported Italian figurines.

Figure 9. Dressed window in Italian neighborhood of south Philadelphia.

Besides showing consistent choices in imagery, dressed windows have a definite sense of design. Figures and vases are carefully placed, with symmetrical and tripartite use of the window as a framing device. Curtains, drapes, and shades are arranged as backdrops or as dramatic accents to the foregrounded composition. These designs are part of neighborhood communication. If a family does not create a window display or if another fails to keep up on window arrangements, it is sufficient cause for neighborly concern and inquiries.[9]

When room permits, people add gardenlike touches to the space outside the house. Wooden barrels or tubs or cast-iron cauldrons filled with flowers appear intermittently on sidewalks through the neighborhood. Window boxes on some houses hold wooden tulips on a stick as well as natural flowers. These small touches and the window adornments mark the boundaries of the Italian neighborhood in South Philly. As one moves further east toward the waterfront, the architecture remains similar, but windows and exterior adornment changes to pink flamingo imagery, American country wreaths and plaques, and lace curtains, signaling the homes of urban sophisticates, not ethnic Italians. Similar changes in outdoor decor occur when second- and third-generation Italians move from the inner city to suburbs like Conshahocken, north of Philadelphia, a place where many Italians from South Philly have found new, more spacious homes. Some ethnic customs persist in altered ways. Yards and porches become the appropriate site for displays rather than front windows. Shrines to the Blessed Virgin appear in niches in the yards along with popular American artifacts: pink flamingos and giant frogs and donkeys pulling carts replace Italian classical figures.[10]

As with the Italians in South Philly, the African-American community on the north side of the city cares for their homes and creates aesthetic displays even when there are no front yards or small ones at best. In an area that is by and large a ghetto, with abandoned and burned-out buildings and much housing stock in disrepair, it is significant to find entire blocks of well-kept housing. Even here, some blocks are entirely owner-occupied, and one can see the signs of care on individual blocks. Adornment is one measure of the care people try to maintain even under difficult social conditions. Along several blocks near Chestnut Street and 57th, brick row houses have been freshly painted. This is a street on which many residents own their homes, so upkeep of houses is encouraged. A stylized painting technique in which white paint outlines each brick makes these houses highly patterned and decorative. Astroturf blankets many front stoops to create an orderly front to the home, and porches are decorated with plants and planters. Car-tire planters have been placed along the sidewalk and painted to match the house with stylized geometric patterns. On one block, tree trunks, telephone poles, garbage cans, and tire planters all have been painted in green and white decorative patterns to spruce up the streetscape. Colorful geometric patterns are an aesthetic echoed in the graffiti found on abandoned buildings in the neighborhood. The graffiti style employs a white or black outline around fields of color to create an image or word, just as nearby home facades and garbage cans have been painted in bold outlines.

Occasionally one house has been more ornately decorated with bright paint and trim and stands out on a block, even while it utilizes similar paint and decorative techniques, only in a more flamboyant manner. The home of John Fields is such a place. Fields lives in the row house with his father and stepmother. They have created a neighborhood landmark with a fanciful fountain in their front yard and iron grill work surrounding the yard and porch, all painted pink. In his late thirties, Fields comments that the decorated home front attracts a lot of attention in the neighborhood, encouraging people to stop by and chat. He especially likes to go all out on Christmas decorations. Neighbors and strangers alike stop frequently to admire his holiday figures and lights.[11]

The Pennsylvania Horticultural Society recognizes the important contribution that efforts like those of John Fields and his neighbors provide a neighborhood. The Society established a program called "Philadelphia Green" to encourage just such small-scale neighborhood projects. In North Philly near John Fields's home, Willie Mae Bullock and her neighbors worked with staff in the Green program to fight urban decay in their area.[12] They added window boxes to their houses and used car-tire planters for ornamental plantings in front. The results revitalized the neighborhood. Next, they took on a corner lot, transforming it into a herb and vegetable garden. Later they renovated the last remaining vacant lot in their area into a flower garden where residents could relax on park benches and enjoy the scenery.

Statuary also appears in suburban yards outside the Philadelphia city limits, where it figures into the conflicts and rivalries between residents of different areas. Similar patterns of design and display as in the inner city neighborhoods can be found in Manayunk, located north of the city on the Schuykill River. Originally a working-class mill town and now a suburb, the Manayunk community still has strong working class ties in its Polish, Italian, German, and Irish populations. There are signs of change today as new groups move in and as gentrification spills over from Philadelphia on the other side of the river. The architecture of Manayunk, like that in the older sections of Philadelphia, is predominantly row houses lining the sides of the hill up from the river and main street. As in South Philly, the front window and the front door are common sites for small statuary or knickknacks and ornamental wreaths. The small front yards, many measuring only about ten by ten feet, are well kept and occasionally adorned with statuary. One Manayunk resident, Florence Adamo, has created a display of ducks in her flower garden matched by duck statuary in her window. She comments that she and her daughter, who lives with her, are "knickknack happy." Two blocks away, Eileen Szewczak has created her miniature flower and sculpture garden featuring wildlife and religious statuary.

Manayunk is changing and upgrading. Nonetheless, its uphill neighbors in Roxborough, always more prosperous and more middle class, look down on Manayunk—topographically and tastewise—calling Manayunk residents low-class "Yunkers." These attitudes are reflected in different choices of yard statuary between Roxborough and Manayunk residents. Marie Fortuna lives in Roxborough but works as a kindergarten teacher in Manayunk. Having grown up in the Kensington neighborhood of Philadelphia, where she had only the cement sidewalk in front of her row house, Fortuna definitely wanted a small yard when she and her husband looked for a home in Roxborough. In this prosperous though not extravagant middle-class suburb, many civil servants like Marie and her husband make their homes in row houses and in single family homes with modest yards. Marie has cultivated a small flower garden in front of her row house home, where she placed two pink plastic flamingos with their necks intertwined. She says they're "tongue in cheek" and thinks they're funny, a sign of her childhood years in the 1950s, when "the flamingo was a symbol of having made it . . . you bought your home and stuck flamingos in the yard."[13] Fortuna's manipulation of pink flamingos shows her greater awareness of taste distinctions, a characteristic of upwardly mobile individuals. This is in keeping with Fortuna's plans to get a master's degree in speech therapy while her husband completes his master's in business administration, so that they can move to a single family home in Roxborough.

Outside of Philadelphia on the way to Lancaster in the central part of Pennsylvania, the crafts of the Pennsylvania Dutch become prominent features of domestic landscapes and of the roadside in general. The Pennsylvania Dutch or Germans have a long history of folk arts and crafts that have had strong impact on rural Pennsylvania. Although the Pennsylvania Dutch live separate from the modern world in many ways, they intersect with contemporary culture at its most intense in the region's tourist trade. Today, the Amish are the most prominent presence, driving horses and buggies along the highways, selling produce at fruit and vegetable stands, hanging out quilts on their porches for sale, and producing a wide range of crafts for tourists. Although they have forsworn contemporary society, living in their own groups and not using modern technology, the Amish in this section of Pennsylvania interact intensively with tourists from the modern world and depend on tourists for income to supplement farming.

In Intercourse, Pennsylvania, a small town on highway 340 out from Philadelphia, Sunday afternoon brings an urban-sized traffic jam to the small town as tourists jockey for parking spaces. They're here to buy Amish crafts—everything from picnic tables and porch swings to gazebos and yard sculpture. The yard art consists primarily of jigsawed cutouts in wood or masonite of bonneted girls, bears, and the popular fleece-covered sheep. One establishment, J.S. Handcrafts, sells "handmade items by the Amish & Mennonite people from the Dutch Country." Their stock includes small outbuildings in barn styles, picnic tables, gazebos, lawn furniture, wishing wells, decorative cupolas, and outdoor yard animals. These objects appear in yards throughout the region. They are not used by the Amish themselves, who create them only for a market of outsiders. In a culture that avoids adornment except for utilitarian or religious purposes, the neatly kept yards of the Amish use only flowers and rocks for decorative borders.

Amish crafts for tourists, nonetheless, have influenced craft practices generally in the area. At Landis' Cackleberry Farms, a short distance from Intercourse, plywood cutouts of cows, bear, geese, and other animals resemble the Amish stock in town. According to Sandy Futty, a member of the family who owns the business, many women make yard sculpture for Cackleberry Farms, working part-time while their kids are in school. For some, the crafts are a family project, worked on with children and husbands during winter months. They openly copy many Amish craft patterns they see at tourist outlets.

In the Midwest, the city of Minneapolis is home to quite different architectural traditions, demographics, and climate from Philadelphia. Domestic residences in this city consist predominantly of single family homes. Few areas of row houses were ever built here, in an urban area that was most heavily settled in post–Civil Wars days. The climate (the so-called "drama of the seasons," as it is called euphemistically by local residents) brings extremes of weather and temperature which can make it relatively hard work to cultivate one's garden. Although Minneapolis is filled with stately trees and home gardens are maintained, lovely gardens and yards do not grow as easily as in more temperate parts of the nation. The population of Minneapolis is composed of people of mixed ethnic descent—primarily old-stock Yankees, and later arrivals of Scandinavians and Germans. African-Americans, Latinos, and Southeast Asians make up low but increasing portions of the current city population.

Northeast Minneapolis continues to be one of the most persistent older ethnic communities in the city.[14] One of the earliest city neighborhoods, located just north of downtown, Northeast is where Polish and German working-class families settled in the late nineteenth century. It continues to be a solid working-class neighborhood, with some upscale housing built recently to attract downtown white-collar workers. The housing stock throughout Northeast consists of modest wood frame homes, many narrow two-story structures on small lots, built in the late nineteenth and early twentieth centuries. One-story ramblers, urban renewal houses built mostly during the 1960s, are scattered throughout the neighborhood. Northeast, known locally as "Nordeast," remains a blue-collar neighborhood, located close to industrial sites and warehouses along the Mississippi River north of downtown.

Yard art at various scales is prevalent throughout Northeast. No one image dominates statuary that includes handmade and store-bought items. Religious shrines appear in many yards in this neighborhood where several small Catholic parishes are located. Other yards display handmade whirligig bottles made from plastic pop containers, hanging from trees. Emily Lambert makes these to hang next to handmade giant wooden butterflies and wooden birds, items that she also sells to friends and neighbors. These crafts are a family affair: her brother-in-law makes the wood cutouts for the animals and she paints them. Northeast is also where Werner and Thekla Muense live in a house surrounded by Werner's handmade sculptures and handpainted cement adaptations from garden stores. Other notable yards here include the German-inspired Hofsteder house. With its yellow and green color scheme for the house and its painted wooden shutters, its backyard fences and garage, and yard sculpture, their home looks like something out of a Technicolor Grimm's fairy tale. A large Dutch windmill serves as a garden centerpiece in their backyard. A shrine to Mary is prominently featured in the front yard, while another to St. Francis is built into the brick wall in the back. Several bird houses in varied architectural styles, built by Mr. Hofsteder, hover on poles in the back yard.

On the other side of the city, the south central neighborhood of Field/ Regina is an integrated neighborhood of African-American and white residents, solid working- and middle-class. Here one finds predominantly homeowners, with some single family homes as rental property. People here take good care of their homes, dominated by Tudor styles built in the 1920s and ramblers of more recent vintage. Even with the diversity of population, home and yard decoration appear consistently throughout the neighborhood, even more so than in Northeast. No one form or image dominates, but the propensity to adorn fronts of homes appears consistently on every block, though not on every home. Door wreaths appear on some doors; pink flamingo pairs in front of other homes; one house displays a handmade miniature Greek temple that serves as a cover for a bird bath; another house features a silver cement lion; and a green milk can serves as a flower holder on the front stoop of a nearby home. The Field/Regina neighborhood may present a case where neighborhood practices encourage neighbors of diverse backgrounds to take part in outdoor adornment. That willingness to participate in a neighborhood practice is also reflected by holiday displays here. Residents on several blocks all place luminaries—paper bags holding lit candles—along their front walks on Christmas Eve and Christmas Day night. These practices seem to connect with the middle-class and working-class nature of the neighborhood, for as one moves further east into upper-middle-class neighborhoods, many of these material objects vanish and flower gardens alone serve as outdoor aesthetic displays.

Plastic flamingos and cement lions are the favored statuary in the Kenwood neighborhood of Minneapolis. This is where wealthy homeowners occupy mansions and other large houses built by the city's elite at the turn of the century on the edge of downtown. Some housing was converted to multi-unit dwellings in the 1950s and 1960s, when the wealthy left the city for roomier suburban living. Today, bohemian

Figure 10. Flamingos in bathtub planter in Kenwood neighborhood of Minneapolis, Minnesota.

artist-types remain nestled into the scattered rental properties that still exist in this upscale neighborhood, located on one of the only hills in Minneapolis and close to picturesque Lake of the Isles. Cement lions flanking the front steps are popular statuary throughout Kenwood. As a sign of aristocratic authority, the lions make the standing and power of the homeowners even more explicit, while they also seem humorous and pretentious. Other homeowners and renters take a more 'thumb your nose" attitude through their prominent displays of pink plastic flamingos. One homeowner had created a bathtub flower garden on their driveway with two flamingos as centerpieces. Thomas Wetzstein, a young renter nearby, comments that he has a fascination with the styles and designs of the 1950s, which attracted him to the pink flamingos he has in his front yard.[15] At Christmastime, evergreen garlands and strings of white lights are the favored decorative schemes in Kenwood, although even here, some mansion owners slum it with lit-up plastic Santas, snowmen, and tin soldiers.

West of Kenwood lies St. Louis Park, a typical post-World War II first-ring suburb filled with neighborhoods of ranch houses built in the same styles. In one section close to the St. Louis Park Junior High School, homeowners have remodeled and customized the houses since they were first built in the 1950s, giving them more individualized appearances with bay windows, room additions, new windows, patios, and porches. As one of the first-ring suburbs of Minneapolis, St. Louis Park has witnessed a great shift in its population, from almost exclusively dad-as-the-bread-winner, mom-at-home-with-the-kids families in the 1950s to a mixed population of young families, middle-aged singles, and older residents today. Once home to a large Jewish community, St. Louis Park now has a more diverse population. Most residents are solid mid-middle-class, though several sections are home to upper-middle-class residents.

As in the Field/Regina area of south Minneapolis, the residents of one St. Louis Park neighborhood bordered by 394 and Franklin Avenue, reveal the tendency to adorn their home exterior with diverse objects. Here, one finds plastic rabbits, chickens, and pheasants, wishing wells, cartire planters, miniature Holsteins, and abstract driftwood sculptures. Some displays are more elaborate, as with one yard that features statuary in the foundation gardens made from old pink plastic flamingos parts and children's toys, all arranged just so. Betty Slice, who has lived in her home for twenty-three years, puts out a changing variety of objects and popular sculpture. A ceramic squirrel climbs up the front of her house near a brown milk can, while a duck windsock flutters in the breeze. A few blocks away, Martina and Gust Olson, also longtime residents of their home, feature a handmade flower pot filled with impatiens on their front patio, made to look like a giant flower. Mr. Olson made the flower-shaped piece, using an old car tire painted yellow for the pot; a garbage can lid for the base, and jig-sawed wood scraps, painted green, for the stem and leaves. A retired construction worker, Gust Olson also built their home back in the 1950s and later constructed a rock garden with cement pond and waterfall in the backyard, home to two cement flamingos. "My husband's pretty good at figuring out how to do things," says Martina.[16] Like the Field/Regina neighborhood in Minneapolis proper, residents of this St. Louis Park neighborhood are ready each year with holiday displays. Next to homes with Christmas lights, plastic Santas, and window decor, Jewish displays appear at many homes in this neighborhood. Most take the form of window decorations celebrating "Happy Chanukah," while some windows feature paper or lit Stars of David or mennorahs. Taken together, the diverse statuary and outdoor decor appearing in St. Louis Park helps to establish the individuality of each home, just as paint color, picture window drapes, foundation shrubs and flowers, and other customized features of these ranch homes help to distinguish one from the other.

The climate in Atlanta nurtures lush vegetation, with its humidity and rare freezing temperatures. Early garden traditions on Georgian plantation estates adopted European classical garden design with linear parterres and ornate floral plantings. In the middle decades of the nineteenth century, some Georgians followed Andrew Jackson Downing's plans for the picturesque landscape, but many rejected his ideas because he was a Northerner. It was not until post–Civil War days when another Northerner, Frederick Law Olmsted, designed the suburb of Druid Hills that Atlantans adapted a "gardenesque" landscape style. Wealthy Druid Hills influenced future domestic landscapes that featured curving roads, natural topography, frequent wooded areas, and lush shrubs and trees surrounding homes. The Olmsted brothers also designed the major recreation area of Piedmont Park in a similar style of lush, overgrown vegetation.[17]

With Atlanta's prosperous growth during the 1980s and with the ascendancy of the "New South," many of its neighborhoods are home to the upwardly mobile. With the self-conscious sophistication which that brings (and the emphasis on resale value of the home), it is not uncommon for many neighborhoods to have restrictive covenants that dictate what residents can display or what colors they can paint their home. Atlanta has a young population that is very cosmopolitan and attuned to popular music and contemporary art. It also is home to a strong gay community. Remnants of older southern culture also persist. In domestic architecture and family life, the front porch continues to function as a focal point of sociability. Porches are commonly decorated and adorned with lush hanging ferns, flags (American and Confederate) furniture, and ornamental objects such as swans, door wreaths, and flower pots.[18] Many Atlanta residents still have strong connections to rural areas and the southern mountains, where they grew up or where family still live. The craft traditions of rural Georgia along with active folk arts traditions and the work of numerous visionary artists like Howard Finster make it a place with a lively mixture of yard art practices.

Nestled next to the massive Fulton Bag and Cotton Mill and neighbor to the once-rural Oakland Cemetery southeast of downtown Atlanta, Cabbagetown today is a poor neighborhood. It evolved from a diverse working-class population in the 1880s to a mill worker's village by the 1930s, after the Cotton Mill was constructed.[19] The small, single-story houses with ubiquitous front porches are home to both black and white residents, some of whom own and some of whom rent the properties. Even here amidst low-income households, where many homes are surrounded by overgrown bushes and weeds, small decorative accents can be found in the washtub planters and the occasional pink flamingo pair near a bird bath. One Cabbagetown resident, Alvin Bentley, sits on his porch enjoying the afternoon sun and the blooming rose bushes in front of his home. He has ornamented his porch with wind chimes and augmented the natural rose bushes with spinning plastic flowers, defiant measures in an area that has problems with thefts and assaults. Having settled in Cabbagetown after living in other parts of Atlanta, he likes being a homeowner in this neighborhood after having only rented properties previously. Planting rosebushes and adding other decorative touches to the front of his home signals he is here to stay, statements backed up by the protection of his pit bull terrier in the rear.[20]

In another section of Cabbagetown, Richard Holland has covered the front of his home with ornate decor, including a large sign salvaged from a junk yard, advertising "Atlanta Zoo." Mannequins sit on the roof of the front porch, waving at passersby; a pink flamingo peeks out from a hole in one of the roof gables, and the porch itself is bedecked with prolific plants. In some ways, Holland's porch is an exaggerated version of the decorated porch common in these parts. In other ways, it reflects Holland's flamboyant aesthetic, which is carried through indoors where vintage advertising signs decorate walls from floor to ceiling. Holland bought the Cabbagetown house two years before: "This is the only place you can buy in Atlanta if you're poor." He likes the area because people are tolerant. He says that they love his decorating, and they seem comfortable having gay neighbors. His found-object aesthetic forms part of his philosophy to live inexpensively. By using some flair he thinks he can make junk and antiques look good.[21]

Nearby Candler Park, a more prosperous neighborhood than Cabbagetown, sports more yard art in its larger yards in front of larger bungalow homes. The area has attracted a lively mix of white and black residents, blue-collar workers and young professionals, settled families and college students. Here, pink flamingo pairs can be found in abundance, mostly in plastic, but occasionally in cement, like the ones Maya Hahn displays in front of her home. Owner of a realty business, Hahn collects flamingos and other Florida memorabilia because she likes the tropics, she says.[22] The flamingos, she also notes, match her azalea bushes when they're in bloom. Hahn has bought flamingo statuettes that decorate the inside of her home at the store Pink Flamingos, located in the nearby business district at Little Five Points. The store fits with the slightly off-beat, bohemian, and artistic nature of Candler Park, characteristics also seen in the Five Points music clubs, art galleries, and inexpensive, hip clothing stores.

Flamingos appear in yards in College Park, a middle-class postwar suburb southwest of Atlanta, but here they are not the dominant garden imagery. Antiques, classical statuary, Halloween harvest figures, and other items are found just as often as flamingos. This is where Estelle Smith moved from a trailer home in the Georgia mountains, where she promptly transformed her suburban yard into a rose and sculpture garden. Manager at the Finley's Greenhouse and Florist, she applies her horticultural, craft, and design skills to her home landscape. Smith terraced her front yard and planted dozens of rose bushes, inspired by large-scale public gardens, like the nearby Calloway Gardens. She also looks at books for ideas, "but most of those are for the big gardens. I just scale it down." She has created a side garden for her corner house complete with garden arch, pink flamingos, classical statues, deer, and frogs. Besides the elaborate permanent display, Smith goes all out at Christmastime: "I have this thing about Christmas decorations," she admits. She installs lights all around the house, puts a star on the chimney, and fills the front yard with Santa in a sleigh, snowmen, tin soldiers, and three animated figures. Forty-five years old and recently divorced, with her children grown, Smith has unleashed her energies and finances on her home, inside and out.[23]

From outlandish buildings like the Big Donut Drive-In, which serves as a base for a twenty-foot-high donut on its roof, to the three-D billboards on Hollywood Boulevard, to the exuberant architecture of the countless gas stations and car washes, Los Angeles is filled with fanciful vernacular commercial architecture that dots the seeming millions of miles of commercial strips lining the streets. Even the buildings meant for the most common, utilitarian functions adopt fanciful forms. Architect Charles Moore has called Los Angeles a series of theme parks, with Disneyland as its prototype.[24] Domestic architecture assumes fantasy styles of the Hollywood sets in references to other time periods and other places.

Given the preponderance of fanciful vernacular architecture, roadside sculpture, and billboard art in Los Angeles, it is surprising to discover that this popular imagery does not spill over into yard art to a great extent. I did find yard art, but not as commonly as I expected. When I did find it, the displays were most often related to ethnic cultures or to older residents who had time to devote to their yards. Perhaps the very preponderance of vernacular sculpture along the roadways makes the home more of a refuge here. The region's lush, colorful, and often sculptural vegetation also may placate the desire for outdoor statuary. Exotic shrubbery frequently assumes fanciful sculptural dimensions bordering on topiary art in the front gardens of many homes. Los Angelenos residents tend toward a more impersonal presentation of the home front, which may be encouraged by their high mobility as well as their fear of crime. Other researchers in the area have noted that Los Angelenos do not encourage interaction at home, and in fact, use fences, alarm system signs, and elaborate entry ways as distancing devices to control interactions with outsiders and even neighbors.[25]

Los Angeles is one of the most multiracial, multiethnic urban areas in the United States, though here, as elsewhere in this country, neighborhoods form around ethnicity, race, and income. The yard art practices apparent in Los Angeles neighborhoods reflect the continued importance and diversity of ethnic culture in the urban landscape. Many white, middle-class areas had neat lawns, sculpted shrubbery, and well-tended gardens but little statuary, even in the San Fernando Valley, a working- and middle-class section of the metropolitan area. In these neighborhoods the front of the home conveyed the overall effect of propriety and anonymity; nothing showed that might provoke response or invite undue notice. Perhaps the very preponderance of extroverted displays focused on the human body, clothing, and behavior common at local beaches and along heavily traveled streets in Los Angeles such as Hollywood Boulevard and Sunset Boulevard make the home less relevant as a place for public display.

One neighborhood in West Los Angeles with a concentration of Japanese-American residents clearly revealed signs of an ethnic community in its domestic landscape. The ranch-style housing resembles surrounding neighborhoods but the landscaping and statuary stand out as Japanese. Sculpted bonsai have been nurtured and pruned in front of many houses. Stone lanterns and bridges, common garden accents in Japan, are arranged in many front yards amid highly designed rock formations. Hiroshi Kobashigawa's yard is representative of many in the neighborhood. Second-generation Japanese-American, Kobashigawa was born in Phoenix, served in the United States Army in World War II, and settled afterwards in Los Angeles. A gardener by trade, he applies those skills to his own yard where he has shaped Japanese pine, juniper, cedar, and cherry trees with bonsai techniques and added a stone lantern or "toro" to the scene. He admits that his garden is only "partly Japanese." In Japan, he says, one wouldn't have a garden in the front yard, only in the back or in an enclosed courtyard.[26]

On the eastern side of Los Angeles is Boyle Heights, a section of East L.A. where more people of Mexican heritage live than anywhere outside of Mexico City. The landscape here reveals a very different aesthetic from the Japanese area of West Hollywood and from most other parts of Los Angeles. Yards more closely resemble yards in Mexico and the American Southwest. The yards surrounding modest one-story homes are work places and, in many cases, resemble barnyards. Fenced-in yards are often barren of turf. Live chickens scratch the dirt rather than plastic or cement ones. Dogs are plentiful and keep their watch, barking at strangers as they pass by. Simple adornments such as pink flamingos are found occasionally, and on

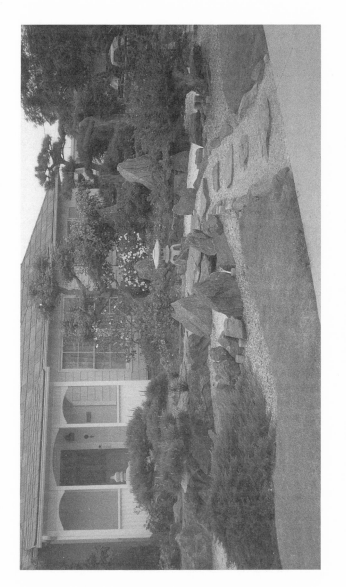

Figure 11. Yard in Japanese-American neighborhood in Los Angeles, California.

certain blocks one house stands out with elaborate sculpture displays. One such Boyle Heights yard was built by Helen Saavedra and her daughter's family. In the midst of their rock-covered yard, Helen has placed a miniature statue of a woman pouring water from an urn, a deer family, and a peasant couple. She created the yard in the 1970s before she came down with emphysema. Now the statuary is in need of fresh paint, which her daughter, Elizabeth Paez, plans to apply soon.[27]

Boyle Heights is predominantly Catholic, and some residents do display shrines to the Blessed Virgin in their front yards. Outdoor religious displays are not seen here on the scale of other Catholic neighborhoods, as in Italian South Philly, for instance. The difference may be purely economic, since this is one of the poorest sections of Los Angeles. But there also may be a cultural aesthetic at work that reserves devotional shrines for home interiors. It could reflect an emphasis on shared public space as appropriate for iconographic displays rather than outdoor domestic space.

Religious objects for domestic shrines can be purchased at the local Mexican market, one of the central public spaces in the neighborhood. People come here daily to meet friends, to chat, to shop, and to listen to mariachi music by the live bands that play here. Customers can buy raw food stuffs for Mexican cooking along with already prepared fare. Numerous booths or stores sell religious statuary and votive candles dedicated to various saints, Jesus, and Mary. Shrines are displayed in many of the market booths themselves. The presence of religious artifacts for sale and the shrines on display suggest that the merchandise is indeed purchased by area residents. Its absence in the outdoor domestic landscape suggests that shrines are probably reserved for home interiors.

Other elements of the Hispanic aesthetic emphasize shared public space and communal expression, as do the many murals in Boyle Heights and in nearby areas of East L.A. These public paintings form part of the Chicano mural movement which began in the late 1960s, arising from the political protests of the United Farm Workers, led by Cesar Chávez, and from the Chicano Movement in general. By 1978, some estimated that nearly one thousand outdoor murals had been created in Los Angeles alone, most of them of Chicano origin and located in Chicano neighborhoods.[28] The murals painted on public housing at the Estrada Courts Housing Project close by the Mexican market are among the most well known from the mural movement. The murals take up entire sides of the two-story housing complexes. Some of their imagery resembles the images of three-dimensional yard statuary. One mural features idyllic scenery where deer graze and bears amble through imaginary forests, and another features Our Lady of Guadeloupe fifteen feet high rather than in the diminutive yard shrine. Much of the imagery draws specifically from Hispanic history and culture, and many murals are pointedly political. A dramatic portrait of Ché Guevara pointing his finger at the viewer appears on one, combined with the verbal message, "We are not a minority." The presence of murals as the dominant visual art form suggests that the Chicano aesthetic focuses on communal space rather than on individual homes, at least in this area.[29]

North of Boyle Heights, Armenian immigrants have settled in areas of East Hollywood and Glendale, most of them first generation. The yardscapes here blend garden traditions from the Middle East with American practices. Neat front yards and gardens incorporate many fountains and imagery from royal gardens: elephants, lions, and aristocratic figures. In their country of origin, these gardens would appear in interior courtyards; in Los Angeles, they are front yards. At Annie Kaputyan's house in Glendale, where she lives with her extended family and two children, she has fixed up the front yard with flower borders, scalloped edging tile, and flanked the front steps with two elephant statues.[30] The elephants remind her of India, a country close to her homeland whose culture she admires.

Other neighborhoods like Mar Vista in the western section of Los Angeles are home to primarily white middle-class residents of diverse ethnic backgrounds. These homes do not feature permanent outdoor displays as often as in ethnic neighborhoods, and when they do, diverse imagery appears: antique wagon wheels, pink flamingos, and farm animals. Holiday displays are favored over permanent outdoor statuary. Halloween is big in Mar Vista. In one section, residents along several streets all put up elaborate displays of store-bought paper skeletons, cats, and witches and create displays of harvest figures. Many adults dress in costumes to pass out candy to trick-or-treaters, antics which entertain the neighborhood children and attract many from nearby areas.

The regions, cities, and neighborhoods surveyed here demonstrate that common traditions and imagery in yard art can be found throughout the Unites States. Some regions show a propensity to more ornamentation than others and some regions display distinctive statuary related to domestic architecture and to ethnic populations. Distinctions between city and suburb are not as much a factor in yard art practices as are class, ethnicity, and religion.

RELIGIOUS SIGHTS AND SITES

As seen in such neighborhoods as South Philly, religious background significantly influences the use of material culture. Roman Catholicism in particular affects choices in yard art, given its long-standing tradition of religious artifacts and images. Shrines to Mary and the saints are the most obvious manifestation of religious practices and beliefs. More generally, Catholics have a propensity to use artifacts for secular as well as religious displays. Roman Catholic residents of diverse ethnic backgrounds—Italian, Polish, German, and Irish—were frequent practitioners of yard art.

Yard shrines of religious statuary are the most obvious and direct connections to religious beliefs. Shrines to the Blessed Virgin are most common in all regions studied except Atlanta, a predominantly Protestant area. Shrines are also dedicated to saints, such as St. Francis (the lover of animals) and St. Theresa, and sometimes to Christ. Religious statuary usually appears at two-foot-high scale, smaller than public or church statuary but larger than pieces used for indoor display. Sometimes statuary is just set in the yard without much fanfare. More often, statues are placed in a homemade grotto made of brick or stone or set inside a wooden garden arch. An old bathtub is sometimes turned on one end and half-buried to create an enclosure. These forms serve as protective niches for the statue and refer to actual grottoes or caves— places where religious revelations are believed to have occurred. While many grottoes make use of vernacular building practices, readymade grottoes also can be purchased at garden supply stores in ceramic, cement, or plastic. Shrines usually function as the central focus of a highly designed portion of the yard, with flower gardens surrounding them and rabbits, deer, flamingos, or butterflies gathering nearby. These public signs of faith correspond to domestic shrines in home interiors. Indoor displays are created on bedroom dressers and on tables or in wall niches, where family pictures, holy cards, rosaries, and other religious artifacts surround a central statue, meant for family devotion and prayer.

People who display sacred images outside their homes consider them a positive contribution to the neighborhood as much as a sign of their own devotion. Rita Sammartino, an Italian woman in the Manoa section of Philadelphia and her husband, put up a prominent outdoor shrine in their side yard where it is visible from the street. Backed by the cement wall of the garage, a fiberglass Virgin statue stands on a pedestal, flanked by dramatic cannas flowers, red sage, and hedges. Sammartino comments, "I hope that when people pass by they'll see her and say a Hail Mary . . . You never know, someone might be feeling bad and walk by and see it and it might make a difference." She hopes that the shrine will be a good influence on children who play in the school yard across the street. Other times Catholic homeowners erect shrines as a public thanks for a specific event or for prayers answered. Once on display, yard shrines demarcate Catholic neighborhoods for both local residents and for outsiders.[31]

Catholic shrines are found in private yards throughout the United States, a shift from their more public locations in European countries where grottoes and shrines were usually found in churches and along the roadside.[32] Some religious grottoes exist as public sites in this country, which have become destinations for travelers as well as local landmarks. One of the most famous of these sites is located in Dickeyville, Wisconsin, where, from 1918 to 1931, Father Mathias Wernerus built the elaborate grounds filled with grottoes and other statuary at his parish of Holy Ghost Church. The Dickeyville Shrine features a central grotto dedicated to the Blessed Virgin. The cavelike structure, large enough to walk into, is constructed from reenforced cement with glass, stones, tile, shells, and other colorful objects embedded in it. In addition to the religious imagery of the Dickeyville Shrine, its relies on imagery of the garden—swans, storybook children, and animals—and of patriotic monuments. Other kinds of public religious displays at a smaller scale persist in the American landscape. Wooden crucifixes and religious statuary commonly appear along highways, for instance, in a Catholic area of Minnesota near St. Cloud.[33]

The American roadside provides a site for Protestant professions of faith, although language and architecture are used to convey and encourage religious reflection more than the overt religious imagery of Catholic displays. Evangelical billboards declare religious messages and remind travelers that "Jesus Loves You So Much It Hurts" or simply, "Jesus Loves You." Roadside chapels serve as outdoor worship environments where travelers can stop to contemplate their spiritual lives. These buildings are usually miniature churchlike buildings where families or individuals can sit on benches, facing a cross or window in the nave. While simple chapels are the most common of these roadside religious sites, some Protestant rest stops do take figurative forms. Lund's Scenic Garden near Maple City, Michigan, for instance, brings many travelers to a stop when they spy the full-scale religious sets displayed in the woods next to the highway. The husband and wife team, E.K. and Ortha Lund, both United Brethren of Christ ministers, were inspired to create thirty-six scenes from the Bible in 1948 after working on theater sets for a church play. At the play's conclusion, the Lunds decided to incorporate the sets into a landscape where travelers could take a break from the road to hike through sixteen acres of woodlands to appreciate nature and the Bible. Another devotional image used in public Protestant displays is the image of praying hands, originally taken from Albrect Durer's engraving. Praying hands appear on many religious billboards and serve as the thirty-two-foot-high evangelical sign at the "Hands in Prayer, World In Peace Memorial" in Webb City, Oklahoma. Handmade praying hands occasionally appear in outdoor domestic settings, like the three-foot-high cement ones in Austin, Minnesota, though most often, praying hands appear in small statuettes or plaques inside the home.[34]

Howard Finster's Paradise Garden in Summerville, Georgia, one of America's most notable examples of evangelical religion in the landscape, merges the public display of the highway shrine with the domestic landscape. Having bought three acres of swampland over thirty years ago, Finster transformed the area into both family home and public park. Daily visitors come from the local community and from across the United States. Finster welcomes all to stop and visit the garden, to listen to his religious messages, and to make a sculpture that they can leave in the garden, which some do.

Finster himself has created most of the myriad sculptures, paintings, signs, and buildings at Paradise Garden. Plywood cutouts of folk figures such as angels, Elvis Presley, John Kennedy, and George Washington, often covered with Biblical texts or Finster's own commentary, commingle with salvaged objects—a dentist's chair, an doctor's examining table, or a commode lid—transformed through paint and applied verbiage into sculptural objects. Next to his modest home and studio building sits the three-story, round building, "Church of Folk Art" and seven other buildings that Finster and his family use and live in. Throughout the garden, signs and sculptures declare his thoughts and messages about the Lord.

Figure 12. Religious assemblage sculpture in Howard Finster's Paradise Garden, Summerville, Georgia.

A Baptist minister, Finster gave up his congregation years ago to concentrate on making art. Now, he says, he reaches more people through his artistic work than he would in church. Commenting on this change in direction, he says,

> I pastored churches up 'til I was about sixty years old. I found out that the people in these churches, you got familiar to 'em, and you preached a good message, and you asked them that night what you preached on that morning, and they had forgot the message, maybe one man remembers the text. Along about that time I resigned from pastoring and worked more on my garden. And then I turned my garden into a ministering garden. See, I got messages all over the garden, I got various kinds of important messages all over the garden. People interview me and take shots of them . . . My sculpture garden has messages and scriptures all through it. And when they take pictures of my sculpture, they have to get my Bible messages.[35]

Paradise Garden is an amazing place. It would have to be. Finster built it because, he says "I was commissioned from God."[36] The three-acre park is full of conventional and unconventional yard art. Visitors can view the rich variety of his creations as they walk down garden paths. Displays of pink flamingos and windmills are interspersed with Finster's original sculpture, most of which have verbal messages and Bible verses painted on them. On the side of one building a red and white cross includes the message, "Get Right With God." Another sign posted next to an old washing machine tub says, "God will not always strive. With Man you can help in this matter by yielding to God." Finster's art resembles and draws on other folk art of hand-painted signs and on evangelism along the road in its references to religious billboards and to roadside shrines and chapels.

AGE, LIFE CYCLES, AND YARD ART

Howard Finster started making art after he had a vision. He was fixing a bicycle one day, when he dipped his finger into a can of paint and then noticed a face appear on his paint-smeared finger. It told him, "Paint sacred art." That was in 1976. Finster was sixty years old. Howard Finster's revelation may be a special case, but it is not unusual for older people, revelations or not, to become highly active in their gardens and enthusiastically engaged with the creation of yard art. Age figures into yard art practices just as does ethnicity, religion, and class. A significant number of residents in all regions of study who created elaborate yard displays and engaged in intensive gardening activities were retired. Increased leisure gives retired folks time to devote to their yards and gardens, especially those who are rooted to their homes. They may go off to visit children and grandchildren every year in other parts of the country, but during most of the year, they stay home. Many of these retired people have lived in their homes for decades and have built gardens and accumulated statuary over many years.

Their involvement in yard art practices serve multiple functions and provide many benefits. Physical activity and creative thought go into building a pleasing display, contributing to more vigorous health. Yard activities are meaningful efforts that occupy much of their time and provide keen enjoyment. When asked why they got so involved, many older folks jokingly dismiss the amount of effort they devote to their yards, commenting, "It keeps me out of trouble," or "It's not that big of a deal," even when their investments in time, money, and energy are substantial.

Americans tend to dismiss the intellectual and creative abilities of older people, to see the later years as a time of diminished intellectual and physical activity. Yet as American society becomes an increasingly older population, scholars have begun to study aging as a multifaceted process, diverging from studies of only pathologies of old age.[37] Some scholars are finding that growing older actually is accompanied by bursts of creativity, when people are given extra leisure and freedom from constraints and responsibilities. Alan Jabbour, Director of the American Folklife Center, has noted that folk artists commonly reach their peaks in old age.[38]

Yard art offers elderly men and women important avenues for creativity and self-expression. Women can design gardens, indulge in flower displays, engage in creative shopping, and create handmade crafts and statuary for the yard and for holiday displays. Men can make use of the skills and materials related to their former occupations. Harold Kaplan in Onamia, Minnesota, has created yard sculptures from his old farm machinery; while C.R. Jordan in Scottdale, Georgia, a landscaper by trade, has created a stunning front yard using his occupational skills. Their publicly oriented landscapes open up opportunities for them to talk with family, friends, neighbors, and strangers about their past occupations as well as their present creations.

Most significant are the opportunities that yards provide for retired people to feel part of their communities. Beautifully designed yards and gardens adorned with sculpture are one way for them to contribute to the upkeep and beauty of their neighborhoods. Yards can earn them social recognition, attracting visits from local news stations, awards from local neighborhood associations, students from local schools to do class projects on them, and journalists who feature them in newspaper articles, all interactions experienced by many older residents in this study. Neighbors might stop by to find out how a sculpture is made or where a person bought it or how to grow roses. Much social interaction engendered by yard art is cross-generational, between elderly homeowners and neighborhood children. Harriet Bagasao in Santa Monica, California, discussed at the beginning of this study, designed her yard with cartoonlike animal statues to please the neighborhood children, many of whom stop by to see the figures. Yard art imagery and practices relate closely to children's attraction and activities, a feature that becomes most vivid at holiday times. Bagasao's motivation to redesign her yard just after her spouse died also intersects with studies showing that grief can spur a burst of creative activities as a way of overcoming loss and getting reinvolved with life.[39]

Harriet Bagasao's lively social life, filled with visits from family and friends and volunteer work, demonstrates a common fact about elderly yard-art creators: these are not people whose social lives revolve only around their yards. Most are closely involved with nearby families as well as with neighborhood and church groups. Mike Schack in Grand Rapids, Minnesota, attends to his children and grandchildren, while also working with local veterans groups and volunteering with other community organizations. These are not isolated loners but vigorous and lively citizens with much to contribute to their communities.

Most of the attention their yards receive is positive in nature, but not all social interactions generated by yard art are positive. The attention some displays attract can be of an unsavory nature. Theft of objects is a common problem. In response to both anticipated and actual theft, older folks try to negotiate and minimize threats by putting up fences, buying dogs, or securing pieces with cement bases. Others consider theft part of the risk and plan to replace objects when necessary. Theft is bothersome to older homeowners, making them feel vulnerable and perplexed that anyone would want to steal their things. Seldom do they talk of abandoning yard displays altogether because of occasional problems. They believe that most people are appreciative of their creations and that it is usually teenagers pulling a prank who are responsible for theft or damage.

Like the elderly today, people in minority groups can often feel that they are without easy means to participate in or to speak as active members of American society. Yard art provides one avenue for them to participate in positive ways in their local neighborhoods and in their larger communities. African-American Lew Harris of south central Los Angeles has created a stunning environment from steel cylinders, industrial fans, and other technological cast-offs. He comments that he might likely be involved in crime if he did not create his sculptures. His creative public works have brought him recognition and have allowed him to contribute something positive to the neighborhood, which Harris acknowledges with the comment, "Once it's been out there for a while it doesn't belong to you anymore, it belongs to the people. People drive by just to see it. It's a love affair."[40]

Yard art in general is testimony of Americans' love affair with material things. The assemblage environment of Lew Harris in Los Angeles, the painted cement animals and children of Werner Muense in Minneapolis, the Virgin Mary shrine of Rita Sammartino in Philadelphia, and the pink flamingos of Richard Holland in Atlanta are not practical, utilitarian objects. Yet they are not frivolous things. They are objects that people need to create some kind of beauty where they live or to make some kind of statement about who they are or simply to communicate that they are there, alive and healthy. In these days when debates rage over what the national culture is and about how subcultures fit—or don't fit—into the cultural fabric, yard art demonstrates one overlooked and humble example of a national culture based on home and neighborhood that can be found from coast to coast, with similarities and variations for different regional, class, ethnic, religious, and age groups. Like any aspect of culture, yard art can divide and distinguish people as well as unite them. Yet the material strikes me as too important to relegate its discussion to taste alone, to minimize the powerful experiences of ethnicity, race, class, and religion that shape displays of pink flamingos and other artifacts in American yards.

NOTES

1. Orson Welles, Director, *The Magnificent Ambersons*, RKO Radio, 1942.

2. Robert Zemeckis, Director, *Back to the Future, Part II*, Universal Pictures, 1989.

3. Tim Burton, Director, *Pee-Wee's Big Adventure,* Warner Communications, 1985.

4. Pierre Bourdieu, *A Social Critique of the Judgement of Taste*, trans. Richard Nice (Cambridge, MA: Harvard University Press, 1984; repr. Paris: Les Éditions de Minuit: La Distinction: Critique sociale du jugement, 1979), 7. Sociologist Herbert Gans produced a polemical analysis of American taste in *Popular Culture and High Culture: An Analysis and Evaluation of Taste* (New York: Basic Books, 1974).

5. See, for instance, Wilber Zelinsky, "General Cultural and Popular Regions" in *This Remarkable Continent: An Atlas of U.S. and Canadian Society and Cultures*, ed. Rooney, Zelinsky; W.F.H. Nicolaisen, "The Folk and the Region," *New York Folklore* 2(Winter 1976): 143-49; and Barbara Allen and Thomas Schlereth, eds., *Sense of Place: American Regional Cultures* (Lexington, KY: University of Kentucky Press, 1990); for a regional approach to material culture studies, see Henry Glassie, *Pattern in the Material Culture of the Eastern United States* (Philadelphia: University of Pennsylvania Press, 1968).

6. In this study I was interested in regional comparisons of yard art practices. I was not attempting to establish folk cultural regions, which some scholars have done with other materials, looking closely at artifacts in one area to determine their distribution and the boundaries of a culture region. That kind of goal would have required a much more detailed study of small geographic areas than I attempted.

7. On the relationship between ethnicity and folklore, see Stephen Stern, "Ethnic Folklore and the Folklore of Ethnicity," *Western Folklore*, 1977, and Stephen Stern and John Allan Cicala, *Creative Ethnicity: Symbols and Strategies of Contemporary Ethnic Life* (Logan, UT: Utah State University Press, 1991); for an example of the relationship between ethnicity and folk arts, see Marion J. Nelson, "Folk Art in Minnesota and the Case of the Norwegian American" in *Circles of Tradition: Folk Arts in Minnesota* (St. Paul: Minnesota Historical Society Press, 1989), 24-44. On the relationship between class and material culture use, see, for instance, Lisabeth Cohen, "Embellishing a Life of Labor: An Interpretation of the Material Culture of American Working-Class Homes, 1885-1915" *Material Culture Studies in America*, ed. Thomas

NOTES

1. Orson Welles, Director, *The Magnificent Ambersons*, RKO Radio, 1942.

2. Robert Zemeckis, Director, *Back to the Future, Part II*, Universal Pictures, 1989.

3. Tim Burton, Director, *Pee-Wee's Big Adventure*, Warner Communications, 1985.

4. Pierre Bourdieu, *A Social Critique of the Judgement of Taste*, trans. Richard Nice (Cambridge, MA: Harvard University Press, 1984; repr. Paris: Les Éditions de Minuit: La Distinction: Critique sociale du jugement, 1979), 7. Sociologist Herbert Gans produced a polemical analysis of American taste in *Popular Culture and High Culture: An Analysis and Evaluation of Taste* (New York: Basic Books, 1974).

5. See, for instance, Wilber Zelinsky, "General Cultural and Popular Regions" in *This Remarkable Continent: An Atlas of U.S. and Canadian Society and Cultures*, ed. Rooney, Zelinsky; W.F.H. Nicolaisen, "The Folk and the Region," *New York Folklore* 2(Winter 1976): 143-49; and Barbara Allen and Thomas Schlereth, eds., *Sense of Place: American Regional Cultures* (Lexington, KY: University of Kentucky Press, 1990); for a regional approach to material culture studies, see Henry Glassie, *Pattern in the Material Culture of the Eastern United States* (Philadelphia: University of Pennsylvania Press, 1968).

6. In this study I was interested in regional comparisons of yard art practices. I was not attempting to establish folk cultural regions, which some scholars have done with other materials, looking closely at artifacts in one area to determine their distribution and the boundaries of a culture region. That kind of goal would have required a much more detailed study of small geographic areas than I attempted.

7. On the relationship between ethnicity and folklore, see Stephen Stern, "Ethnic Folklore and the Folklore of Ethnicity," *Western Folklore*, 1977, and Stephen Stern and John Allan Cicala, *Creative Ethnicity: Symbols and Strategies of Contemporary Ethnic Life* (Logan, UT: Utah State University Press, 1991); for an example of the relationship between ethnicity and folk arts, see Marion J. Nelson, "Folk Art in Minnesota and the Case of the Norwegian American" in *Circles of Tradition: Folk Arts in Minnesota* (St. Paul: Minnesota Historical Society Press, 1989), 24-44. On the relationship between class and material culture use, see, for instance, Lisabeth Cohen, "Embellishing a Life of Labor: An Interpretation of the Material Culture of American Working-Class Homes, 1885-1915" *Material Culture Studies in America*, ed. Thomas

Districts of Minneapolis and Saint Paul (Minneapolis: University of Minnesota Press in Association with the Center for Urban and Regional Affairs, 1983).

15. Fieldwork in Kenwood and conversation with Kenwood residents, 1986-1989.

16. Interview with Betty Slice, St. Louis Park, Minnesota, August 5, 1990; Interview with Martina and Gust Olson, St. Louis Park, Minnesota, August 5, 1990.

17. Catherine M. Howett, *Land of Our Own: 250 Years of Landscape and Gardening Tradition in Georgia* (Atlanta: Atlanta Historical Society, 1983),14-23; 26-27.

18. On restrictions on home display, see "Restrictive covenants keep plastic flamingos at bay," *Twin Cities Star Tribune,* 1 June 1991, pp. 1R-2R. Sue Beckham discusses the development of the porch in the southeastern United States and its role in sociability in "The American Front Porch: Women's Liminal Space" in *Making the American Home: Middle-Class Women & Domestic Material Culture 1840-1940,* edited by Marilyn Ferris Motz and Pat Browne (Bowling Green, OH: Bowling Green University Press, 1988), 69-89.

19. On early history of Cabbagetown, see Stephen W. Grable, "Cabbagetown-A Working-Class Neighborhood in Transition During the Early Twentieth Century," *The Atlanta Historical Journal* 26, Nos. 2&3(Summer/Fall 1982): 51-66; No one is exactly sure how the area was named. Some stories say that outsiders called it Cabbagetown as a derogatory comment on the poor families who lived there and subsisted on a diet of cabbage; others say that once a truck full of cabbages broke down there and vandals made off with the vegetables; see Grable, 66.

20. Interview with Alvin Bentley, Atlanta, Georgia, October 20, 1988.

21. Interview with Richard Holland, Atlanta, Georgia, October 22, 1988.

22. Interview with Maya Hahn, Atlanta, Georgia, October 20, 1988.

23. Interview with Estelle Smith, College Park, Georgia, October 23, 1988.

24. Charles Moore, Peter Becker, and Regula Campbell, *The City Observed: Los Angeles* (New York: Random House, 1984), xiii-xiv; 35-38.

25. Barbara Mathieu Altman noted the anonymous face presented by residents in a Los Angeles neighborhood compared to neighborhoods in other regions and by a Hutterite community in her study of the front door and related attitudes toward privacy. Los Angelenos she interviewed were generally suspicious of contact with outsiders, even neighbors, and used adornment in front of and on their homes to limit and control the interaction with outsiders.

See her dissertation, "The Door as Cultural Symbol: A Contrast of Hutterian Community and Middle-Class Society," UCLA, 1987.

26. Interview with Hiroshi Kobashigawa, Los Angeles, California, November 5, 1988. The profession of gardener has been a significant one for Japanese settling in southern California. See Nobuya Tsuchida, "Japanese Gardeners in Southern California, 1900-1941" in *Asian Immigrant Workers and Communities*, 435-69.

27. Geographer Daniel D. Arreola argues that Chicano housescapes in Texas use enclosure, color, and yard shrines to express an idealized Mexican aesthetic with a long history in Europe and in the New World; see his article "Mexican American Housescapes," *Geographical Review* , 78, no. 3 (July 1988): 299-315. Interview with Helen Saavedra and her daughter, Elizabeth Paez, November 7, 1988, Los Angeles. See also Seymour Rosen, *In Celebration of Ourselves* (San Francisco: San Francisco Museum of Modern Art, 1979), 169.

28. On Chicano murals, see Eva Sperling Cockcroft and Holly Barnet-Sanchez, *Signs from the Heart: California Chicano Murals* (Venice, CA: Social and Public Art Resources Center, 1990); on murals at Estrada Court, see 45-46.

29. On importance of interior domestic shrines to Chicano art and sensibilities, see Tomás Ybarra-Frausto, "Arte Chicano: Images of a Community" in *Signs from the Heart: California Chicano Murals*, 59-62.

30. Interview with Annie Kaputyan, Los Angeles, November 3, 1988.

31. Interview with Rita Sammartino, Philadelphia, Pennsylvania, September 27, 1988. Folklorist Joseph Sciorra has studied yard shrines in New York City; see his article "Lawn Shrines and Sidewalk Altars of New York's Italian-Americans," *New York Folklore Newsletter*, 6 (December 1985): 3-4. In some cities, shrines are devoted to deities other than Catholic figures; see James R. Curtis, "Miami's Little Havanna: Yard Shrines, Cult Religion and Landscape," *Journal of Cultural Geography*, 1(Fall/Winter 1980): 1-15. On shrines demarcating Catholic neighborhoods, see Manzo, 122-23 and Vogeler, 71-83. I am grateful to John Banasiak of the Fine Arts Department at the University of South Dakota-Vermillion for sharing with me his slides of religious shrines found in that area.

32. On Old World shrines, see Sciorra, 3. There is a longstanding history of grottoes in spectacular or sacred European landscapes, and eventually, in aristocratic gardens; see Naomi Miller, *Heavenly Caves: Reflections on the Garden Grotto* (New York: George Braziller, 1982). Miller focuses on European high-style gardens. On shrines as the mark of a culture region, see Voegler, 79.

34. See Betty MacDowell, "Religion on the Road: Highway Evangelism and Worship Environments for the Traveler in America," *Journal of American Culture*, 5 (Winter 1982): 63-73; Robert L. Gambone, "The Folk Culture of Praying-Hands Souvenirs," *International Folklore Review*, 5 (1987): 96-100. While Protestants generally do not use religious imagery, a common exception in the domestic landscape occurred with the figure of St. Francis. Numerous instances of St. Francis yard shrines were found in Atlanta, for instance, at Protestant homes. St. Francis, the patron saint of animals, seems to have been generalized to become a more generic sign of the garden. Praying hands are not common in domestic landscapes. I have seen one handmade version of this image in Austin, Minnesota.

35. Interview with Howard Finster, Summerville, Georgia, October 19, 1988; see also J.F. Turner, *Howard Finster: Man of Vision* (New York: Alfred A. Knopf, 1989). Finster is one of the best-known visionary artists working today. He was one of the American artists represented at the 1984 Venice Biennale; the American Folklife Center at the Library of Congress has done a film on him. His most well-known painting appears on the album cover for the rock group The Talking Heads' 1985 *Little Creatures*.

36. Turner, 54.

37. On aging and creativity, see John A.B. McLeish, "The Continuum of Creativity" in *Perspectives on Aging*: *Exploding the Myths*, edited by Priscilla W. Johnson (Cambridge, Mass.: Ballinger Publishing Company, 1981),95-115.

38. Alan Jabbour, "Some Thoughts from a Folk Cultural Perspective," in *Perspectives on Aging;* on aging and folk arts, 143-46; see this essay also on symbiotic relationship between old and young in relation to folk art traditions, 146-49.

39. On grief and creativity, see Michael Owen Jones, *The Handmade Object and Its Maker* (Los Angeles: University of California Press, 1975), 163-66.

40. Telephone interview with Lew Harris, Los Angeles, California, November 10, 1988.

Selected Bibliography

Allen, Barbara and Thomas Schlereth, eds. *Sense of Place: American Regional Cultures*. Lexington: University of Kentucky Press, 1990.

Allen, Frederick Lewis. *Only Yesterday*. New York: Bantam Books, 1931.

Altman, Barbara Mathieu. "The Door as Cultural Symbol: A Contrast of Hutterian Community and Middle-Class Society." Ph.D. dissertation. University of California, Los Angeles, 1987.

Ames, Kenneth. *Beyond Necessity: Art in the Folk Tradition*. New York: W.W. Norton with The Winterthur Museum, 1978.

————. "Material Culture as Nonverbal Communication: A Historical Case Study." *Journal of American Culture* 3 (Winter 1980): 619-41.

————. "Meaning in Artifacts." In *Material Culture Studies in America*, edited by Thomas Schlereth, 206-21. Nashville, Tenn.: American Association for State and Local History, 1982.

Andrews, J.C. *The Well-Built Elephant and Other Roadside Attractions*. New York: Congdon & Weed, Inc., 1984. With an introduction by David Gebhard.

Arreola, Daniel D. "Mexican-American Housescapes." *Geographical Review* 78, no. 3 (July 1988): 299-315.

Axelrod, Alex, ed. *The Colonial Revival in America*. New York: W.W. Norton, 1985.

Babcock, Barbara A., ed. *The Reversible World: Symbolic Inversion in Art and Society*. Ithaca: Cornell University, 1978.

Barnett, James. *The American Christmas: A Study in National Culture*. New York: Macmillan, 1954.

Barrett, Helena, and John Philips. *Suburban Style: The British Home, 1840-1960*. London: MacDonald & Co., 1987.

Barron., Leonard. *Lawns and How to Make Them*. New York: Doubleday, Page & Co., 1914; rpt. 1906.

Barth, Jack, et al. *Roadside America*. New York: Simon & Schuster, 1986.

Beardsley, John. *Art in Public Places: A Summary of Community-Sponsored Projects Supported by the National Endowment for the Arts*. Washington, D.C.: Partners for Livable Places, 1981.

_____. *Gardens of Revelation: Environments by Visionary Artists*. (New York: Abbeville Press, 1995.

Beecher, Catherine E., and Harriet Beecher Stowe. *The American Woman's Home*. Watkins Glen, N.Y.: Library of Victorian Culture American Life Foundation, 1979; rpt. 1869.

Beecher, Catherine E. *Treatise on Domestic Economy*. New York: Harper & Bros., 1848.

Bellah, Robert, et al. *Habits of the Heart: Individualism and Commitment in American Life*. Berkeley: University of California, 1985.

Benedict, Burton. *The Anthropology of World's Fairs: San Francisco's Panama Pacific International Exposition of 1915*. Berkeley: University of California with the Lowie Museum of Anthropology, 1983.

Bender, Thomas. "The 'Rural' Cemetery Movement: Urban Travail and the Appeal of Nature." In *Material Life in America*, edited by Robert Blair St. George and Dell Upton. Boston: Northeastern Univeristy, 1988.

Blasdel, Greg. "The Grass-roots Artist." *Art in America* (September/October 1968): 24-41.

Bishop, Robert. *American Folk Sculpture*. New York: Bonanza Books, 1985.

Blockson, Charles L. "Escape from Slavery: The Underground Railroad." *National Georgraphic* (July 1984): 3-39.

Bogart, Michele H. "Barking Architecture: The Sculpture of Coney Island." *Smithsonian Studies in American Art* 2 (Winter 1988): 3-17.

_____. "The Development of a Popular Market for Sculpture in America, 1850-1880." *Journal of American Culture* 4 (spring 1981).

_____. *Fauns and Fountains: American Garden Statuary, 1890-1930*. Southampton, N.Y.: The Parrish Museum, 1985.

_____. *Public Sculpture and the Civic Ideal in New York City, 1890-1930*. Chicago: University of Chicago, 1989.

Bourdieu, Pierre. *A Social Critique of the Judgement of Taste*. Trans.lated by Richard Nice. Cambridge, Mass.: Harvard University, 1984; repr. 1979.

Bronner, Simon, ed. *American Material Culture and Folklife: A Prologue and A Dialogue*. Ann Arbor: UMI Press, 1985.

_____. *The Chain Carvers: Old Men Crafting Meaning*. Lexington: University Press of Kentucky, 1985.

————, ed. *Consuming Visions: Accumulation and Display of Goods in America, 1880-1920*. New York: W. W. Norton, 1989.

————. *Grasping Things: Folk Material Culture and Mass Society in America*. Lexington: University of Kentucky, 1986.

Burg, David F. *Chicago's White City of 1893*. Lexington: University Press of Kentucky, 1976.

Calkins, Carroll C., ed. *Great Gardens of America*. New York: Coward-McCann, Inc. 1969.

Cerwinske, Laura. *Tropical Deco: The Architecture and Design of Old Miami Beach*. New York: Rizzoli, 1981.

Clark, Clifford Edward, Jr. *The American Family Home, 1800-1960*. Chapel Hill: University of North Carolina, 1968.

Clifford, Derek. *A History of Garden Design*. New York: Frederick A. Praeger, 1963.

Cockcroft, Eva Sperling, and Holly Barnet-Sanchez. *Signs from the Heart: California Chicano Murals*. Venice, Calif.: Social and Public Art Resources Center, 1990.

Cohen, Lisabeth. "Embellishing a Life of Labor: An Interpretation of the Material Culture of Working-Class Homes, 1885-1915." *Material Culture Studies in America*. Edited by Thomas Schlereth, 289-305. Nashville: American Association for State and Local History, 1982.

Core, Philip. *Camp: The Lie That Tells the Truth*. New York: Delilah Books, 1984.

Corn, Wanda. *Grant Wood: The Regionalist Vision*. New Haven: Yale University, 1983.

Cromley, Elizabeth. "Modernizing: Or, 'You Never See a Screen Door on Affluent Houses.'" *Journal of American Culture* 5, no. 2 (Summer 1982): 71-79.

Csikszentmihalyi, Mihaly, and Eugene Rochberg-Halton. *The Meaning of Things: Domestic Symbols and the Self*. Cambridge: Cambridge University, 1981.

Curtis, James R. "Miami's Little Havana: Yard Shrines, Cult Religion and Landscape." *Journal of Cultural Geography* 1 (Fall/Winter 1980): 1-15.

Doell, Christine Klim. *Gardens of the Gilded Age: Nineteenth-Century Gardens and Homegrounds of New York State*. Syracuse, N.Y.: Syracuse University, 1984.

Doss, Erika. *Spirit Poles and Flying Pigs: Public Art and Cultural Democracy in American Communities*. Washington, D.C.: Smithsonian, 1995.

Downing, Andrew Jackson. *The Architecture of Country Houses*. New York: Dover, 1969; rpt, D. Appleton & Co., 1850.

————. *Victorian Cottage Residences.* New York: Dover Publications, 1981; rprt 1842.

Edwards, Paul. *English Garden Ornament.* London: G. Bell & Son, 1965.

E.I. du Pont's Garden at Eleutherian Mills. (brochure) Wilmington, Del.: Hagley Museum and Library, n.d.

Ewen, Stuart. *Captains of Consciousness: Advertising and the Social Roots of Consumer Culture.* New York: McGraw-Hill, 1976.

Fabos, Julius G, et al. *Frederick Law Olmsted, Sr., Founder of Landscape Architecture in America.* Amherst, Mass.: University of Massachusetts, 1968.

Fairmount Park and the International Exhibition at Philadelphia. Philadelphia: Claxton, Remsen & Haffelfinger, 1876.

Fiske, John. *Reading Popular Culture.* Boston: Unwin Hyman, 1989.

————. *Understanding Popular Culture.* Boston: Unwin Hyman, 1989.

Fine, Gary Alan. "The Goliath Effect: Corporate Dominance and Mercantile Legends." *Journal of American Folklore* 98, no. 387(January-March 1985): 63-85.

Foster, Hal, ed. *The Anti-Aesthetic: Essays on Postmodern Culture.* Port Townsend, Wash.: Bay Press, 1983.

Forty Years of California Assemblage. Los Angeles: University of California with the Wight Art Gallery, 1989.

Fox, Richard Wightman, and T.J. Jackson Lears. *The Culture of Consumption Critical Essays in American History 1880-1980.* New York: Pantheon Books, 1983.

Friedman, Martin. *Oldenburg: Six Themes.* Minneapolis: Walker Art Center, 1975.

Gambone, Robert L. "The Folk Culture of Praying-Hands Souvenirs." *International Folklore Review* 5 (1987): 96-100.

Gans, Herbert. *The Levittowners: Ways of Life and Politics in a New Suburban Community.* New York: Pantheon Books, 1967.

————. *Popular Culture and High Culture: An Analysis and Evaluation of Taste.* New York: Basic Books, 1974.

Glassie, Henry. *Pattern in the Material Culture of the Eastern United States.* Philadelphia: University of Pennsylvania, 1968.

Gowans, Alan. *The Comfortable House: North American Suburban Architecture, 1890-1930.* Cambridge, Mass.: MIT Press, 1986.

Graburn, Nelson. "Tourism and the Sacred Journey." In *Hosts and Guests: An Anthropology of Tourism.* Edited by Valene Smith, 17 - 32. Philadelphia: University of Pennsylvania Press, 1977.

Grable, Stephen W. "Cabbagetown—A Working-Class Neighborhood in Transition During the Early Twentieth Century." *The Atlanta Historical Journal* 26, Nos. 2 & 3 (Summer/Fall 1982): 51-66.

Grattan, Patricia. *Flights of Fancy: Newfoundland Yard Art.* St. John's, Newfoundland: Art Gallery of Memorial University, 1983.

Green, Harvey. *The Light of the Home: An Intimate View of the Lives of Women in Victorian America.* New York: Pantheon, 1983.

Griebel, Helen Bradley. "Worldview on the Landscape: A Regional Yard Art Study." *Pennsylvania Folklife* 36 (Autumn 1986): 39-48.

Greenfield, Verni. *Making Do or Making Art: A Study of American Recycling.* Ann Arbor: UMI Research Press, 1984.

Groves, Derham. "Walt Disney's Backyard," *Exedra: Architecture, Art & Design* 5, no. 1 (1994): 29-38.

Grover, Catherine, ed. *Hard At Play: Leisure in America, 1840-1940.* Amherst: Massachusetts Press with The Strong Museum, 1992.

Hall, Michael D. and Eugene W. Metcalf, Jr., eds.*The Artist Outsider: Creativity and the Boundaries of Culture.* Washington, D.C.: Smithsonian, 1994.

Handlin, David. *The American Home: Architecture and Society, 1815-1915.* Boston: Little, Brown & Co., 1979.

Harrison, Helen. *Dawn of a New Day: The New York World's Fair, 1939/40.* New York: New York University Press with the Queens Museum, 1980.

Hayden, Dolores. *The Grand Domestic Revolution: A History of Feminist Designs for American Homes, Neighborhoods, and Cities.* Cambridge, Mass.: MIT, 1981.

———. *Redesigning the American Dream: The Future of Housing, Work and Family Life.* New York: W.W. Norton, 1984.

Hebdige, Dick. *Subculture: The Meaning of Style.* London: Methuen, 1979.

Hillier, Bevis. *The World of Art Deco.* New York: E.P. Dutton, 1971.

Hollis, Richard, and Brian Sibley. *The Disney Studio Story.* New York: Crown Publishers, 1988.

Home and Yard: Black Folk Life Expressions in Los Angeles. Los Angeles: California Afro-American Muusem, 1988.

Horowitz, Daniel. *The Morality of Spending: Attitudes toward Consumer Society, 1875-1940.* Baltimore: Johns Hopkins University Press, 1985.

Howett, Catherine M. *Land of Our Own: 250 Years of Landscape and Gardening Tradition in Georgia.* Atlanta: Atlanta Historical Society, Press, 1983.

Hummon, David M. "House, Home, and Identity in Contemporary American Culture." In *Housing, Culture, and Design: A Comparative Perspective.*

Edited by Setha M. Low and Erve Chambers, 207-28. Philadelphia: University of Pennsylvania Press, 1989.

Ingram., J.S. *The Centennial Exposition Described and Illustrated.* Philadelphia: Hubbard Brothers, 1876.

Jabbour, Alan. "Some Thoughts from a Folk Cultural Perspective." In *Perspectives on Aging: Exploding the Myths.* Edited by Priscilla W. Johnson. Cambridge, Mass.: Ballinger, 1981.

Jackson, J.B. *American Space: The Centennial Years: 1865-1876.* New York: Norton & Co., 1972.

———. *Discovering the Vernacular Landscape.* New Haven: Yale University Press, 1984.

———. "Ghosts at the Door." *Landscape* (Autumn 1951): 3-9.

———. *The Necessity for Ruins and Other Topics.* Amherst: University of Massachusetts Press, 1980.

———. "The Popular Yard." *Places* 4 (Spring 1989): 26-31.

Jackson, Kenneth T. "A Nation of Suburbs." *Chicago History* (Summer 1984): 6-25.

———. *The Crabgrass Frontier: The Suburbanization of the United States.* New York: Oxford University Press, 1985.

Jakle, John. *The Tourist: Travel in Nineteenth-Century North America.* Lincoln, Neb.: University of Nebraska Press, 1985.

Jekyll, Gertrude. *Garden Ornament.* London: George Newnes, Ltd., 1918; rpt. by Antique Collectors Club., 1982.

Jenkins, Virginia Scott. *The Lawn: A History of an American Obsession.* Washington, D.C.: Smithsonian, 1994.

Jones, Michael Owen. *Exploring Folk Art: Twenty Years of Thought on Craft, Work, and Aesthetics.* Ann Arbor: UMI Research, 1987.

———. *The Handmade Object and Its Maker.* Berkeley: University of California Press, 1975.

———. "L.A. Add-Ons and Re-dos." In *Perspectives on American Folk Art,* Edited by Ian M.G. Quimby and Scott Swank, 325-363. New York: Norton with the Henry Francis du Pont Winterthur Museum, 1980.

Kaplan, Sidney, and Emma Nogrady. *The Black Presences in the Era of the American Revolution.* Amherst: University of Massachusetts Press, 1989.

Kasson, John. *Amusing the Millions: Coney Island at the Turn of the Century.* New York: Hill & Wang, 1978.

Kenworthy, Richard G. "Bringing the World to Brookline: The Gardens of Larz and Isabel Anderson." *Journal of Garden History,* II, 4 (1991): 224-41.

Kirschenblatt-Gimblett, Barbara. "The Future of Folklore Study in America: The Urban Frontier." *Folklore Forum,* 16 (1983): 175-234.,

Kitchener, Amy. *The Holiday Yards of Florencio Morales*. Jackson: University Press of Mississippi, 1994.

Kroger, Earl, Sr. *Jocko: A Legend of the American Revolution*. Englewood Cliffs, N.J.: Prentice-Hall, 1976.

Lears, T.J. Jackson. *No Place of Grace: Antimodernism and the Transformation of American Culture, 1880-1920*. New York: Pantheon Books, 1981.

Leibs, Chester H. *From Main Street to Miracle Mile: American Roadside Architecture*. Boston: Little, Brown, 1985.

Leighton, Ann. *American Gardens of the Nineteenth Century*. Amherst: University of Massachusetts Press, 1987.

————. *Early American Gardens: "For Meate or Medicine."* Boston: Houghton Mifflin, 1970.

Levi-Strauss, Claude. *The Savage Mind*. Chicago: University of Chicago Press, 1966.

Levine, Lawrence. *Highbrow and Lowbrow: The Emergence of Cultural Hierarchy in America*. Cambridge: Harvard University, 1988.

Limerick, Jeffrey, et al.. *America's Grand Resort Hotels*. New York: Pantheon Books, 1979.

Linden, Blanche M.G. "Death and the Garden: The Cult of Melancholy and the 'Rural' Cemetery." Ph.D. dissertation. Harvard University, 1981.

Linden-Warden, Blanche. "Strange but Genteel Pleasure Grounds: Tourist and Leisure Uses of Nineteenth-Century Rural Cemeteries." In *Cemeteries and Grave Markers: Voices of American Culture*. Edited by Richard E. Meyer. Ann Arbor: UMI Research Press, 1989.

Lippard, Lucy. "Making Something from Nothing (Toward a Definition of Women's Hobby Art). *Heresies* 1, no. 4 (1978): 62-65.

Lipsitz, George. *Time Passages: Collective Memory and American Popular Culture*. Minneapolis: University of Minnesota, 1990.

Lynd, Robert, and Helen Lynd. *Middletown: A Study in Contemporary American Culture*. New York: Harcourt Brace, 1929.

Lynch, Kenneth. *The Book of Garden Ornament*. Canterbury, Conn.: Canterbury Publishing, 1979.

Lynch, Kevin. *What Time Is This Place?* Cambridge, Mass.: MIT Press, 1980.

Lynes, Russell. *The Domesticated Americans*. New York: Harper and Row, 1957.

————. *The Tastemakers: The Shaping of American Popular Taste*. New York: Dover Publications, 1949.

MacCannell, Dean. *The Tourist: A New Theory of the Leisure Class*. New York: Schoken Books, 1976.

MacDowell, Betty. "Religion on the Road: Highway Evangelism and Worship Environments for the Traveler in America." *Journal of American Culture* 5 (Winter 1982): 63-73.

Manley, Roger. *Signs and Wonders: Outsider Art Inside North Carolina.* Raleigh, N.C.: North Carolina Museum of Art, 1989.

Manzo, Joseph T. "Italian-American Yard Shrines." *Journal of Cultural Geography* (Fall/Winter 1983): 119-25.

Marchand, Roland. *Advertising the American Dream: Making Way for Modernity, 1920-1940.* Berkeley: University of California Press, 1985.

Marcus, Greil. *Lipstick Traces: A Secret History of the Twentieth Century.* Cambridge: Harvard University Press, 1989.

Margolies, John, and Nina Garfinkel. *John Margolies's Miniature Golf.* New York: Abbeville Press, 1987.

Marling, Karal Ann. *Colossus of Roads: Myth and Symbol Along the American Highway.* Minneapolis: University of Minnesota Press, 1984.

———. *George Washington Slept Here: Colonial Revivals and American Culture, 1876-1986.* Cambridge: Harvard University Press, 1988.

———. *Wall-to-Wall America: A Cultural History of Post-Office Murals in the Great Depression.* Minneapolis: University of Minnesota Press, 1982.

Marsh, Margaret. "Suburban Men and Masculine Domesticity, 1870-1915." *American Quarterly* 4 (June 1988): 165-86.

Martin, Judith A., and David A. Lanegran. *Where We Live: The Residential Districts of Minneapolis and St. Paul.* Minneapolis: University of Minnesota Press, 1983.

Marx, Leo. *The Machine in the Garden: Technology and the Pastoral Ideal in America.* New York: Oxford University Press, 1964.

Mathews, Glenna. *"Just A Housewife": The Rise and Fall of Domesticity in America.* New York: Oxford University Press, 1987.

Mathieu, Barbara Altman. "The Door as Cultural Symbol: A Contrast of Hutterian Community and Middle-Class Society." Ph.D. dissertation. UCLA, 1987.

Mays, Alan E. "The Welded Chain Mailbox Support: A Study in Material Culture." Unpublished paper from course at Pennsylvania State University, Harrisburg. November 25, 1985.

McCracken, Grant. *Culture and Consumption: New Approaches to the Symbolic Character of Consumer Goods and Activities.* Bloomington: Indiana University Press, 1988.

McKinstry, E. Richard. *Trade Catalogues at Winterthur: A Guide to the Literature of Merchandising, 1750 to 1980.* New York: Garland Publishing, 1984.

Meinig, D.W., ed. *The Interpretation of Ordinary Landscapes: Geographical Essays.* New York: Oxford University Press, 1979.

Meyer, Melissa, and Miriam Shapiro. "Waste Not, Want Not: An Inquiry into What Women Saved and Assembled." *Heresies* 1, no. 4(1978): 66-69.

Miller, Naomi. *Heavenly Caves: Reflections on the Garden Grotto.* New York: George Braziller, 1982.

Motz, Marilyn Ferris, and Pat Browne, ed. *Making the American Home: Middle-Class Women and Domestic Material Culture, 1884-1940.* Bowling Green, Ohio: Bowling Green University Press, 1988.

Naives and Visionairies. New York: E.P. Dutton and Minneapolis: The Walker Art Center, 1974.

Nelson, Marion. "Folk Art in Minnesota and the Case of the Norwegian American." In *Circles of Tradition: Folk Arts in Minnesota*, 24-44. St. Paul: Minnesota Historical Society Press with the University of Minnesota Art Museum, 1989.

Nicolaisen, W.F.H. "Distorted Function in Material Aspects of Culture." *Folklore Forum* 12, nos. 2 & 3 (1979): 223-35.

———. "The Folk and the Region." *New York Folklore* 2 (Winter 1976): 143-49.

Noyes, Dorothy. *Uses of Tradition: Arts of Italian Americans in Philadelphia.* Philadelphia: Philadelphia Folklife Project and Samuel S. Fleisher Art Memorial, 1989.

Nye, David. *Electrifying America: Social Meanings of a New Technology 1880-1940.* Cambridge, Mass.: MIT Press, 1991

Nye, Russel B. "Eight Ways of Looking at an Amusement Park. *Journal of Popular Culture* 15(Summer 1981): 63-65.

Nunes, Jadviga M. Da Costa. "The Naughty Child in Nineteenth-Century American Art," *Journal of American Studies* 21 (August 1987): 225-47.

O'Donnell, Georgene. *Miniaturia: The World of Tiny Things.* Chicago: Lightner Publishing, 1943.

Passing Time and Tradition: Contemporary Iowa Folk Arts. Des Moines: Iowa Arts Council and Ames, Iowa: Iowa State University Press, 1984.

Patoski, Christina. *Merry Christmas America: A Front Yard View of the Holidays.* Charlottesville, Va.: Thomasson-Grant, Inc. 1994.

Perin, Constance. *Everything in Its Place: Social Order and Land Use in America.* Princeton, N.J.: Princeton, 1977.

Peters, Richard. "Light and Public Places." *Places* 1 (Winter 1984): 41-47.

Peterson, Mark Tory, and Virginia Marie Peterson, eds. *Audubon's Birds of America.* Facsimilie edition of the baby elephant folio. New York: Abbeville Press, 1981.

Potter, Burton Willis. *The Road and the Roadside*. Boston: Little, Brown, and Co., 1893.

Quimby, Ian M.G., ed. *The Craftsman in Early America*. New York: Norton with the Henry Francis du Pont Winterthur Museum, 1984.

Ramsey, Eonidas W., and Charles H. Lawrence. *The Outdoor Living Room*. New York: Macmillan Co., 1932.

Rapoport, Amos. *The Meaning of the Built Environment: A Nonverbal Communication Approach*. Beverly Hills, Calif.: Sage, 1982.

Robbins, Bruce, ed. *The Phanton Public Sphere*. Minneapolis: University of Minnesota, 1993.

Rosen, Seymour. *In Celebration of Ourselves*. San Francisco: San Francisco Museum of Modern Art, 1979.

Rosenzweig, Roy, and Elizabeth Blackmar. *The Park and the People: A History of Central Park*. Ithaca, N.Y.: Cornell University Press, 1992.

Rowe, Anne. *The Idea of Florida in the American Literary Imagination*. Baton Rouge: Louisiana State University Press, 1986.

Rubin, Barbara. "Aesthetic Ideology and Urban Design." In *Common Places: Readings in American Vernacular Architecture*. Edited by Dell Upton and John Micheal Vlach. Athens, Ga.: University of Georgia, 1986.

Santino, Jack. "Halloween in America: Contemporary Customs and Performance." *Western Folklore* XLIII, 1 (January 1983): 1-20.

Schickel, Richard. *The Disney Version: The Life, Times, and Commerce of Walt Disney*. 2nd ed. rev. New York: Simon & Schuster, 1985.

Schuyler, David. *The New Urban Landscape: The Redefinition of City Form in Nineteenth-Century America*. Baltimore: Johns Hopkins University Press, 1986.

Schroeder, Fred. "The Democratic Yard and Garden." In *Outlaw Aesthetics: Art and the Public Mind*, 94-122. Bowling Green, Ohio: Bowling Green State University Press, 1977.

_____. *Front Yard America: The Evolution and Meanings of a Vernacular Domestic Landscape*. Bowling Green, Ohio: Bowling Green State University Press, 1993.

Sciorra, Joseph. "Lawn Shrines and Sidewalk Altars of New York's Italian-Americans." *New York Folklore Newsletter* 6 (December 1985): 3-4.

Scott, Frank Jessup. *Victorian Gardens: The Art of Beautifying the Suburban Homegrounds*. Watkins Glen, N.Y.: American Life Books, 1982; rpt. D. Appelton & Co., 1870.

Sears, John. F. *Sacred Places: American Tourist Attractions in the Nineteenth Century*. New York: Oxford University, 1989.

Seitz, William C. *The Art of Assemblage*. New York: Musem of Modern Art, 1961.

Siebert, Wilbur Henry. *The Mysteries of Ohio's Underground Railroads.* Columbus, Ohio: Long's College Book Co., 1951.

Sennett, Richard. *The Fall of Public Man*. New York: Alfred A. Knopf, 1977.

Sheehy, Colleen J. "American Angling: The Rise of Urbanism and the Romance of the Rod and Reel." In *American Play, 1840-1914*. Edited by Catherine Grier, 77-92. Amherst: University of Massachusetts Press, 1992.

————. "Giant Mosquitoes, Eelpout Displays, Pink Flamingoes: Some Overlooked and Unexpected Minnesota Folk Arts." In *Circles of Tradition: Folk Arts in Minnesota*, 45-59. St. Paul: Minnesota Historical Society Press, 1989.

Slovic, David, and Ligia Rave. "Building of the Month Awards: Philadelphia." *Places* 1 (Spring 1984): 44-59.

Smith, Henry Nash. *Virgin Land*. Cambridge: Harvard University, 1950.

Smith, Mary Ann. *Gustav Stickley: The Craftsman*. Syracuse, N.Y.: Syracuse University Press, 1983.

Snyder, Ellen Marie. "Victory Over Nature: Victorian Cast-Iron Seating Furniture." *Winterthur Portfolio* 20 (Winter 1985): 221-242.

Snyder, Phillip V. *The Christmas Tree Book*. New York: Viking, 1976.

Sontag, Susan. "Notes on Camp." *Partisan Review* (Fall 1964): 515-30.

Stilgoe, John R. *Common Landscapes of America, 1580 to 1845*. New Haven: Yale University Press, 1982.

Stern, Stephen, and John Allan Cicala, eds. *Creative Ethnicity: Symbols and Strategies of Contemporary Ethnic Life*. Logan, Utah: Utah State University Press, 1991.

Stern, Stephen. "Ethnic Folklore and the Folklore of Ethnicity." *Western Folklore* XXXVI, no. 1 (January 1977): 7-32.

Stillinger, Elizabeth. *The Antiquers*. New York: Knopf, 1980.

Sutton, S.B. *Civilizing American Cities: A Selection of Frederick Law Olmsted's Writings on City Landscape*. Cambridge, Mass: MIT Press, 1971.

Swanson, Mary T. *From Swedish Fairy Tales to American Fantasy: Gustaf Tenggren's Illustrations, 1920-1970*. Minneapolis: University of Minnesota Art Museum, 1986.

Thacker, Christopher. *The History of Gardens*. Los Angeles: University of California Press, 1979.

Thompson, Michael. *Rubbish Theory: The Creation and Destruction of Value*. Oxford: Oxford University Press, 1979.

Tice, Patricia. *Gardening in America, 1830-1910*. Rochester, N.Y.: The Strong Museum, 1984.

Trachtenberg, Alan. *Brooklyn Bridge: Fact and Symbol.* Chicago: University of Chicago, 1965.

Tuan, Yi-Fu. *Dominance and Affection: The Making of Pets*. New Haven: Yale University Press, 1984.

————. *Landscapes of Fear*. Minneapolis: University of Minnesota, 1979.

————. *Space and Place: The Perspective of Experience*. Minneapolis: University of Minnesota Press, 1977.

————. *Topophilia: A Study of Environmental Perception, Attitudes, and Values*. Englewood Cliffs, N.J.: Prentice Hall, 1974.

Turner. J.F. *Howard Finster: Man of Vision*. New York: Alfred A. Knopf, 1989.

Turner, Patricia. *Ceramic Mammies and Celluloid Uncles: Black Images and Their Influence on Culture*. New York: Anchor Books, 1994.

Van Bruvand, Jan. *The Vanishing Hitchhiker: American Urban Legends and Their Meanings*. New York: W.W. Norton, 1981.

Veblen, Thornstein. *The Theory of the Leisure Class*. New York: New American Library, 1953; rpt MacMillan, 1899.

Venturi, Robert, Denise Scott Brown, and Steven Izenour. *Learning from Las Vegas: The Forgotten Symbolism of Architectural Form*, rev. ed. Cambridge, Mass.: MIT Press, 1977.

Vlach, John Michael, and Simon Bronner, eds. *Folk Art and Art Worlds: Essays Drawn from the Washington Meeting on Folk Arts*. Ann Arbor: UMI Research Press, 1986.

Vogeler, Ingolf. "The Roman Catholic Culture Region of Central Minnesota." *Pioneer America* 8, no. 2 (July 1976): 71-83.

Wampler, Jan. *All Their Own: People and the Places They Build*. New York: Oxford University Press, 1978.

Ward, Daniel, ed. *Personal Places: Perspectives on Informal Art Environments*. Bowling Green, Ohio: Bowling Green, 1984.

Warner, Sam Bass. *Streetcar Suburbs: The Process of Growth in Boston, 1870-1900*. 2nd ed. Cambridge: Harvard University, 1980.

Westmacott, Richard. *African-American Gardens and Yards in the Rural South*. Knoxville, Tenn.: University of Tennessee Press, 1992.

Wright, Gwendolyn. *Building the Dream: A Social History of Housing in America*. Cambridge, Mass.: MIT, 1981.

Zelinsky, Wilbur. "General Cultural and Popular Regions." In *This Remarkable Continent: An Atlas of United States and Canadian Society and Cultures.* Edited by John F. Rooney, Jr., Wilbur Zelinsky, and Dean R. Louder, 3-24. College Station, Tex.: Texas A&M University Press, 1982.

Zuckerman, Lord, ed. *Great Zoos of the World: Their Origins and Significance.* Boulder, Colo.: Westview Press, 1980.

INTERVIEWS

Adamo, Florence. Manayunk, Penn. September 23, 1988.

Bagasao, Harriet. Santa Monica, Calif. November 9, 1988.

Barbula, Donna. St. Louis Park, Minn. August 5, 1990.

Bentley, Alvin. Atlanta, Ga. October 20, 1988.

Bruce, Iris. Decatur, Ga. October 17, 1988.

Bushinsky, Tony and Emily. St. Paul, Minn. January 20, 1983; Emily only August , 1991.

DiGiantomasso, Constantino. Phil., Penn. September 27, 1988.

Erickson, Alberta. Grand Rapids, Minn. August 6, 1987.

Fields, John. Phil., Penn. September 29, 1988.

Finster, Howard, Summerville, Ga. October 18, 1988.

Flurschutz, Bonnie. College Park, Ga. October 22, 1988.

Fore, Julie Hetman. Minneapolis, Minn. Nc ember 11, 1983.

Fortunato, Marie. Roxborough, Penn., September 23, 1988.

Futty, Sandy. Gap, Penn. September 23, 1988.

Garren, Elizabeth. Minneapolis, Minn. January 29, 1983.

Gaffney, Janet. Atlanta, Ga, October 17, 1988.

Goldstein, Fredrika. Mar Vista, Calif. November 10, 1988.

Hahn, Maya. Atlanta, Ga. October 20, 1988.

Harris, Lew. Los Angeles, Calif. November 10, 1988.

Higgins, Molly. Scottdale, Ga. October 26, 1988.

Holland, Richard. Atlanta, Ga. October 21, 1988.

Jacobs, Jeffrey, Minneapolis, Minn. January 29, 1983.

Jordan, C.R. Scottdale, Ga. October 24, 1988.

Kaplan, Harold and Ethel. Onamia,Minn. August 5, 1987; June 24, 1991.

Kaputyan, Annie. Glendale, Calif. November 3, 1988.

Kaspersak, David. Minneapolis, Minn. February 17, 1985.

Kobashigawa, Hiroshi. West Los Angeles, Calif. November 5, 1988.

Lambert, Emily. Minneapolis, Minn. August 20, 1990.

Manoukien, Harry. East Hollywood, Calif. November 10, 1988.

McCormack, Judy. Anaheim, Calif. November 11, 1988.

Muense, Werner and Thekla. Minneapolis, Minn. January 6, 1983; August 20, 1990.

Nachtwey, Chester. Los Angeles, Calif. November 5 & 10, 1988.

Noel, Martha. Mar Vista, Calif. November 9, 1988.

Olson, Martina and Gust. St. Louis Park, Minn. August 5, 1990.

Pattern, Frances. Phil, Penn. September 26, 1988.

Polnasek, Joe and Marcie. Minneapolis, Minn. January 29, 1983.

Powers, Tony. Atlanta, Ga.. October 27, 1988.

Pyne, Thomas. Minneapolis, Minn. January 22, 1983.

Saavedra, Helen. Boyle Heights, Calif. November 7, 1988.

Sammartino, Rita. Phil., Penn. September 27, 1988.

Schack, Mike. Grand Rapids, Minn. February 2, 1988; August 18, 1988.

Slice, Betty. St. Louis Park, Minn. August 5, 1990.

Smith, Estell. College Park, Ga.. October 22, 1988.

Smith, Valerie. Jackson, Ga.. October 22, 1988.

Stanowich, Al. Manayunk, Penn. September 23,1988.

Szewczak, Eileen. Manayunk, Penn. September 23,1988.

Tolleson, Joan. Venice, Calif. November 10, 1988.

Truitt, Maria Cotton. College Park, Ga.. October 22, 1988.

Verbugge, Mark. Minneapolis, Minn. March 10, 1985.

Weidert, Clarence. Minneapolis, Minn. January 2, 1990.

Wetzstein, John. Minneapolis, Minn. June 10, 1985.

Index